Contemporary Nationalism

Contemporary Nationalism provides a clear and illuminating framework for understanding nationalist politics. It builds upon the core theories of nationalism so as to explain their differing approaches, and develops a coherent understanding of the contemporary nation-state and the challenges it faces.

This outstanding book shows why and how nation-states are being challenged by the tensions between contending civic, ethnocultural and multicultural nationalist visions, and examines their varying responses. The analysis is illustrated throughout by case studies, which include examinations of nationalist politics in Singapore, Ghana, Spain and Australia. The tensions in Northern Ireland, Rwanda and Kosovo are also discussed.

This book brings a fresh and topical international focus to the study of nationalism. It is a valuable resource for all students of nationalism and politics.

David Brown is Senior Lecturer in the School of Politics and International Studies at Murdoch University, Australia. He has published widely on nationalism and ethnicity. He is the author of *The State and Ethnic Politics in Southeast Asia* and co-author of *Towards Illiberal Democracy in Pacific Asia*.

D1328997

Contemporary Nationalism

Civic, ethnocultural and multicultural politics

David Brown

London and New York

First published 2000
by Routledge
11 New Fetter Lane, London EC4P 4EE

Simultaneously published in the USA and Canada
by Routledge
29 West 35th Street, New York, NY 10001

Routledge is an imprint of the Taylor & Francis Group

© 2000 David Brown

Typeset in Baskerville by Keystroke, Jacaranda Lodge, Wolverhampton

Printed in the United Kingdom at the University Press, Cambridge

British Library Cataloguing in Publication Data
A catalogue record for this book is available from the British Library

Library of Congress Cataloguing in Publication Data
Brown, David,
    Contemporary nationalism : civic, ethnocultural, and multicultural politics / David Brown.
     p.   cm.
    Includes bibliographical references and index.
    1. Nationalism. 2. Ethnicity. 3. Ethnic relations—Political aspects. I. Title.
JC311 .B764 2000
   320.54—dc21   00–020053

ISBN 0–415–17138–5 (hbk)
ISBN 0–415–17139–3 (pbk)

For Diana, and in memory of my mother

Contents

Acknowledgements   ix

Introduction: unravelling nationalism   1

1   The conceptual languages of nationalism   4

2   New nations for old?   30

3   Are there two nationalisms?: good–civic and
    bad–ethnocultural   50

4   Constructing nationalism: the case of the Basques   70

5   Globalisation and nationalism: the case of Singapore   89

6   Reactive nationalism and the politics of development:
    the case of Ghana   107

7   Contentious visions: civic, ethnocultural and multicultural
    nationalism   126

8   How can the state respond to nationalist contention?:
    Corporatist and pluralist approaches   135

9   Epilogue: nationalist ideologies in conflict   152

    Appendix: case studies   155
    David Brown with Natalia Norris
    Australia   155
    Northern Ireland   158

Rwanda	160
Kosovo	164
Notes	168
Bibliography	182
Index	193

Acknowledgements

Various sections of the book have benefited from discussions with Anthony Sayers and Ian Cook, and from the assistance of Natalia Norris, Kate Badgery-Parker and Sarah Farnsworth. Natalia's involvement in the development of the case studies in the Appendix, is much appreciated, and is acknowledged in the joint authorship.

Some of the chapters of the book have been adapted from the following articles:

'Why is the Nation-State so Vulnerable to Ethnic Nationalism?', (1998) *Nations and Nationalism* 4(1) :1–16. (Revised for Chapter 2.)

'Are there Good and Bad Nationalisms?', (1999) *Nations and Nationalism* 5(2): 281–302. (Revised for Chapter 3.)

'Globalisation, Ethnicity and the Nation-State: The Case of Singapore', (1998) *Australian Journal of International Affairs* 52(1): 35–46. (Revised for Chapter 5.)

'The Politics of Reconstructing National Identity: A Corporatist Approach', (1997) *Australian Journal of Political Science* 32(2): 255–69. (Revised for part of Chapter 8.)

Introduction

Unravelling nationalism

> Why do the nations so furiously rage together, and why do the people imagine a vain thing?
>
> (Handel's Messiah, from Psalm 2: 1)

Nationalism is unravelling in the sense that the nationalist legitimacy of many existing states is under challenge from the nationalist claims of ethnic and regional minorities, thus generating new contentions. Nationalism needs unravelling analytically therefore, so that by isolating and examining its conceptual ingredients we can more clearly understand the resultant changes – the ethnic conflicts, the emergence of new nation-states, the uncertainties of national identity and the restructuring of multicultural nations.

When told about the projected book on nationalism, which would develop an explanation of the upsurge of nationalist conflicts, a friend responded in tones of bemused regret. 'But you're missing the point, David. They are *not* nationalist conflicts at all, they are disputes caused by economic disparities and élite power rivalries. Write a book about class, not about nationalism.' The tone of regret was because any analysis based on the concept of nationalism, however brilliant, would not just be a marginal academic pursuit, it would also be misleading. It would add to intellectual obfuscation by promoting what we used to pithily call 'false consciousness'; thereby legitimating the conflicts which it purported to analyse. Reading this book would therefore be more than a waste of time, it would be dangerous.

For those readers who choose to remain, the first response of this book to the pre-emptive criticism is to accept that nationalism is indeed a form of false consciousness, a 'vain thing', in the sense that it is an ideology offering a distorted perception of reality, containing selective simplifications and elements of myth. Neverthless, it is also a particularly powerful and pervasive ideology which convinces large numbers of people, and structures their political behaviour. Thus, while nationalism may indeed be stimulated by competing interests relating to disparities of access to power, status and wealth, it is also a major causal factor in politics; a belief in the grievances and destiny of nations which means that negotiable differences of interest become translated into non-negotiable confrontations between opposing national rights.

The present work begins by suggesting that debates concerning nationalism are sometimes rendered incoherent or confusing because of the mutual incomprehension arising from the use of different analytical languages. Nationalism may be viewed either as an embedded loyalty tying individual identity to the organic community; as a political resource used to mobilise individuals for the rational pursuit of common interests; or as an ideological myth appealing to confused individuals who seek simple formulas for the diagnosis of complex situations. But discussions of nationalism which mix primordialist ideas of instinctual loyalty, situationalist ideas of rational interest and constructivist ideas of non-rational ideology, are unlikely to be conducive to clear thought. It is suggested, then, that the constructivist view is most fruitful as the basis for the examination of nationalism; and it is this approach which is developed in the remainder of the book.

The second chapter outlines a constructivist explanation for the rise of the nation-state, and for the present contentiousness of nationalist politics. The suggestion is that, until recently, state élites were able, in varying degrees, to legitimate themselves as the agents of equitable development. The nation was portrayed as the vision of the social justice community, promising ethnocultural assimilation and civic integration. The erosion of developmental optimism, and thence the growth of disillusionment with these state élites, have exposed tensions between the previously intertwined visions offered by civic nationalism and ethnocultural nationalism. Ethnic minorities and regional peripheries have therefore begun to heed new promises of social justice which can reintwine ideas of civic and ethnocultural community in the context of minority rights claims. In the British case, for example, the cohesion of the United Kingdom as a 'nation-state' was previously manifested in the degree of interchangeability of the terms 'English' and 'British'. But such ambiguities seem to have given way to a clearer differentiation between 'English' perceived increasingly in ethnocultural terms, and 'British' perceived in predominantly civic terms.[1] This differentiation has arisen, particularly since the 1960s, out of the erosion of 'never had it so good' developmental optimism, and the consequent growth of accusations of 'English supremacism' by the emergent minority nationalisms in the UK.

The concepts of civic nationalism and ethnocultural nationalism are discussed in more detail in the third chapter, in order to examine why nationalism is portrayed as sometimes promoting the freedom and development of the individual, and sometimes generating their suppression. It is suggested that the political character of nationalism, its liberalism or illiberalism, is linked not to its civic or ethnocultural basis, but rather to the status position of those who articulate it, and to the developmental optimism or pessimism which underlies its construction.

The first three chapters thus suggest a series of propositions linking the construction of nationalist ideologies with the strength and cohesion of the nation. These propositions are examined in the following three chapters, in case-study discussions. Chapter 4 indicates how the constructivist view of nationalism, and the civic–ethnocultural distinction, might be applied to explain the changing politics of Basque nationalism in Spain. Chapter 5 uses the Singapore case to show how the ideologies of civic and ethnocultural nationalism might each be employed by state élites so as to strengthen the nation-state in the context of economic globalisation. Chapter 6 looks at the case of Ghana in order to indicate how the illiberal implications of reactive civic nationalism might vary, depending upon the type of enemies against which it is constructed.

If the strength of nation-states was in the past built upon the intertwining of civic nationalism and ethnocultural nationalism, then one of the major consequences of their unravelling has been the emergence of the new vision of multicultural nationalism – the vision of a national community which promises autonomy and integrity to its component ethnic minority segments. The three nationalist visions – civic, ethnocultural and multicultural – are summarised in chapter 7, in order to draw attention to the tensions between them. Chapter 8 then reflects on some of the political implications of attempts by state élites to manage or accommodate these tensions. Managerial (corporatist) responses, where the state seeks to resolve the tensions, are compared to pluralist responses, where the state seeks to blur the distinctions between divergent nationalist visions. It is suggested that the latter strategy might be the more fruitful basis for reconstructing cohesive nation-states in which visions of civic nationalism, ethnocultural nationalism and multicultural nationalism, might be reintwined.

The final chapter reminds us that there is as yet more unravelling than reintwining in contemporary nationalist politics. The examples of Northern Ireland, the Aboriginal issue in Australia, Rwanda and Kosovo, are used to illustrate how competing ideological visions of the nation are constructed, so as to resist attempts at reintwining, and to perpetuate the politics of nationalist confrontation.

1 The conceptual languages of nationalism

In 1963 Clifford Geertz referred to the 'stultifying aura of conceptual ambiguity' surrounding the subject of nationalism (Geertz 1963: 107). Since then, there has been a remarkable growth of perceptive works on the topic, but in the opinion of several influential writers on nationalism, the concept still refers to an 'unsteady mixture [of ideas] . . . unsuitable for clear analytical thought' (Dunn 1995: 3. Also Periwal 1995).[1]

The problem is sometimes explained as arising from the fact that nationalism is a 'category of practice', as well as a 'category of analysis' (Brubaker 1996:15). This implies that it is the very conceptual ambiguities which make it so useful for mobilising or manipulating political action in a wide variety of situations, which undermine its utility for clear explanation. Nations are often defined as communities united by their 'moral conscience' or their consciousness of themselves as a nation. This faces analysts of nationalism with a particular problem. Should they accept these self-definitions as their defining criterion of nationhood: should they accept these self-definitions only when they coincide with other 'objective' criteria (linguistic or genetic, for example); or should they depict these self-definitions as interesting symptoms in need of diagnosis?

Given the varying responses of different writers on nationalism to this problem, it is evident that we need a map of the terrain. One possibility is to seek such a map by tracing the 'historical evolution of nationalist thought' (Dahbour and Ishay 1995: 1), and guiding a reader down this evolutionary road; examining the major contributions, from both practitioners and analysts, along the way. Unfortunately, the evolutionary road begins to look rather like a maze, as similar conceptual approaches keep reappearing. The aim in this first chapter, therefore, is to offer clarification by disentangling three conceptual languages, which each generate distinct stories as to the nature of contemporary nationalist politics. The first story explains such politics as the assertion of the natural *primordial* rights of ethnic nations against contemporary multi-ethnic states; the second sees contemporary nations as in the process of being transformed by *situational* changes in the structure of the global economy; and the third sees assertions of nationalism as arising out of the search for new myths of certainty, *constructed* to resolve the insecurities and anxieties engendered by modernisation and globalisation.

These three conceptual languages, which see nationalism as, respectively, an instinct (primordialism), an interest (situationalism) and an ideology (constructivism), provide the nodal points within which the various writers on nationalism may be located (Figure 1). They are outlined here to show how they each generate differing stories as to the relationship between ethnicity and nationalism, the rise of nation-states, and the problematical character of contemporary nationalist politics. But they are also outlined in order to support the suggestion that one of these languages, the constructivist language which portrays nationalism as an ideology, might be preferred because it seems to answer some of the unresolved questions raised by the other approaches. The comparison of the three conceptual languages in this first chapter, thus paves the way for a more extended development and application of the constructivist approach in subsequent chapters.

The different approaches have sometimes been used to refer to different *types* of identity, contrasting an instinctual and primordial identity in less-developed societies, usually labelled 'tribalism', with an allegedly more rational form of affili-ation in the developed west, deserving of the title 'nationalism'; and distinguishing also between the authentic nationalist sentiment of the masses, and the xenophobic nationalist fictions sometimes articulated and manipulated by élites. No such distinctions are made here. Members of all national communities tend to believe that preferential loyalty to their communities is in some sense natural. The primordialist approach seeks to validate and specify that perception; the situationalist approach depicts it as the manifestation of rational interests; and the constructivist approach sees it as a politically constructed myth. Hitherto, the distinction between the three

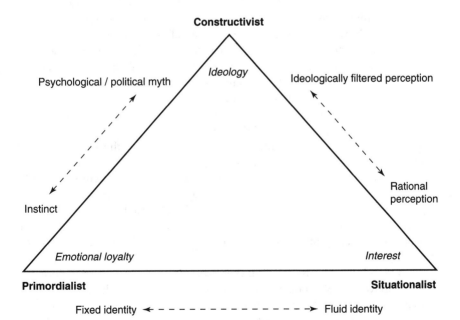

Figure 1 National identity – the three conceptual languages

approaches has been made most explicit in discussions of ethnicity, but since the concepts of ethnicity and nationalism are so closely intertwined, it seems likely that the disentangling of the three approaches might also clarify debates on nationalism.[2]

A primordialist approach to the study of nationalism

Primordialist approaches depict the nation as based upon a natural, organic community, which defines the identity of its members, who feel an innate and emotionally powerful attachment to it. Natural nations have natural rights to self-determination.

We need to begin by recognising the confusion which surrounds the term 'primordialism', and which persists because few writers on ethnicity and nationalism make their primordialist assumptions explicit.[3] The problem arises because the term is used sometimes to refer to a sense of identity, and sometimes also to refer to a particular kind of explanation for that sense of identity.[4] The belief that one is born into a particular linguistic, racial or homeland community, and therefore inevitably feels an overwhelming emotional bond with that community, is sometimes referred to as the 'primordial bond'. The primordialist explanation for this belief is, in effect, that it is true. The argument is that humanity has indeed evolved into distinct, organic communities, each with their own language and culture, with each individual's sense of identity derived from their location within one such community. When nations claim to be communities of common ancestry, they are, from the primordialist perspective, essentially correct. Primordialism thus explains the conflict and violence which characterises much of modern nationalist politics as arising from the discontinuity between the boundaries of the natural national communities which deserve and seek political autonomy, and those of the modern states. The fact that these modern states are usually called, and call themselves, 'nations', is regarded from this perspective either as a mistake, or as a politically motivated trick (Connor 1994: 90–117).

It is immediately apparent that, from this perspective, the only authentic nationalism is ethnic nationalism. The ethnic group is that community which claims common ancestry and sees the proof of this in the fact that its members display distinctive attributes relating to language, religion, physiognomy or homeland origin. The ethnic community is also characterised by the belief on the part of its members that there exists a natural emotional bond between the individual and the community, and that ethnic consciousness is indeed a central component of individual identity. The ethnic community thus constitutes an ethical community, whose members see themselves as having prior moral obligations to each other, over and above any obligations they owe to other communities. Ethnic identity may in some circumstances be taken for granted by those concerned, and need not necessarily generate claims to political rights. But once it is actively and self-consciously mobilised in order to legitimate claims that the ethnic community has some rights of self-determination, then ethnicity has become transformed into nationalism.

Primordialism recognises that the complex and opaque histories of contemporary national communities mean that we cannot show the factual truth of their claims to common ancestry. Indeed, most would accept Walker Connor's formulation that the nation is 'a group of people who *feel* that they are ancestrally related. It is the largest group that can command a person's loyalty because of *felt* kinship ties' (Connor 1994: 202, emphasis added). But the primordialist suggestion is that such beliefs are likely to be strongest when they are most authentic. Their transmission through the generations may indeed involve some distortion and simplification; they may well be adopted by assimilating minorities; and they may well be embroidered and elaborated by intellectuals and political élites. But it is suggested that kinship ideologies articulated by élites will only engender nationalist sentiment where they resonate with the collective memories of the wider populace, and where they refer to myths of common ancestry which are substantially true.

The primordialist approach has been criticised for being unable to offer any explanatory proof as to the basis for this bond between the individual and the ethnonational community. It does however offer several lines of thought which might be insightful, if unprovable. In its simplest version, primordialism claims that nations are organic communities united by the fact of common ancestry. This view is given some support by a significant literature on sociobiology, which suggests that there might be a genetic or instinctual mechanism leading us to favour kin over non-kin; a mechanism which is functional in biological terms for the survival of the genes of the individual and of their genetic relatives (Shaw and Wong 1989, Reynolds *et al.* 1987). Although such a mechanism would initially seem to apply only to communities defined on a racial basis, Pierre Van den Berghe has suggested that we are programmed to favour those who *appear* to be genetically related, on the basis of clues in the form of similarities of language and culture (Van den Berghe 1995). This gives rise to a more subtle version of primordialism which suggests that the natural, organic basis for nations derives, not from a genetic basis, but from the innate power of cultural affinities of language, religion and custom. Karl Jung gives support for this in his suggestion that primordialism might refer to the inheritence of a collective memory, an 'archetype of the collective unconscious' (Jung, in Campbell 1976: 56).

Many psychologists, and some contemporary communitarian theorists, suggest, however, that such 'group memories' are better explained in terms of the over-whelming influence of the primary socialisation processes, whereby the culture of a society is transmitted through the generations, in part from parents to children, but also in part through the public channels of religion, literature, education and the arts, so that the identity of the adult is moulded and fixed by the experiences of childhood (Black 1988, Sandel 1982). This kind of social psychological argument paves the way for what Anthony Smith has called the 'perennialist' variant of primordialism, exemplified in the work of Walker Connor and Donald Horowitz, in which ethnic and national groups whose pre-existence is assumed, are socialised into political consciousness by modern formulations of their common ancestry:

In this view, there is little difference between ethnicity and nationality: nations and ethnic communities are cognate, even identical phenomena. The perennialist readily accepts the modernity of national*ism* as a political movement and ideology, but regards nations either as updated versions of immemorial ethnic communities, or as collective identities that have existed, alongside ethnic communities, in all epochs of human history.

(Smith 1998: 159)[5]

All these formulations of primordialism agree that the development of individual identity is necessarily embedded in and defined by the culture of the community of birth and childhood, which has belief in common ancestry as its focal point.

Frequently, however, primordialist approaches to nationalism do not try to specify the precise nature of the ethnonational bond, and do not indeed overtly label themselves as primordialist. One strategy is simply to claim that ethnicity and nationalism refer to an emotional and spiritual bond which is 'ineffable' and 'unaccountable' (Geertz 1973: 259); which 'can not be explained rationally . . . [but only] obliquely analyzed by examining the type of catalysts to which it responds' (Connor 1994: 204). Alternatively, the primordialist approach is sometimes indicated only briefly, as if it were self-evident, by merely asserting that 'all peoples have the right to self-determination', and leaving it implied that the oppressed, minority or indigenous people referred to, do constitute in some sense an authentic and 'natural' community, with a correspondingly 'natural' right.

The awakening of the ethnic bond, and its development into the nationalist claim, is not usually depicted as being inevitable. So long as the ethnic community retains its autonomy, ethnic identity may remain at the 'taken for granted' level; a 'sleeping beauty' until awakened by the perception that the culture, cohesion or autonomy of the community is in some way threatened. But this awakening is unlikely to be spontaneous. Ethnic consciousness, and the formulation of nationalist responses to ethnic grievances, needs to be articulated and transmitted by activists who can show the link between the present threats, the authentic past, and the future destiny. These activists act therefore as historicists (Smith 1981) who help the community to rediscover its ethnic past and therefore its continuity and destiny, so as to turn the 'taken for granted' ethnic identity into a conscious national pride, which can be mobilised for the defence of its right to autonomous development. Such 'historicists' (the storytellers, the intelligentsia, the media) can dramatise and embroider, but cannot invent, the ethnic past of the nation.[6] Any attempt at invention would fail to resonate in the culture and collective memory of the society, and so would lack the power to mobilise. The success of the mobilisation is thus proof of the authenticity of the ethnic past.

Adrian Hastings (1997) offers an argument on these lines. He recognises, with Anthony Smith, that modern nations, whose roots go 'a very long way back indeed' (1997: 181), are 'constructed' only in the sense that they are 'an almost inevitable consequence of the interaction of a range of external and internal factors' (1997: 31), with the development of a vernacular literature, and religion, being seen as the key ingredients. It is these factors which lead some ethnic communities to 'naturally' develop into the integral element within nations. Anthony Smith and Adrian Hastings are important because they combine primordialist and constructivist themes so as to offer subtle explanations of the continuities between modern nationalism, whose conscious collective identity and memories are generated and carried in their literature and religion; and their core ethnic roots, whose myths of common genetic descent contain, in Hasting's words, 'a necessary core of original truth' (1997: 169. See n. 6 in the Notes section).

During the 1950s and1960s, primordialist approaches were applied most explicitly to the discussion of ethnic conflict in less-developed societies, on the assumption that political behaviour in such 'backward' societies was most likely to be based on emotion and instinct, and on ancestrally based 'tribal' affiliations. By the same token, it was widely assumed, at that time, that the processes of modernisation would lead to more rational forms of political behaviour as development occurred, promoting either a universalistic rationality, or at least an intrinsically democratic form of civic nationalism focused upon identification with the modern state, rather than with the community of common ancestry. But any such optimism was eroded from the late 1960s onwards, when ethnic and nationalist conflict escalated, with the onset of civil rights unrest in the USA, the conflicts of Biafra and Bangladesh, and the upsurge of violence in Northern Ireland and the Basque country. In the face of such apparent failures of the modernisation process to integrate the current nation-states in either the developed or the developing countries, primordialist approaches have revived. But, in the process, the moral evaluation of the primordialist ethnic bond has undergone some reassessment. Primordialist explanations of ethnic assertions in the third world tended in the 1950s and 1960s to depict them in negative terms, as outbursts of inward and backward-looking irrational intolerance. However, the application of this approach to the study of contemporary ethnic minority claims has depicted ethnic assertions as ethically valuable bases for individual self-fulfilment and collective self-determination.

The primordialist explanation of contemporary nationalist politics rests on the claim that the history of state-formation has been primarily one of conquest and migration. This means that virtually all modern states contain societies which are ethnically heterogeneous. The pattern of such multi-ethnicity, and the nature of their nationalist claims, varies greatly, depending upon whether the state contains several homeland communities, as in Russia; several communities claiming the same homeland, as in Israel; or several migrant communities, as in Singapore.

Such disparities in ethnic structure generate differences in the resultant politics, but from the primordialist perspective these are all variations on a common theme, which is stated most clearly in the plural society model of politics (Kuper and Smith 1969). Nationalist thinkers such as Herder and Fichte had suggested that each distinct linguistic nation ought to enjoy political self-determination by forming its own sovereign state. This was not just a moral right, it was also a prudential move – since only states formed on such an ethnic basis would be held together by the necessary common values, so that they could develop as harmonious, stable and democratic societies. States which were not ethnically homogeneous would lack such normative consensus, and would therefore tend to fragment into ethnic rivalries if they were not held together by some form of state force. The ethnocentric loyalties and disparate values of each ethnic segment would necessarily generate political tensions as to the allocation of resources and power. In Walker Connor's words:

> it is evident that for most people the sense of loyalty to one's [ethno-]nation and to one's state do not coincide . . . [W]hen the two loyalties are perceived as being in irreconcilable conflict – that is to say when people feel they must choose between them – [ethno-]nationalism customarily proves the more potent.
>
> (Connor 1994: 196)

There are two formulations of the resultant politics. One possibility is that those aspects of the modernisation process which promote integration might be actively engineered by the 'nation-building' activities of state élites, so that primordial ethnic sentiments can be either eroded, or accommodated within an encapsulating sense of nation-state identity. This process does make two assumptions which are, from the primordialist perspective, highly unlikely. The first is that new rational attachments to nation-states become more powerful than the emotional and instinctual primordial bonds. The second is that the state has sufficient legitimacy and managerial capacity to modify or manipulate people's sense of identity in this way.

The other, more likely possibility, is that the élites of one of the ethnic segments in such a plural society – the largest, best organised, best educated, or the one which dominates the armed forces – manage to infiltrate or capture the state institutions of government and administration, so as to ensure that their ethnic segment retains higher cultural, economic and political status. This may be done overtly through policies of ethnic discrimination and exclusion, or more covertly by the promotion of ethnocultural assimilation whereby entry into high-status positions is opened to those who acquire the cultural attributes of the dominant ethnic segment.

It is this latter tendency, in which ethnic domination is disguised as national integration, which seems to offer the most widely applicable and feasible explanation of ethnic tensions. In Anthony Smith's and Adrian Hastings's formulations, previously noted, modern states have only been able to generate a strong sense of national identity among their people to the extent that intelligentsia have been able to link the sense of nationhood to its authentic ethnic roots. This process implies that citizens of the state who are of ethnic minority background thus come to believe that they can culturally assimilate into the dominant ethnic community and can therefore celebrate their adoption of, and association with, its history. Over time, they will even adopt its myths of common ancestry as their own.

> Though most latter-day nations are, in fact polyethnic, or rather most nation-states are polyethnic, many have been formed in the first place around a dominant *ethnie*, which annexed or attracted other *ethnies* or ethnic fragments into the state to which it gave a name and a cultural charter . . . The presumed

boundaries of the nation are largely determined by the myths and memories of the dominant ethnie.

(Smith 1991: 39)

But the success of the enterprise might be unlikely. The primordialist approach has stressed that it is the authenticity of the claim to common kinship which gives it its emotional power. This means that the attempt by a dominant ethnic core to persuade the ethnic minorities to assimilate by adopting an objectively false kinship myth, is unlikely to succeed. This doubt is reinforced by the reality that citizens who belong to minority ethnic segments face barriers to assimilation, and are thereby marginalised. So long as the state employs authoritarian controls, it can hope to suppress minority ethnic claims in order to maintain national unity and order, but modern states have recently faced various problems in maintaining such authoritarian controls. The end of the cold war reduced the ideological certainty and cohesion of some state élites, so that these states became corroded by internal factional rivalries and therefore became less effective as agencies of social control. This was the case for example with the state élites of Yugoslavia and South Africa in the 1980s. Moreover, the spread of democratisation since the 1970s has provided new legitimate channels through which minority ethnic claims can be made. Such weakening or democratisation of the state serves, therefore, to take the political control 'lid' off the tensions which have hitherto been contained in the multi-ethnic states claiming to be nations.

The primordialist view indicates that solutions to such political issues must be sought in the granting of maximum autonomy to each ethnic community, with the ideal being that of a world divided into ethnically homogeneous nation-states. But since migrations have made this unattainable – or rather have meant that attempts at its attainment might involve some form of 'ethnic cleansing', primordialists have begun to argue for various forms of limited or non-territorial forms of sovereignty – modifying previous ideas of the absolute sovereignty of the state so as to ensure special international legal protections for ethnic minorities. Primordialist views are frequently also referred to in arguments for 'multiculturalism', when the state is called upon to give institutional recognition to the claims of the authentic ethnic communities within its society, whose cultural distinctiveness and cohesion is proclaimed as being an essential source of identity for its individual members (Lijphart 1977).

Evaluation

The primordialist argument that ethnic and national identities are emotionally powerful and ascriptively fixed, is probably so widely accepted because it accords with the consciousness of those involved. Individuals who claim an ethnic or national identity know the emotional power of their ethnocentricity, and believe that it refers to objective attributes deriving from common ancestry; though they may be hard-pressed to specify which of those attributes are the decisive markers of identity. As a description of perceptions of identity, primordialism is rather good; but various critics have suggested that it is less satisfactory as an explanation of the causes of such perceptions (Eller and Coughlan 1993). Indeed, the core criticism is that it offers no explanation at all, merely taking such identities as (primordially) given. But this does not necessarily make it wrong.

The test is rather whether it turns out, in practice, to offer useful insights. My own evaluation of its limitations can best be explained by describing the particular case where I first sought to apply it. I was doing fieldwork in the 1970s, studying local-level politics in an Ewe-speaking community in Ghana, West Africa.[7] I went there armed with the knowledge that West Africa was one of the most ethnically divided areas of the third world, and that the Ewe were one of the most 'tribalistic' communities of West Africa. These preconceptions were supported by the fact that the most recent elections in Ghana (1969) had split the country on ethnic lines, with the Akan majority overwhelmingly supporting the Akan candidate for Prime Minister, and the Ewe minority supporting the Ewe candidate; the latter, not surprisingly, losing. Primordialist preconceptions were further reinforced by the knowledge that the Ewe community, divided by the international border between Ghana and Togo, maintained an active Ewe unification movement; and that Togolese politics were also dominated by an ethnic split – with the Ewe-based government having recently been removed by a *coup* of the northern (mainly Kabre) military. I went into the study of this politics armed with the assumption that, although the forces of modernisation might be progressively weakening these ethnic bonds as national integration progressed, the contemporary political tensions were nevertheless precisely the kind of 'direct conflict between primordial and civil sentiments', which Clifford Geertz had identified as the main problem facing new states (1963: 111).

But the more I found out about the details of Ghanaian nationalism and 'Ewe tribalism', the less they seemed to fit the primordialist assumptions. It soon became clear, from archival documents and interviews, that the idea of an Ewe ethnic community was a twentieth-century phenomenon. Prior to this time, the only communities which were politically salient were those relating to local-level clan, village and chiefdom communities, and to the rivalry between the southern (Anlo) chiefdoms, and northern (Krepi) chiefdoms, which had been stimulated by invasion of the area from the neighbouring Ashanti empire. It was indeed the case that all of the present-day Ewe community shared a common myth of origin and migration (involving flight from the oppressive rule of King Agorkoli at Nuatja), but the story in each case was of flights by each family, to establish distinct chiefdoms each with their own dialect, identity, and histories of mutual rivalry. The sense of Ewe identity was clearly something new, which had developed after the introduction by the colonial rulers of the international border. Second, investigation showed that several of the clans whose elders were interviewed and who initially recounted the Nuatja migration myth as their own, were actually of Akan origin, having fled to this area during the Ashanti wars. They regarded themselves, and were regarded by their neighbours, fully as Ewes, despite the fact of their Akan origins. Third, the view that contemporary politics was dominated by inter-ethnic rivalry, was soon shown to be superficial and misleading. Not only were the Ewe deeply divided by factional, village and chiefdom rivalries over almost every twentieth-century political issue, but, for the large majority, their commitment to the Ewe unification movement was either latent or remained at the symbolic level, while their commitment to Ghanaian nationalism was both conscious and integrated into their daily lives. But instead of finding any clash between primordial and civil sentiments, it became clear that the political perceptions of individuals were structured so that attachments to clan, village, faction, chiefdom, administrative region, ethnic community, political party and nation-state, were complementary and intertwined. Finally, it seemed likely that the 1969 election result in Ghana might not reflect any deep-seated ethnic tension; but was rather a situational response to the contingencies of the nomination process, which gave voters the choice only between an Ashanti and an Ewe candidate. In a situation where those from each village and each administrative region knew from past experience that the best way of getting development resources was by having a 'home boy' in power, it seemed more likely that it was rational self-interest, rather than primordial ethnic bias, which dictated voting behaviour.

Such doubts concerning the ability of the primordialist approach to illuminate this particular case led, therefore, towards consideration of an alternative approach in which Ewe nationalism was depicted more as a resource for the pursuit of self-interests, than as an ascribed emotional loyalty.

A situationalist approach to the study of nationalism[8]

Situationalism explains ethnic and national identities, not as natural instinctual ties to organic communities, but rather as resources employed by groups of individuals for the pursuit of their common interests. As the type of threats and opportunities with which people are faced change, so do their options and their responses. Thus, both the utility of ethnicity and nationalism, and the form which they take, will vary in response to changing situations.

Perhaps the dominant situationalist explanation of the rise of modern nation-states, and of the contemporary politics of contending nationalist claims, is to see these as responses to changes in the economic environment; thus the modernist variant, discussed in Chapter 2, argues that nation-states emerged because they were useful economic units for the earlier stages of industrialisation, but that the further globalisation of the economy makes such national units less appropriate, so as to weaken the contemporary nation-states.

The argument begins with the liberal assumption that individuals seek in general to promote their freedom, self-fulfilment or self-realisation; and that this is manifested in their pursuit of particular self-interests. At both levels – the pursuit of self-realisation and the pursuit of particular interests – individuals frequently find it useful to ally with others in 'interest groups', or what Dov Ronen calls 'functional aggregations' (1979: 54–62). The extent to which these interest groups become central to the individual's sense of identity (in Ronen's terms, the extent to which they become 'conscious aggregations') varies, and depends both on the type and extent of the interests to which they refer, and on the type and intensity of the threats or opportunities with which the individual is faced. In general terms, we would expect that the more central the interests are to the pursuit of self-realisation, and the more intense the threats, the greater would be the conscious sense of individual identification with the interest group. The argument is sometimes presented in structuralist terms, indicating that the options open to individuals might sometimes be restricted by external structures, as in confrontational situations, to such an extent that group behaviour is largely determined. But instead of taking the primordialist route of depicting such structures as the 'ineffable' and 'coercive' powers which trigger instinctual responses, the situationalist approach stresses both the extent to which such situations are changeable and manipulable, and also the extent to which individual responses do vary. As Hechter explains:

> Rational choice considers individual behaviour to be a function of the interaction of structural constraints and the sovereign preferences of individuals. The structure first determines, to a greater or lesser extent, the constraints under which individuals act. Within these constraints, individuals face various feasible courses of action. The course of action ultimately chosen is selected rationally.
>
> (1986: 268)

Thus, individuals align in ways which seem to them to provide the most useful resource for the pursuit of their interests, in the prevailing circumstances. Faced with a threat, individuals will vary, depending upon their preferences, as to whether they exit, fight, align with the enemy, appeal to religion, or turn to alcohol etc. But where their preferences are similar, as is more likely for those brought up in a common culture, it may become more possible to predict aggregate behaviour. Thence the general assumption that beneficial and equal interactions with others are likely to lead individuals to identify with the interactive community. This was Karl Deutsch's explanation of why increasing social interactions within a state-territory would promote national integration. By the same token, unequal interactions with threatening others will tend to lead individuals to identify reactively, into 'us' and 'them' communities; thence Michael Hechter's view that unequal interactions between core and peripheral regions within a country would promote reactive peripheral nationalism. The most pithy statement of this situationalist approach is that by Dov Ronen, to the effect that it is the 'them' which determines the 'us' (1979: 56).

It is clear that individuals do in fact identify in varying degrees and in varying situations, with a wide range of groupings based on affiliations of, for example, ideology, occupation, class, gender or locality; as well as on affiliations of ethnicity and nationalism. The particular prevalence of the latter ethnic and national affiliations cannot, from the situationalist perspective, be explained by arguing that they have any innate priority over other possible affiliations. Instead, it is argued that they are prevalent because they appear to offer particular utility to individual and group interests in the context of contemporary situational opportunities and threats. They do this in various ways. Ethnicity and nationalism often refer to easily identifiable identity markers, such as language or clothing, which facilitate political mobilisation. They also frequently refer to the social interaction networks within which individuals develop their 'way of life', so that it might seem rational for such individuals to defend the interests connected with that way of life. Ethnic and national claims also have an important advantage over other attachments which cannot so easily portray themselves as natural, in that they can more easily clothe the interests being defended in the language of natural rights, and thereby provide particularly effective ways to strengthen a bargaining position.

From the situationalist perspective, the term 'ethnicity' is sometimes used to refer to communities making claims for cultural autonomy, whereas the term 'nationalism' is used where territorial homeland claims are being made; but the distinction is a permeable one since both refer to the political defence of rational attachments to the interactive community.

There seem, however, to be several problems with trying to provide a rational-choice explanation for political affiliations which are not perceived as rational choices by those involved, which are emotionally powerful, and which clearly sometimes impel people to acts of irrational prejudice and hatred. But the problems might be more apparent than real. First, emotions may surely be either irrational or non-rational in the sense that they can either distort our perceptions of the world, or can comprise reactions which complement rationality. It would be difficult to argue, for example, that it is irrational for us to become afraid in the face of attack, or to become emotionally involved in the defence or pursuit of those interests which we consider to be most central to our life goals.

Second, it is clear that I may have little or no choice in the kind of language, racial or religious attributes which I possess, or in the territory of my birth and upbringing. But the degree to which any of these is central to my sense of identity is not similarly fixed, and their significance as a basis for group consciousness may vary enormously. My religion may be politically irrelevant in one situation, but politically salient in another. My sense of identity may refer to my place of birth in some contexts, but to my place of current residence in others. Similarly, the graded variations among humanity of physiognomy or dialect or sect do not, of themselves, provide clear boundary markers which demarcate the 'us' from the 'them'. But when people in threat situations perceive that there is some differential clustering of such attributes among the confronting communities, it may well become pragmatically useful for them to employ such attributes as alignment markers and mobilising devices.

Third, it is evident that in the face of external threats or challenges, individuals frequently make choices in line with peer-group, or authority pressure, such that they do not in fact feel to be making rational individual choices. It is, however, often neither functional nor sensible for each individual to try to interpret a new situation in isolation. It might be more rational, in the face of potential danger, to trust in the judgements of others, the many or the experts, who we believe are likely to have already arrived at diagnoses of the situation.[9] Individuals thus frequently rely upon information from élite activists who can explain the nature of the situational threats or opportunities to them, and who can mobilise support for an appropriate group response. Such élite activists may indeed dramatise the situation so as to explain it in simple comprehensible terms, and may sometimes offer misleading information to their audiences, but false diagnoses are unlikely to be given credence. Situationalism and primordialism agree on this point. In John Dunn's words, 'No lies will deceive either speaker or audience so effectively when necessary, as lies which are largely or usually true' (1980: 59). Thus the more extreme the situational pressures, the less likely is the perception of free choice on the part of the individual subject to those pressures. But the decision to react in the way which common sense, conformity, or authority figures seems to indicate, is, none the less, a rational decision, even if, on occasion, a mistaken one.

Fourth, if situational explanations of ethnic and national identities depict them as fluid responses to changing circumstances, how are we to explain why they are perceived by those involved as being fixed and even ascriptive? Part of the answer is simply that some of the situations to which these identities are a reaction, relate to structures of power which are embedded in the state system or the economy, and are therefore of long-standing. But it is also a feature of ethnic and national consciousness that even though the decision to grant social and political significance to a particular attribute (language, territory, religion, etc.) as an identity marker, is an act of choice, the fact of the permanence of that marker means that the new identity consciousness may become perceived as correspondingly permanent. Thus an Australian citizen might choose to portray their identity, to themselves and others, by reference to their place of origin (e.g. Italy), or their present homeland (Australia) or their race or religion (e.g. Jewish). But once chosen, this identity can be portrayed as fixed and natural because the attribute to which it refers is itself permanent.

Finally, it may be noted that the situationalist explanation for ethnic and national identities, is, at several points, comparable to the Marxist explanation of class identity. The term 'class' is used in Marxism to refer both to an individual's objective location in the production process, and also to a sense of identity and group consciousness, which, in that it involves perceptions of exploitation, is manifested in emotional terms. Class consciousness, like ethnic and national consciousness, frequently develops only after being mobilised by vanguard activists who can explain the true structure of the situation to their followers. Both are regarded as rational reactions to the perception of a threatening other, and also as emotional attachments to an ethical community. The linkages between the two forms of identity are indeed such that, in some formulations of situationalism, ethnic and national identities are depicted as a form of class consciousness; as with the 'cultural division of labour' approach discussed below (see p. 18).

The situationalist approach claims to provide a straightforward explanation both for the rise of modern nation-states, and also for the contemporary upsurge of nationalist contention, by seeing both as arising fundamentally out of interest-based responses to changes in the structure of the global economy. It is possible to identify such situationalist threads in the rich literature on modern nationalism, without implying that the explanations offered by such important writers as Benedict Anderson or Ernest Gellner, for example, are consistently or solely situationalist in focus. But isolating the situationalist aspects of their arguments may help to show how their differing formulations relate to, and in some respects complement, each other.

Theories of modernisation, which flourished between the 1950s and the 1970s, suggested that modernisation and national integration were intrinsically connected. The general argument was that the emergence of the modern centralised state with effective and sovereign control over a demarcated territory, facilitated the socio-economic integration of the society within that territory. The resultant development of economic interdependence, and of social interactions, led to a new awareness of common interests and common values which manifested itself as a growing sense of 'national' community, so that the state became the nation-state, and thereby became more centralised, effective and sovereign.

The situational core to such arguments is most explicit in those formulations which focused upon industrialisation as the core component of modernisation. The development of modern nation-states, which occurred in Europe around the late eighteenth century, was depicted as being both generated by the development of industrial capitalism, and also conducive to its growth. Two processes were involved. First, capitalism generated new bourgeoisies who sought political power in new states, which could provide the political and legal framework for the new economies. Second, the spread of industrialisation led to distinct networks of economic and social interaction, which generated a corresponding development, among the wider populace in each emergent economic region, of perceptions of common identity. Thus Ernest Gellner argues that the industrialisation process, which was uneven in its impact and emerged in particular centres, required new autonomous and efficient political units to replace the decentralised and weak medieval empires of Europe (Gellner 1983). These new states could promote social mobility between groups of differing dialects and cultures by training workers and managers into a common culture and common language. Eric Hobsbawm similarly argued that capitalism required new political units which could provide the necessary legal frameworks, political control and markets (Hobsbawm 1990). It was therefore in the interests of the dominant bourgeoisies to promote the spread of new nationalist cultures. Karl Deutsch located the growth of industry and commerce as the key factors generating new networks of social communication, which provided the basis for the mobilisation of new feelings of nationalism (1966). Benedict Anderson located the core precondition for the emergence of modern nation-states in the development of 'print-capitalism' which facilitated the spread of a common vernacular language and literature, so that the modern nation could develop as a new imagined community (1983).

The subsequent spread of the modern nation-state, beyond its western European home, is then usually explained partly in terms of the global spread of industrialisation and commerce, and partly as a political reaction to colonialism. Such nationalism is thus understandable in situational terms as the new sense of community engendered by social and economic interactions within the new states, and also as the reactive communities engendered by unequal interactions with the West. Nationalism then became a resource which new political élites could employ to mobilise support for themselves. Since it is rational for individuals to identify with the social, economic and political unit which appears to them to best promote their interests, this unit thereafter develops also as a corresponding cultural unit. The modern nation-state thus emerges as a socio-economic community, a political community, and a cultural community.

If it was indeed the early phases of the spread of industrialisation and commerce which gave rise to the development of modern nation-states; then it would be consistent to argue that the present problems of these nation-states might also be explainable in similarly situationalist terms, as the outcome of changes in the global economy. Indeed, the argument that economic globalisation is irretrievably weakening the nation-state, is frequently depicted, these days, as merely common sense (Ohmae 1995).

There are two main formulations of the argument that changes in the economic situation have weakened contemporary nation-states. The first such argument to emerge was the 'internal colonialism' theory associated particularly with the work of Michael Hechter. Building upon the insight that it was the uneven spread of industrialisation in distinct territorial centres which had led to the emergence of modern nation-states, Hechter suggested that the subsequent uneven development of industrialisation within and across these nation states, whereby metropolitan areas developed by extracting resources from peripheral regions, led to the emergence of new peripheral nationalisms directed against the state. Since cultural variations between those in the core and peripheral regions of the nation-state are extremely likely, this economic disparity tended to engender a 'cultural division of labour', such that those whose cultural attributes identified them as members of the peripheral region found themselves clustered in low-status occupations, while those with the cultures of the core region dominated the high-status positions. This clustering engendered the belief on the part of each community that their economic position derived from their cultural attributes – the peripheral community perceiving themselves as discriminated against because of their low-status culture; and the core community perceiving their higher economic status as proof of their cultural superiority. The result was the development of ethnic consciousness among each regional community, and thence of ethnic rivalry. In those cases where the peripheral community had access to political élites and intelligentsia who could articulate and mobilise their ethnic identity in support of claims to regional resource and autonomy claims, then their ethno-regional consciousness could provide a basis for nationalist movements.

The second situational approach to explaining the contemporary upsurge of ethnic and regional nationalist claims against existing nation-states emerges out of the proliferating literature on economic globalisation. If nation-states developed because they were the appropriate economic units for the early stages of industrialisation, then it follows that, as the capitalist networks expand beyond national boundaries to become global in scope, and the distinctiveness of the national economies erode, so will the corresponding sense of national identity decline. It is frequently suggested that in the long run, this will lead to new larger regional senses of identity, with the European Union sometimes being depicted as a model. But in the short term, the erosion of the economic management capabilities of state élites exposes peripheral communities in each state to new economic-competition threats, and thereby engenders various types of reactive nationalism as marginalised communities, within existing nation-states, seek sufficient autonomy to protect their economic self-interests.

Evaluation

The situationalist approach offers an important insight in its recognition that the sense of community based on ethnic or national identity can be a response to commonalities of interest; and that ethnic and nationalist movements can be vehicles for the defence of such interests in the face of economic or power disparities. It makes it clear that ethnic and national identities which depict themselves in the primordialist language of historical continuity, might nevertheless involve fluid and rational responses to changing situations.

But the attempt to incorporate both structuralist and rational-choice elements into the situationalist approach does open up a problem. As Michael Hechter has recognised, individuals within a community who make choices in response to similar situational constraints, may nevertheless vary in the range and order of the preferences from which they choose; unless there exists some mechanism for 'the systematic limitation and distortion of information about alternatives existing beyond the group's boundaries' (1986: 275). This explains why some formulations of the situationalist approach offer rather ambiguous depictions of the role of the élite activists who mobilise support for nationalist movements (Brass 1985). Should we interpret their behaviour as offering simplified but accurate diagnoses of situations, or are they telling lies? Or are they themselves likely to believe the misleading information which they articulate? Also, is it indeed the case that lies will fail to effectively mobilise followers, and will not be believed, if they do not accord with other data? If we were to accept that mobilising élites sometimes either deliberately or unwittingly act as inventors of lies rather than as communicators of the situation, and that followers sometimes accept these lies even in the face of countervailing evidence, then the core assumption of situationalism – that nationalist politics can be understood in terms of functional and rational responses to situational changes – would appear to be called into question.

In order to examine this, it might be useful to return to my problem of interpreting the nature of ethnic politics regarding the Ewe community of Ghana. It soon became clear that while national politics were dominated, in the 1970s, by rivalry between Ewes and Akan élites, this could not be fully explained by the extent of the status, power or economic disparities between the two communities; or by the degree of boundedness between their respective interaction networks. Such disparities and distinctions were much more marked between the southern Akan and various ethnic communities of the northern regions; and yet this did not apparently generate politically salient ethnic tensions. The answer seemed to be that the Akan élites, who dominated the state, repeatedly depicted the Ewes as tribalists, oppositionists, and secessionists. Ewe élites, for their part, depicted the Akans as aggressive and arrogant tribalists. These stereotypes were not validated by the everyday experiences which arose from the frequent interactions between the two communities; but they were none the less influential and powerful myths, since they could be validated by selective reference to the known histories of nineteenth-century Ashanti invasion, the known agitation of some Ewes for unification with neighbouring Togo, and the known support of many Ewes for those political parties which had failed to gain governmental power. The conclusion seemed to be that 'Ewe tribalism' should be explained primarily as a kind of ideological myth propagated by politically dominant Akan élites, rather than simply as a sense of community which derived either from the rational responses of individuals to situational options; or from the primordial givens of their common ancestry.[10] This observation of the perceived limitations of the situational approach to explain fully the Ewe case, should not be seen as an attempt to deny its insights. Indeed, the recognition that ethnic and national identities are mobilised as responses to situational factors, is crucial as the starting point for seeking to understand the ways in which the ideological myths of ethnic and national identity are constructed and employed by political élites. But this needs a shift away from the assumption of rational choice, and towards a focus on the politics of how identities are ideologically constructed.

A constructivist approach to the study of nationalism

Constructivist approaches suggest that national identity is constructed on the basis of institutional or ideological frameworks which offer simple and indeed simplistic formulas of identity, and diagnoses of contemporary problems, to otherwise confused or insecure individuals.

Why do so many people feel an emotionally powerful sense of national consciousness and loyalty? The primordialist answer was to say that the feeling must be innate, and derive from the fact that nations are based on real substantive groups which are natural organic entities preceding social interactions. The situationalist answer was to say that they are indeed real substantive groups, but are formed as a result of social interactions and gain power from their utility in the defence and pursuit of crucial 'way of life' interests common to those involved. The constructivist answer begins by denying that nations are real substantive entities, and suggesting that the perception by those involved that they *are* real should be understood as a form of ideological consciousness which filters reality, rather than reflects it.

It has been noted in the preceding discussions that national identity may vary in the primary attributes to which it refers; it may refer to place of personal birth;

place of parental or ancestral birth; place of current residence; the governmental regime one inhabits; the language of public or private use; the religious group one is born into or converts to; or some aspect of biological attributes. No one of these is essential to national identity, and the selected attributes do not themselves determine the level or label by which they are identified. Similarly, it is clear that the 'sociological temptation' to find the 'real' factors which comprise the general causes of nationalism, in the authenticity of an ethnic core or in the industrialisation process for example, seems to point rather to the variability of its causality (Kedourie 1993: 140). But it does not necessarily follow from this that the concept of nationalism should be dismissed for its 'conceptual ambiguity'. Its conceptual rigour may lie, not in the external attributes to which it refers and the external causes which generate it, but rather in the functions which it performs and the way in which it performs them.

The core function of nationalism is most usually stated as being that of offering individuals a sense of identity; and the suggestion that such a sense of identity might be neither rationally chosen nor innately given, but constructed largely unconsciously or intuitively as a category of understanding, is offered in its most straightforward form by some formulations of 'new institutionalism' (March and Olsen 1989, Koelble 1995). This suggests that the institutional arrangements which an individual inhabits may become the defining categories of political understanding concerning their identity, interests and goals. Thus when the state organises parliamentary representation, regional structures, interest associations or identity documents specifically on a racial, ethnic or nationality basis, such institutionalisations come to define the ideological parameters for those who function within them. They provide, in Rogers Brubaker's words:

> a pervasive system of social classification, an organizing 'principle of vision and division' of the social world, a standardized scheme of social accounting, an interpretative grid for public discussion, a set of boundary-markers, a legitimate form for public and private identities, and . . . a ready-made template for claims to sovereignty. Institutional definitions of nationhood . . . constitute basic categories of political understanding, central parameters of political rhetoric, specific types of political interest, and fundamental forms of political identity.
>
> (1996: 24)

But Brubaker is referring here specifically to the situation of the Soviet Union, in which the Communist political élites created the institutions of national republics and national identity classifications in order to try to co-opt, contain, and emasculate the political expression of nationalism. By the late 1980s, it became clear that their impact had been the opposite one, of ensuring that individuals of minority nationalities identified their own status with that of their nationality, and their own aspirations for freedom with the goal of national liberation. But it is clear that assertions of national identity sometimes flourish precisely because of their suppression by the state, rather than their institutionalisation, so that we need to examine the issue of identity-formation more closely.

Since all approaches to the study of nationalism agree that it is an idea – whether a sense of identity, a form of consciousness, a rights belief, or a feeling of affiliation – it might be sensible to begin by looking at its psychology. The approach here is to depict it as one of several psychological mechanisms which individuals employ to provide simple formulas for locating themselves in relation to others. Rather than being paralysed by the philosophically and sociologically difficult question 'who are you?', we seek simple labels which quickly communicate to others those aspects of our attributes or thoughts which we wish to highlight. We define ourselves as young or old, male or female, black or white, left-wing or right-wing. Such labels are not (often) false, but they are never merely descriptive, in that their purpose is precisely to simplify selectively.

But such ideological labels are rarely freely or consciously chosen, nor are they usually constructed in isolation. They sometimes feel more like 'old clothes' than consciously selected uniforms (Nairn 1997: 183) in that in some circumstances at least we take them for granted as habitual or apparently natural aspects of ourselves. But this is only so when they seem to be validated by the others with whom we interact. When we interact with others for whom our identity label evokes hatred or disdain, then we become more conscious of it so as to either assert it strongly, or deliberately retreat from it. But when we interact with others who merely find our identity label confusing, because it does not fit with their mental maps of the world, then we are led to look within ourselves or our social environment for an alternative label which will better ease our sense of isolation. (My self-label as 'agnostic' was quickly replaced by 'Christian' while in Singapore, when the former label evoked mainly confused silence.)

Nationalism is thus one of several formulas which solve problems relating to my feelings of isolation by defining me as a member of one distinct community demarcated from other such communities. It offers me 'an escape from triviality, [and] gives a sense of immortality' (Minogue 1967: 32). It also provides me with an instant diagnosis of contemporary ills, a prescription for their remedy, and a vision of a world in which 'everyone will live happily ever after' (Kedourie 1994: xiii). It offers me a moral legitimation, in the language of rights, for the defence of a range of my personal interests, which might otherwise be regarded as merely selfish. But nationalism is not alone in making such promises of ideological support, so why is it so successful?[11]

The answer is in two parts. First, nationalism is particularly able to offer individuals the ideological myths of ancestry, kinship, permanence and home, which promise a sense of identity, security and moral authority to individuals faced with the complexities and uncertainties of modernity. Second, individuals are more likely to need this form of ideological support if their face-to-face communities and authority structures of family and locality are being attenuated or disrupted by various aspects of the 'modernisation' process.

Nationalism as a psychological ideology

Nationalism clearly has a rational basis in the concern of individuals to defend the 'way of life' in which they grew up and feel at ease. But the consequent development of prior ethical obligations to the 'us', and the exaggeration and stereotyping of distinctions between the 'us' and the 'them', indicate that there is also a non-rational aspect. In most discussions of the politics of nationalism, this latter element seems to be given cursory treatment. Brief references tend to be made to some instinctual herd instinct for affiliation with in-groups against out-groups, or to the psychological need for a sense of identity. But the psychological dimension demands more attention. Explanations of nationalism in terms of its functionality for the industrial-isation process must surely recognise, as Ernest Gellner does, the individual's search for a resolution of the stress and 'perpetual humiliation' which the incongruences of modern life engender (1996: 626).[12] Similarly, those who depict nationalism as an ideological doctrine propagated by élites, must recognise, as Elie Kedourie does, that the 'metaphysics' of this doctrine 'cannot adequately account for the frenzy they conjure up in their followers' (1993: 96). The same applies to those who portray nationalism as a sense of community based on shared memories and myths, since they must explain why individuals seek such collective remembering. As Anthony Smith indicates, nationalist myths fulfil 'intimate, internal functions for individuals in communities', providing 'a powerful means of . . . enabling us to "rediscover" ourselves, the "authentic self", or so it has appeared to many divided and disoriented individuals' (1991: 17).

It is thus widely recognised that nationalism is powerful because it fulfils emotional functions for individuals. But if we are to specify these functions, we need an appropriate language which can give some precision to ideas of 'humiliation', 'frenzy' and 'divided and disoriented individuals'. This needs concepts which explain the non-rational aspects of mythical representations of reality, and the ways in which individual identities are in turn constructed by those myths. As Stephen Frosh has noted,

> it demands a language able to grapple with psychological phenomena which are more extensive than those of consciously willed acts . . . A language, therefore, of the unconscious – of the impulses, anxieties, wishes and contradictory desires that are structured and restructured by our immersion in the social order. Such a language is, of course, the central component of psychoanalysis.
>
> (1991: 1–2)

There are several studies of nationalism from a partly or predominantly psycho-analytic perspective (Finlayson 1998, Volkan 1998; Group for the Advancement of Psychiatry 1987; Kristeva 1993; Kecmanovic 1996; Salecl 1990).[13] The aim here is not to summarise these, but rather to indicate briefly two of the psychological mechanisms, examined in psychoanalysis, which elucidate the construction of nationalism's primary myths. The first myth refers to the belief that the community is authentic because of its objective permanence, defined by national character, territory and institutions, and by its continuity across the generations. The second myth refers to the belief that the community is authentic because of its common ancestry.

The nationalist myth of permanent, fixed, homeland community, derives its emotional power, according to psychoanalysis, from the anxieties generated by the fragility of the sense of self, the ego, in the face both of the complex ambiguities inherent in relationships with the external modern world, and also of the disintegrative incoherence of the inner, psychological world. In an attempt to escape the resultant anxiety, the individual engages in an act of self-labelling and self-construction which is essentially static, inserting him or herself into the institutions of society, so as to 'seek out a name' and thence attain an imaginary sense of stability (Frosh 1997: 165).[14] In Melanie Klein's formulation of this argument, the construction of national categories emerges as one example of how adults may seek to contain their destructive impulses by retreating into an infantile 'splitting' of the world into the loved us and the hated other (Holbrook 1971). In Lacan's formulation, it offers an example of how external structures are incorporated to construct a specious sense of identity. In both formulations, but particularly in Lacan's, such attempts to find refuge from feelings of insecurity in a myth of categorised identification, are unlikely to succeed (Frosh 1997: 162–5). The implication is that a sense of national identity is not subject to final, definitive attainment, but emerges rather as the pursuit of a 'mirage' nationalist vision.

The second core nationalist myth is that the members of a national community are united by their distinctive culture and attributes because of their common ancestry. The emotional power of this belief is explained in psychoanalysis, as a form of 'regressive narcissism', a longing for a return of the feeling of oneness which the infant experienced in the womb, and in dependence upon the parents (Frosh 1991: 63–87). If the nation is conceived as a natural kinship community of common ancestry (as the parental family writ large), then it is more likely to evoke the feelings of security which the infant found in dependence on the mother. Moreover, if the national character is perceived as inherited from the common ancestors, then it is more likely to provide the sense of strong moral authority which the insecure individual seeks, evoking the internalisation of the authority of the infant's father. In Erich Fromm's formulation, nationalism is thus an escape from freedom into 'a new idolatry of blood and soil' (1955: 59). The point is not that belief in the nation resolves the problems arising from the individual's loss of the real mother and father, but rather that it involves an attempt to recreate a sense of 'oneness' by denying difference (seeing the nation as a community of cultural sameness), rather than by accepting and grappling with difference. Fundamentally, 'narcissism is regressive because it prefers the imaginary over the real' (Frosh 1991: 920).

Nationalism is certainly not alone in providing a repository for myths of permanence and myths of sameness, and individuals clearly do seek their sense of identity, security, and moral authority in various other forms of identity. But the prevalence of nationalism would seem to indicate that it has a particular appeal. This is explained first, in the claim by psychoanalysis, noted above, that it is the family and home which provide the unconscious models employed by individuals who seek relief from insecurity in a sense of identification with community. Nationalism, more than other identity constructions, is able to portray itself as the family, in all its symbolism of ancestors, forefathers, national character, homeland, motherland, and fatherland. This symbolism of kinship seeks to combine, in most cases, the kinship and home of common ancestry (the parental kin), with the kinship and home arising out of common commitment and love of the demarcated homeland territory, akin to the kinship bond created by matrimonial contract. This combining of the myth of common ancestry and the myth of home-land community strengthens the potential psychological appeal of nationalism, but also generates potential tensions, which will be explored later.

Second, nationalism is particularly useful in employing psychological myths as the basis for political ideology, since it is able to grant public legitimacy to private neuroses by depicting the community as a whole as having the attributes which are sought by its individual members. In asserting the uniqueness and permanence of the national community; the emotional and physical security provided within the homeland; and the right of the moral community to self-determination, nationalism thereby translates the psychological needs of individuals into the public-rights claims of the authentic community, thus raising the insecure individual to the status of the proud nation.

The rational basis for nationalism, relating to the interest in defending a way of life, is thus intrinsically linked with its non-rational basis, as a political attachment of identity and belonging. No other form of identity and belonging relating, for example, to gender or race or family, is secure unless I have a nation to protect me. The sense of being in my own homeland, among people who speak my language and who effortlessly understand me, begins to make me feel significant, secure, and certain (Ignatieff 1993: 6–7). The fact that I nevertheless am haunted by feelings of insignificance, insecurity and uncertainty, makes me vulnerable to the siren calls of further myths of permanence and family, and thence to repeated reformulations of the nationalist vision.

Nationalism and social disruption

The argument that nationalism might rest in part on the reversion of adult individuals to infantile ideological formulas, might initially seem a rather implausible basis for the political analysis of nationalism. It perhaps becomes more acceptable once it is recognised that such reversion occurs in the context of social, economic, and political processes which have disruptive impacts on individuals, and which are not always clearly comprehensible to those affected, and thence not so amenable to more rational solutions.

One formulation of the link between disruptive social forces, the psychology of individuals who feel disempowered in the face of those forces, and the emergence of nationalism, is that offered by Marx. Marxism does depict some nationalisms in situational terms, as offering attachments which might promote human well-being and provide arenas or programmes which can be employed by class groups to deal with the 'specific interests, threats or deprivations' which they face (Benner 1995: 234). But Marxism also offers an alternative formulation which depicts some nationalisms as 'ideologies' in the Marxist sense of a fiction masking the recognition of real interests and real class conflicts.

In an illuminating discussion, Erica Benner notes that

> Marx was not perhaps the most sensitive analyst of this problem [of individual identity] but he was aware that the breakdown of pre-modern social structures and the rise of competitive individualism made freedom terrifying for many; and his writings on alienation reflect a keen appraisal of the value people place on having satisfactory social and political identities.
>
> (1995: 246)

Thus, in the case of Germany,

> the pressures of international competition had engendered a distinctly alienated form of nationalist ideology [which was] wrong-headed ... A misplaced obsession with Germany's uniqueness or, indeed, its superiority to other nations, came to disguise the social causes of German weakness, thereby impeding efforts to address them directly.
>
> (Benner 1995: 82)

Nationalism, in this form, constituted a retreat from freedom into a fundamentally irrational identification with a unique community. But this type of alienative response is fed, as Marx recognised, not just by capitalism but also by political repression, which 'encourages irrational behaviour because it doesn't allow people to make their own considered choices out of a range of policy options. Where people have scant control over their own destinies, they feel helpless; and helpless people will cheer nationalist promises of protection if no other credible protectors are available' (Benner 1995: 235).

This Marxist view, that the alienating impact of capitalism and authoritarianism might promote nationalism, is echoed by the suggestion that there are various aspects of globalisation which have tended to weaken face-to-face family and locality communities. Colonialism frequently disrupted local rural communities through the introduction of education and the related migration of youths to urban areas in search of employment. In the industrialised societies, the nuclear family and the sense of locality community has apparently been weakened by the increased social mobility and individualistic cultures associated with modernity (Lasch 1977). Contemporary economic and cultural globalisation are frequently depicted as weakening existing ties of community so as to expose individuals to new insecurities. These changes have various implications for nationalism, but one probability is that the weakening of the face-to-face communities within which individuals sought a sense of security and meaning, might make it more likely that they look for such significance in affiliation to alternative imagined communities. If ideas of a global community are too weak and shallow to offer a sense of 'collective faith, dignity and hope', then nationalism might be the beneficiary. 'It is [the] promise of collective but terrestrial immortality, outfacing death and oblivion, that has helped to sustain so many nations and national states in an era of unprecedented social change and to renew so many ethnic minorities' (Smith 1995: 160).

It might be possible, moreover, to make this suggested link between the disruptive impact of 'unprecedented social change' and the resurgence of nationalisms more precise. When functioning kinship and locality communities are weakened, either by economic forces or by political interventions, one result is to disrupt social cohesion so as to make anomic people susceptible to visions of harmony and unity embodied either in nostalgic myths of an ideal past, or Utopian dreams of an ideal future. The other frequent impact is to dislocate the authority structure of such communities so that incumbent or aspiring élites lose both their power and their authority and thus begin to search for new ways to re-establish authority. In such circumstances, nationalism becomes an attractive ideological formula since it can provide both ideological legitimacy to élites in search of authority, and visions of community to masses in search of social cohesion. It promises that contemporary social disruptions can be resolved by restoring a mythical state of communitarian harmony, attainable by granting political support to élites claiming autonomy for the authentic cultural or homeland nation. This process, where nationalist myths appeal both to élites in search of authority and masses in search of community, is illustrated in Chapter 4 in the case of Basque nationalism, formulated in the nineteenth century initially by a rural gentry displaced by the centralising Spanish state, and then adopted by those sections of Basque society disrupted by rapid industrialisation. The model has also been illustrated elsewhere in an attempt to explain the roots of ethnic rebellion in Burma (Brown 1994: Ch. 2). Nineteenth-century British colonialism dislocated the Buddhist-authority structure of the Burman empire and engendered massive social disruption. The displaced Buddhist monkhood and the aspiring educated élites created new leadership roles for themselves by articulating new myths of Burman ethnic nationalism, so as to give a new sense of direction to peasant unrest. The resultant Burman nationalist movement succeeded in dominating and controlling the independent Burmese state, and forming the basis for Burmese state nationalism. Subsequent attempts by the independent Burmese state to impose Burman control over the non-Burman minorities had a parallel impact on these minority and peripheral communities, dislocating the authority structure and the social cohesion of the existing locality and kinship communities. This led their displaced traditional élites, as well as their aspiring educated élites, to unite around new myths of minority ethno-regional nationalism. These assertions of Shan, Karen, Kachin and other nationalisms thus clashed head on with the assertions of Burman nationalism employed by the Burmese state, engendering the current ideological, and military, stalemate.

As the brief reference to the Burma case indicates, this interpretation of the constructivist approach to nationalism implies that the distinction between ethnic nationalism and state nationalism begins, at the conceptual level, to become blurred. In Margaret Canovan's words:

If ethnic groups themselves are not actually primordial kin groups, but involve a greater or lesser element of fiction in their claim to common blood; if nations, though built around some core ethnic group, are built through the blurring of boundaries and the adoption of ancestors; if the political mobilization of populations through the use of evocative fictions is inescapable from nationalism, then should we perhaps be looking at a different, more sceptical account of nations, which understands them in terms of the use of myths . . . ?

(1996: 59)

Evaluation

Once nationalism was understood as based on ideological myths constructed by displaced or aspiring élites, and appealing to societies whose social structure and political autonomy had been disrupted, it became feasible to understand the changes in ethnic and national consciousness which had taken place among the Ghanaian Ewes during the twentieth century, and particularly during the period of decolonisation. From the late 1930s onwards, new ideas began to develop of unifying the Ewe nation, of reunifying the (German) Togo nation which had been divided by League of Nations Trusteeship, and of building a Ghanaian nationalism. These ideas were variously promoted by traditional chiefs being marginalised by new state institutions: by the first generation of German-educated "young men" whose careers and status positions had been disrupted by the bifurcation of Togoland, and by a new generation of English-educated "Standard VII boys" who aspired to new leadership positions in state institutions, but who felt uncertain of their limited educational qualifications. The ordinary villagers found their lives and village communities increasingly disrupted, not only by the rapid changes in the economic and social structure of their societies, but also by the political chaos arising from attempts by a misguided colonial administration to manage the factional rivalries between these various aspiring and marginalised élite groups. Visions of nationalist harmony immediately appealed to the disrupted societies and offered new myths of community beyond the village and chiefdom. But the Ewe people were offered a confusing choice of nationalist visions – of a united Eweland, a reunified Togo, and an enlarged Ghana. They were also offered uncertainty as to whether these would build upon, or displace, the traditional communities. Quite sensibly, their dominant response was to say that they wanted them all; they wanted an end to the factional disputes which were destroying their local community, and they had a vision of a nation which could unite all Ewes within a united Ghana and Togo. The problem which has dominated Ghanaian politics since decolonisation has been that rivalries between competing élites means that the actual nationalisms on offer did not interweave these different promises of community. Instead they counterposed them.

If the constructivist view of nationalism is insightful in focusing attention on the use of visions of territorial certainty and common ancestry, to resolve the insecurities engendered by rapid change, then it seems to demand elaboration, since nationalisms frequently manifest themselves in new situations of conflict and rivalry, which threaten to generate new insecurities and uncertainties. The tensions of nationalist politics do not just arise because of clashes between the competing kinship and homeland visions of different societies, each marginalising or demonising the other. They also repeatedly emerge, as in the Ghanaian Ewe case, as disunity within nationalist movements, with competing élites promoting different visions of nationhood. Ewe nationalism has been riven by tensions between those promoting a vision of an ethnic nation for all Ewes, and those promoting a vision of an enlarged Togolese state. Ghanaian nationalism also has uneasily combined two visions; that of modern Ghana as built upon a traditional Akan ethnic core, around which non-Akan peripheries are clustered; and that of Ghana as a new community which must, at least politically, break with its 'tribalistic' past so as to unite all citizens on the basis of a new civic pride.

If these tensions or ambiguities were merely associated with the competing interests of rival élites, then they would be amenable to negotiation. But ideological myths are less easy to manage. If nationalism is an ideologically constructed myth of kinship and home, then it seems to refer to two rather different communities. I have two homes, the parental home of my birth and upbringing, and the marital home of my current family and residence. Both offer images of security, but I probably cannot combine them so as to live in both at once, and the attempt to combine the two might turn out to be uncomfortable. Various aspects of the problematical politics of nationalism which arise from this potential tension, will be examined in the ensuing chapters.

2 New nations for old?

The upsurge of ethnic and ethno-regional conflict means that we need to reassess our understanding of nationalism. It had been widely assumed that the capacities of established nation-states were strong enough to resist challenge from their peripheries and minorities, but it has suddenly become conventional wisdom to assert their fragility and in some cases their demise. Nation-states which used to be regularly described as assimilated (or at least assimilating) cultural communities, integrated socio-economic communities, and sovereign political communities, are now regularly portrayed as struggling unequally with the realities of cultural pluralism, economic globalisation, and competing sovereignties.

When Dankwart Rustow wrote *A World of Nations* in 1967, he saw progress towards the modern nation-state as

> the only political framework within which [the] principles of equality and of achievement [could] be maintained [. . .] Only societies transformed into nations have shown themselves capable of attaining the more advanced forms of modernity, and only modernising nations are likely to retain their identity in the present era of modernisation.
>
> (1967: 30–1)

His optimism that the dynamics of the modernisation process were pushing in the nation-state direction was tempered by the recognition that some state boundaries might not be the most suitable for successful modernisation, and that at some time in the future, modernisation would require 'political institutions that transcend and transform the nation-state' (1967: 31). There was a 'margin for human choice' as to whether the modern nation-state would become 'the God-appointed instrument for the welfare of the human race' (Mazzini), or would produce 'a multitude of miserable and wretched nations' (Carpenter, in Rustow 1967: 282). More than thirty years later, a sense of crisis seems to have replaced Rustow's tempered optimism. Is the nation-state still 'the God-appointed instrument', or is the pursuit of this goal merely generating 'a multitude of miserable and wretched nations'? Is it the nation-state which is under threat, or is it merely that established nation-states are under threat from new potential nation-states? Should we be using the 'margin for human choice' to pursue the vision of a world of nations, or to envision and construct 'political institutions that transcend and transform the nation-state'? (Rustow 1967: 280–2). The purpose here is to employ a constructivist approach to nationalism in order to examine, and perhaps clarify, these issues.

The constructivist element in nationalism

Theories of nationalism concur in recognising that the strength of the nation-state arose in part from its employment as a legitimatory ideology by new state élites seeking new sources of legitimacy.

While the major theories of nationalism have apparently incompatible starting points, deriving in part from their differing primordialist, situationalist or constructivist approaches, there is nevertheless a degree of overlap in one respect: in their recognition of the crucial role played by élites in promoting nationalism. This constitutes the explicit focus of the constructivist approach indicated here. In this approach, nationalism is depicted as an ideology, invented and employed by new political élites aspiring to power in the modern state, who seek alternative sources of legitimacy to replace appeals to divine right or colonial mandate. Such élites construct new myths of unity for the control of societies characterised by socio-economic complexity and cultural diversity. This view of nationalism as a legitimatory ideology has been argued, in differing ways and in differing contexts, by Elie Kedourie (1993), John Breuilly (1982), with a Marxist twist by Eric Hobsbawm (Hobsbawm and Ranger 1983), and by Paul Brass (1991). State élites are seen to construct ideas of the natural nation by selectively reinterpreting historical symbols so as to portray the society within the state in largely mythical terms of historical continuity, as a community of common ancestry, kinship, homeland, and destiny. The organic basis of pre-modern communities is thus attributed to the contemporary society, so that the invented or constructed community can be disguised as natural. The legitimatory and mobilising power of this invented nationhood does not depend upon its factual accuracy (which may vary enormously), but rather on the power of the state élites to select and deploy symbols which resonate with aspects of contemporary culture, and to inculcate skilfully myths of organic unity through appropriate institutional channels.

Such an explanation of nationalism as a manipulatory ideology employed by state élites, is frequently counterposed to two other approaches. The first sees the nation in terms of its (situational) functionality for the modernisation process; while the second stresses the primordial origins of the nation, or at least the 'remarkable continuity' between the pre-modern kinship-based ethnic community and the modern nation. There is no doubt that the focus and stress of these two approaches differ markedly from each other, and from the constructivist approach, as indicated in Chapter 1. Nevertheless, examination of the two literatures shows that both the situationalist and primordialist views of nationalism generate a recognition, among some if not all their proponents, of the independent role played by state élites in articulating and mobilising national identity. The apparently incompatible theories do not converge, but they do complement each other in this key area.

The 'modernist' theories of nationalism, which employ mainly situationalist language, depict the nation-state as the political, economic and cultural unit which was conducive to, and was in turn generated by, the spread of commerce and industry. While much of this literature stresses the causal impact of economic change, several writers see the link between modernisation and nationalism in terms of the power of cultural ideas, the most notable being Benedict Anderson (1983) and Liah Greenfeld (1992). There are three variants of this modernist approach. Diffusionist theorists stress that the growth of commerce and industry both generate and require the spread of a common language and a common culture among societies hitherto characterised by local dialect and cultural differences. The achievement of one language and culture within the sovereign polity facilitates social communication (Deutsch 1966), economic mobility (Gellner 1983), the diffusion of a literature in which the new sense of national community can be imagined (Anderson 1983), and the democratic mobilisation of the community (Greenfeld 1992). But this functional fit between modernisation and nationalism does not itself explain, or ensure, their mutual development. Only the emergence of the strong, bureaucratic, centralised state could remove barriers to mobility, create new institutional arenas for political participation, and introduce a common educational system (Gellner 1983). The emergent national identities were then imagined in part also by state élites, who frequently moved to adopt and adapt the idea of nationalism. They reinterpreted it as a collectivist ideology which is 'inherently authoritarian' in that it 'introduces (or preserves) fundamental inequality between those of its few members who are qualified to interpret the collective will and the many who have no such qualifications; the select few dictate to the masses who must obey' (Greenfeld 1992: 11). As Greenfeld notes, the imagining of the nation in civil society is, in all cases, accompanied, and necessarily modified, by the ideological invention of the nation by state élites.

The second variant of the modernist approach is the Marxist argument which explains the origins and aims of nationalism in terms of the interests of conflicting classes.[1] For Marxists, the nation is, in part, the objective arena of capitalist development within which class contention occurs. However, the origins and aims of all nationalist movements are 'driven forwards or backwards by class struggles, and can be analysed in terms of the class interests they aim to promote or obstruct' (Benner 1995: 96). Nationalism is thus also a prescriptive ideology employed by all social classes 'as the building blocks with which [they] must work in their efforts to preserve or redesign existing communities' (Benner 1995: 96). Nationalism is not solely the ideological weapon of the dominant class, but it is nevertheless frequently employed, pragmatically and selectively, by the dominant bourgeoisie as an ideology to promote their prudential class interests in ameliorating class tensions and facilitating alliances with other classes (Benner 1995: 104–14).

Third, the 'uneven development' literature previously referred to, explains how regional disparities between economic centre and economic periphery, engendered by industrialisation, lead to the racial or cultural division of labour, and thence to the development of reactive national consciousness among peripheral communities. This process explains both how internal colonialism engenders ethno-regional nationalism against existing state nationalisms (Hechter 1975, Nairn 1977), and also how imperialism engendered anti-colonial nationalisms in the third world (Amin 1980, Blaut 1987). In both cases however, reactive nationalism is never the automatic result of uneven development. This outcome requires not only the distinctive culture of the peripheral community, but also the emergence of political leaders who mobilise support by employing a nationalist ideology depicting the peripheral regional community as a potential nation (Hechter and Levi 1979).

Thus the three variants of the modernist approach to nationalism have in common not only their explanation of the nation-state as the social, cultural and political unit appropriate for modernisation and industrialisation; but also their recognition that this functional fit is facilitated by the push of political élites promulgating ideological myths and symbols of nationhood.

These modernist arguments are usually counterposed to explanations of the nation-state which stress its roots in pre-modern natural kinship communities. For Anthony Smith (1981, 1986), the modern nation is lineally descended from the ethnic community which has its own distinct origin, and this claim to common descent is politicised by the intelligentsia seeking to mobilise support. Smith stresses that modern nations can best legitimate themselves by reference to ethnic myths which are authentic and which already exist in the group memories. Nevertheless, the intellectuals who resuscitate and ideologise ethnic identities have important discretion and autonomy in terms of their choice of ethnic myths, their interpretations of historical continuity and their visions of the identity and destiny of the community. Their manipulation of such myths thus involves important elements of invention, even if the scope for such invention is relatively constrained. While the intellectuals who translate ethnic sentiments into nationalism are not themselves members of the state élite, they nevertheless see the modern state as the main agency for their ideals, and they rely on the professional intelligentsia who comprise the state bureaucrats to disseminate their ideas (Smith 1981). In this way, arguments which stress real continuities between nation and *ethnie* do recognise that 'much of the history will have to be rediscovered, even "invented"' (Smith 1981: 67).

There is, in much of the writing on nationalism, an attempt to distinguish between 'the real thing' – nationalism as an actual sentiment of community ('the dog'), and its political manifestation, nationalism as a manipulative ideology ('the tail'). This distinction arises because of the variation between different states as to the extent to which their claims to authority are believed by the people they purport to govern. As Kenneth Minogue notes, 'Nationalism . . . began by describing itself as the political and historical consciousness of the nation, and came in time to the inventing of the nations for which it could act . . . Instead of a dog beginning to wag its political tail, we find political tails trying to wag dogs' (1967: 154). If, in the case of England, nationalism did indeed 'spring more or less spontaneously out of mass feeling and sentiment', then England stands as the exception rather than the model. Elsewhere, as in Germany and Italy 'The inhabitants . . . had fairly to be galvanised into nationalist activity by purposeful currents of propaganda' promoted by middle class activists (Hayes 1949: 293–4).

The first point, then, is that the nation is never merely the imagined community, it is also always the invented community, so that explanations of both the rise and the fall of the nation-state must focus on explaining not only why state élites articulated the ideology of nationalism, but also why these invented nationalist ideologies resonated in the imaginings of civil society, and then why this resonance subsequently began to weaken.

The construction of civic and ethnocultural nationalisms

Nationalist ideologies contain two myths which are potentially in tension with each other; the ethnocultural nationalist myth of common ancestry, and the civic nationalist myth of common commitment to the residential homeland.

It has been suggested in Chapter 1 that the emotional power of nationalism might be explained, in psychoanalytic terms, as arising from the claim of nationalism to offer a community within which individuals can find the sense of identity, security and authority which is associated with family and home relationships. Nationalism offers this, in that it claims to denote the community united by common kinship, but the claim is contained in two different types of nationalist myths; those which focus on offering a sense of categorised permanence in a territorial home, and those which focus on offering a sense of cultural sameness in the claim to common ancestry.

The oldest formulation is that which is denoted here as *civic nationalism*, but which had earlier been designated by the term 'patriotism'.[2] In this formulation, the nation is defined in terms of a shared commitment to, and pride in, the public institutions of state and civil society, which connect the people to the territory that they occupy. The nation is thus depicted as united by a common public culture, a way of life, a national character, which is shared by all citizens irrespective of ethnic origin. Civic nationalism thus portrays itself as a voluntaristic political community formed by the recognition that the self-interest of each citizen is promoted by commitment to the common good (Viroli 1995: 47). But these images of the open, voluntaristic community based on rational choice coexist with less rational ideas of 'love of country', loyalty and self-sacrifice which have their origin in religious ideas of the sacred soil of the ancestors (the homeland, the motherland, the fatherland) and ideas of a community of ethical obligation where 'citizens owe to their *patria* . . . a benevolent love similar to the affection that they feel for their parents and relatives, a love that expresses itself in acts of service and care' (Viroli 1995: 20 and n. 7). The nation portrays itself as the kinship home which welcomes new members who are willing to commit themselves, as in matrimonial contract, to the institutions and way of life of the home which they enter, and who consequently become kin. Civic nationalism thus offers a sense of permanence in the territorial home.

The more recent formulation is that of *ethnocultural nationalism*, sometimes denoted as ethnic or cultural nationalism, in which the nation is portrayed as a community united by its ethnocultural sameness, which stems from the common ancestry of its members.[3] Thus, whereas civic nationalism stresses the imagery of home and matrimonial kinship, ethnocultural nationalism stresses the imagery of the biological family. The ethnocultural nation is depicted as a unique, natural organic entity, a 'single body with its own spiritual soul, faculties and forces' (Viroli 1995: 118). It promises the security of membership in a genetic family.

It has sometimes been asserted that civic nationalism is intrinsically weaker than ethnocultural nationalism, as in Walker Connor's assertion, noted above (see p. 10), that when they compete for the allegiance of the individual, ethnocultural nationalism invariably proves the most potent.[4] But Connor argues this by depicting ethnocultural nationalism (for him, 'ethnonationalism') as a particular type of kinship bond, based on a 'sense of consanguinity', and civic nationalism (for him 'patriotism') as loyalty to the state (1994: 196). This ignores the aspects of civic nationalism which refer to commitment to the institutions of civil society, to love of land and way of life, and to the perceived links between security, territory and continuity, all of which enable civic nationalism to employ the myths of kinship and home. Kinship and ancestry are not the same. The kin are not merely those to whom I am related by blood ties, but also those who I invite into my home on the basis of contractual commitment, as in adoption and marriage. If the nationalist ideology is emotionally powerful because of its ability, in the kinship myth, to mimic the infant's bond to family and home; then the beneficiaries are likely to be both communities portraying themselves primarily as the genetic family (ethnocultural nationalism), and also communities portraying themselves primarily as homeland kin (civic nationalism). It is not self-evident, for example, that the predominantly civic British and American (USA) nationalisms are weaker than predominantly ethnocultural Welsh and black American nationalisms. Connor's classic example of the defeat of civic nationalism by ethnocultural nationalism is the collapse of the Soviet Union, but this did not employ either vision of nationalism as its dominant unifying ideology, and it broke up, not simply into ethnic nations, but into regional units whose contested identities have a partially civic nationalist basis (Brubaker 1996).[5]

The two myths of nationhood, ancestral kin and homeland kin, are usually intertwined. National communities tend to be depicted, therefore, as united by civic pride and by ethnocultural attributes, as having ethnic cores and as accommodating ethnic diversity, as being in some respects natural and in some respects political, as being partly ascriptive communities and partly voluntaristic ones. Nationalism is powerful precisely because it can combine the different ideas of kinship and homeland in this way so as to unite individuals to form communities. But this mix of civic and ethnocultural elements in the nationalist ideology also explains its potential fragility.

The distinction between the two aspects of nationalism relates to a parallel distinction between two aspects of statehood which need to be briefly outlined. One of the main distinctions in definitions of the state is between those which focus upon the character of their institutional structures, and those which focus on the composition of the individuals who occupy those institutions. But the behaviour of all actual states is likely to reflect in part the interests and values embedded in their institutional structures, and in part the interests and values of whichever social groups in society control or 'capture' those institutions.[6] Individuals may well become politicians or army officers or civil servants in order to try to implement the goals and interests which derive from the particular class, occupational, ethnic, gender, locality or other interest group with which they identify. They may well succeed in this regard in some degree, so that the policy outcomes of government do indeed come to reflect the interests and values of whichever majority or minority groups have dominated in recruitment to the ranks of the powerful. But there is also a countervailing force at work. Recruitment involves socialisation. Individuals who are elected to parliament, or trained in the army or who rise to power as dictators, are under pressure to become housetrained; to adopt the values, interests and demeanour which are embedded in the institutions which they enter. The institutional culture may well, in part, derive from the history of the institution itself, as with many of the Western parliamentary rules of behaviour; but it is also related to the particular functions which each institution performs – judges are under pressure to adopt judicial demeanours; army officers to adopt commanding demeanours. Moreover, each institution has an interest in preserving or enhancing its autonomy and status. These institutional interests and values may well come to dominate the interests and values of the individuals who occupy the institutions so that, for example, even if an individual with liberal impulses gets to the top in an authoritarian regime, he or she might find that the institutions of absolute power push him or her to act in illiberal ways. States vary then, as to which of these aspects of statehood – agency or institutionalist – becomes dominant; and this in turn influences the character of nationalism.

If the state were viewed simply as the whole set of institutions relating to the administration of public affairs in a given territory, then we might wish to regard nationalism as the development within that territorial society, of a sense of identification with, and collective pride in, those institutions. This sense of community might be initiated by the state or emerge within civil society, but, in either case, governments seeking to defend and enhance the authority and status of the society's public institutions, are likely to articulate legitimatory nationalist ideologies. The nationalism which emerges, whether as a real sentiment or an ideological lever to generate such a sentiment, is civic nationalism.

But if the state were viewed from the alternative perspective – as the agency of whichever social group in society captures it, then ethnocultural nationalism seems to be implied. Any such group, however pernicious their intentions, will wish to claim that they represent the whole society. It is possible, but not likely, that they may do this by showing how the internal diversity of their own interests and values reflect the diversity of interests and values of the wider society.[7] But if they do in fact represent themselves as one cohesive group, then they will need to claim that their will should hold sway because it embodies the common will of the whole society.[8]

This claim, that there is a 'general will', is most easily comprehensible if 'the people' are depicted as one organic community. Indeed, since the only entity which can have a conscious will is an individual, the idea that a collectivity of individuals could have one collective will, demands that the collectivity be depicted as a single organic entity, a singular 'people'. This concept of an organic community is embodied most clearly in the kinship group which claims that its common values derive from the fact of its common ancestry; and that its common history underlies its claim to common destiny. Thus the term 'nation' comes, in this usage, to refer to a community whose common will is a reflection of the links of common ancestry, and is denoted in the objective similarities which derive from such links, most notably a common language and a common traditional culture. The term 'ethno-cultural nationalism' refers to this tendency.[9]

Both visions of community, civic and ethnocultural, can emerge either within civil society, or can be inculcated and engineered by élite ideologies; similarly, both can emerge either in a liberal form which stresses civil society freedoms and individual self-fulfilment, or in an illiberal form which suppresses individual freedom and sustains state controls over civil society.[10] Moreover, both visions of community portray themselves in the language and imagery of family and home. The family of the ethnocultural nation is the family of common ancestry, and the home is that of the ancestral homeland. The family of the civic nation is the community of non-sanguine kinship entered into through voluntary commitment, and the home is the territory of residence. They thus refer to two different communities, with two different, though overlapping, memberships. Entry into the ethnocultural nation depends upon a process of inheritance or assimilation, whereby the ethnocultural values and attributes which define the community, including the belief in common ancestry, are acquired. The civic nation refers to all citizens of a state, who are perceived as forming a community, irrespective of any differences in their place of origin, racial or ethnic backgrounds, on the basis of their shared pride in the institutions of the homeland.

The distinction between the agency and institutionalist views of the state is an analytical one only, in that the behaviour of all actual states will reflect elements of both aspects of statehood; and this is directly reflected in the character of nationalism. All actual nationalisms combine elements of ethnocultural nationalism and elements of civic nationalism. All depict themselves partly in the language of parenthood and ancestry – forefathers, motherland, fatherland; and partly in the language of matrimonial kinship – contract, commitment, union, loyalty.

But this means that there is a potential tension, within all actual nation-states, between the community referred to by civic nationalism, and the community referred to by ethnocultural nationalism. Most nation-states are, in varying degrees, multi-ethnic, in the sense that the community of citizens is different from the community of those who have been born into, or been fully assimilated into, the dominant ethnic culture. This disparity is not new, even if it has been exacerbated in some cases by recent migrations, and it means that the success of the nationalist ideology has depended upon its ability to unite the two different communities to which it refers. It has succeeded, not by resolving the disparity, but by distracting attention from it.

The 'social justice' vision of the nation

During the twentieth century, nationalist élites have portrayed themselves as the agents of equitable development, so that the image of the nation has been reconstructed as the social justice community. The forward-looking optimism implied in this vision has ameliorated the tension between the community of civic nationalism and the community of ethnocultural nationalism.

There is an important link between the development of modern nation-states, and the fact that these nation-states have been built on the two intertwined forms of nationalism, the civic and the ethnocultural. This has been indicated, in general terms by Anthony Smith but a similar point has recently been stated more explicitly by Margaret Canovan:

> nationhood is a *mediating* phenomenon, the strength of which is that it holds together . . . the political and the familial [and so] creates an enduring 'we' that can form the basis of a strong and stable politic and give the state unity, legitimacy and permanence because it is 'our' state.
>
> (1996: 69 and 71)

Those modern states which have been most successful in providing social harmony and political stability to their societies, have done so because they have managed to persuade these societies that the gap between the community denoted by civic nationalism, and that denoted by ethnocultural nationalism, was not a significant one, since it was in the process of being bridged. Michael Mann (while not using the terms 'civic' and 'ethnocultural' nationalism in the same sense as here) has indicated how this was achieved in the case of pre-twentieth-century European nationalisms. He shows how modern nationalism has been built on the interlinking of nationalist ideologies 'which assert the moral, cultural and political primacy of an ethnic group (real or constructed)' (Mann 1996: 147), with ideas of 'loyalty to the strong state' (1996: 163). These linked ideas were then diffused beyond the confines of the core ethnic community, by the 'infrastructural' development of various institutions of 'discursive literacy', including church, civil administration, universities, legal profession and the mass media.[11]

During the twentieth century, the strength of nation-states has increasingly depended on the perception that both political integration and ethnocultural assimilation are progressing and converging. The potential tension between the two has thus been defused by a forward-looking optimism which looks towards an ideal where the political community and the ethnocultural community coincide in the one 'nation-state'. This forward-looking optimism has been facilitated by economic development. The emergence of new nation-states in nineteenth-century Europe occurred when centralising political élites were able to achieve sufficient administrative control to integrate politically and culturally assimilate their peripheral regions and ethnic minorities. But nationalist success has subsequently relied on the fact that when the élites in the peripheries and minorities found their authority positions disrupted by the centralising state, it became both possible and advantageous for them to assimilate culturally so as to gain access to new status, power or authority positions in the centralising state, or its emergent civil society. Otherwise, they were likely to become politically oppositionist. Thus it was economic development which ensured that political integration and ethnocultural assimilation could successfully interweave so as to generate the new nation-state.

This successful interweaving of civic and ethnocultural nationalism has in some cases been instigated by a strong centralising state, and in other cases it has occurred more through the development of a vibrant civil society focused at the ethnic core. In both cases, the consequent development of civic pride – in the institutions of the state or in those of civil society (or both) – becomes sufficient to generate a sense of common citizenship (civic nationalism) which is strong enough to persuade those citizens who are not yet assimilated into the culture of the dominant ethnic segment, that this is not particularly politically salient. This is so, partly because the status of citizenship does not depend upon it, and partly because avenues to assimilation into the ethnocultural nation remain open. Specifically, the fact that the state and/or civil society employ the language of the dominant ethnic segment is not perceived as an attempt at cultural domination. Rather (and again ambiguously), it is perceived both as a means of entry into the assimilating ethnocultural nation, and also as a potentially ethnically neutral means of communication within the civic nation.

This linking of the civic and ethnocultural visions of community through the agency of economic development, generated a change in the basis of state legitimacy. Prior to the twentieth century, the dominant trend had been for governments to claim authority on Hobbesian grounds, as the guarantors of order within the state territory. The liberal view was that the advancement of society, the spread of social justice and the growth of the economy were to be generated primarily by civil society, rather than by the state. This had begun to change by 1931, however, when Carlton Hayes wrote his classic text on nationalism, and asked himself what the fundamental causes were of its 'vogue' in the twentieth century. He considered that ideas of democracy and of religiosity both played a role, but then suggested that the main impetus came from 'the growth of a belief that the state, particularly the nation-state, can and should promote human progress' (Hayes 1949: 300).

This new reliance on the state as the engine of development was argued most explicitly by eastern European Communist regimes which legitimated extensive state control and coercion as being necessary for the attainment of the Communist vision of economic prosperity and social justice. In the industrialised West, the statist view of development eventually appeared in Keynesian and socialist variants, which concurred in recommending state interventions in the economy as the means to both economic growth and redistributive justice. In the third world, Kwame Nkrumah's dictum of 'Seek ye first the political kingdom and all else will be gathered unto you' pointed the way for the mobilisation systems of the new post-colonial states to rely on state-led programmes to achieve the rapid transition to equitable industrialisation. In differing contexts, therefore, the legitimacy of the state came to be closely tied to its promise that it would deliver social justice and development. This shift in the proclaimed role of the state, from the guarantor of order and unity, to the engineer of progress and development, implied a corresponding modification in the depiction of the nation. A state 'needs to create a national sentiment . . . It . . . therefore has to create its own symbols, mythology and sense of sacredness and belonging' (Rex 1994: 210). Previously, it could do this by depicting the society as a natural community of unequal citizens, bonded by tradition, on the lines indicated by Edmund Burke. But its new developmental role implied the need to specify the egalitarian vision of the nation as a social justice community (Miller 1995, Canovan 1996). This is recognised in Elie Kedourie's definition of nationalism as an ideology which offers a 'vision of justice, virtue and happiness' (Kedourie 1993: xiv). Once the state élites began to define the nation in terms of equitable development, the legitimatory and mobilising power of nationalism would come to depend upon their ability to sustain, and then to deliver, this promised vision of social justice, in which the ideas of civic community and ethnocultural community converged.

The resonance of the national community 'invented' by the state in the imagining of civil society

The 'invented' ideology of the nation-state resonated with the 'imagining' of civil society, as the impact of industrialisation and colonialism disrupted the face-to-face communities of family and locality. Individuals sought imagined communities which could mimic the kinship group in offering a sense of identity, security and authority. The promises of state élites to provide equitable development in the social justice nation seemed to fulfil these societal needs.

Not all states were successful in their attempts to interweave the civic and ethnocultural forms of nationalism so as to convince their minority and peripheral communities of the virtues of national integration. Occasionally, as was the case with the Soviet Union, this was because they did not try to do so, seeking unity in ideologies other than nationalism. More frequently, attempts at national integration failed because the state machinery was inadequate for the attainment of effective centralised control over the territory. The state's cultural policies were seen to promote ethnic exclusion rather than ethnocultural assimilation, or its economic policies failed to generate a flourishing civil society. In such cases, state élites resorted to authoritarian measures. These made it more likely that peripheral and minority élites would see the state's attempts at political integration as disruptive administrative centralisation which threatened the authority structure of their society and promoted their cultural marginalisation. The consequence of this failure of nationalist vision was that the tensions between the civic claim that all citizens of the state's territory constituted the nation, and the ethnocultural claim that all who had inherited or assimilated the core ethnic culture constituted the nation, remained politically salient. Such states have remained battle grounds for competing nationalisms, with regionalist nationalisms reacting against attempts at political centralisation, and ethnic minority nationalisms reacting against attempts at ethnocultural assimilation or exclusion.

Other states did succeed, however, in becoming established nation-states. In these cases, nationalism proved powerful because the nation invented in the ideologies of state élites corresponded to, and resonated with, the nation imagined in civil society. The assumption, as indicated in Chapter 1, is that individuals would have little psychological need of an imagined kinship community if they were able to fulfil themselves within real face-to-face communities such as those offered by family and locality in pre-modern societies. Only to the extent that such face-to-face communities have been dislocated or attenuated, or prove inadequate, do individuals seek imagined alternatives. Such dislocations and attenuations were indeed provided by the major modernisation processes of industrialisation and colonialism. The more that social cohesion was disrupted by these processes, the more individuals looked for new sources of identity, security and authority. Thus when state élites portrayed the society within the state boundaries in 'family' terms, as an ethnocultural community united by common ancestry and a civic community of kinship created by commitment to the common homeland, they were seeking to deploy the emotional power of the family in the service of the state. The nationalist ideology provided nostalgic appeals to a past period of national unity and cohesion, a diagnosis of contemporary ills as arising from the invasion of national autonomy, and a vision of a destiny of future autonomy which might be secured through support for the political movement led by the nationalist élites.

This depiction of the disaggregated society as the mythical kinship community, the nation, was more likely to succeed in capturing the imagination of the society if the state élites could claim that they were indeed fulfilling the 'parental' role, in that they could provide the moral and physical security which the real family previously offered. It is in this regard that the claim by state élites to be the agents of develop- ment and social justice becomes crucial in explaining the rise of the nation-state. By articulating a vision of the nation as embodying the developmental promise of economic security and social justice (in addition to the Hobbesian promise of order), the state élites were able to tap into the emotional and moral needs of individuals undergoing the disruptive impact of modernisation. This suggestion of a perceived connection between individual needs and the proclaimed goals of the state is reflected in the recent concern of social theorists to expand, and in some respects to merge, the key normative concepts of political science. 'Rights' are redefined to include individual and minority claims to development, participation and welfare (UN 1993); 'citizenship' is expanded to include the social and self-determination rights of individuals and communities (Held 1984); 'democracy' is interpreted as individual and group empowerment (Held 1994); 'development' is expanded to refer to local community autonomy and empowerment (Escobar 1992); and 'security' and 'sovereignty' are widened to encompass concern for human rights, basic needs, self-determination and democracy (Makinda 1996). The identity, emotional and moral needs of individuals here become linked, in the new definitions of such concepts, with membership of community, and thence with the normative values which contemporary states are expected to espouse.

The search for a mythical kinship community able to offer identity, security and authority to the dependent individuals in society, was thus satisfied by the ideological vision, constructed by state élites, of the nation-state as the unique ethnocultural and civic community, secure in its own sovereign homeland, with its own destiny of development and social justice. Thus, so long as state élites were seen to be delivering on their promises of progress towards equitable development, the strength of the nation-state was assured. It was only when state élites, in various countries and contexts, began to appear to act more as the causes of social disruption, inequity and insecurity, than as their solution, that faith in the state élites, and in their nationalist claims, began to weaken.

Development and the crisis of state legitimacy

From the late 1960s onwards, disparities between the developmental promises of state élites and their performances began to engender disillusionment, so that state élites began to be seen increasingly as the source of insecurity and disruption. In these circumstances, marginalised individuals began to look for alternative imagined communities able to promise security in the form of social justice.

By the late 1960s, doubts were beginning to spread as to the capacity of the state to deliver on its variously formulated development and social justice promises. These doubts have probably been weakest in the USA, where developmental optimism remains high and the resilience of its contemporary nationalism remains strong. But elsewhere in the democratic industrialised countries, the widespread 'crisis of legitimacy' (Held 1984) has been generated by the failures (or abandonment) of Keynesian economic management, which left governments with a credibility gap between the redistributive social justice promised to subordinate classes, and the capacity both of the state bureaucracies to deliver it and of the middle classes to pay for it. In many parts of the third world, and particularly in Africa, the crisis of the state was much more intense, as impatient efforts at statist development led into the dependency trap and thence into governmental autocracy, instability, incompetence and corruption. This culminated in the collapse of some states, and the retreat or erosion of others. In eastern Europe, the failures and inequities of central state planning to fulfil developmental promises produced the disintegration of the Communist vision. In each case, though in varying degrees, the failures of the state to fulfil its promise as the agency for the delivery of equitable development has generated a widespread cynicism about government and a weakening of its legitimacy.

The implications of this for an explanation of nationalism were recently pointed out by Jack Snyder in the context of the collapse of the USSR:

> Nationalism reflects a need to establish an effective state to achieve a group's economic and security goals. The most aggressive nationalist movements arise when states fail to carry out those tasks, spurring people to create more effective states. Today, nationalism is flaring up where old states have collapsed and where mobilised populations are consequently demanding the creation of effective new states.
>
> (1993: 81)

Nevertheless, it is important to note that increased disillusionment with the capacities of the state does not depend on any generalised decline in those capacities. While a few states such as the USSR, Liberia, Somalia or Afghanistan have indeed collapsed, most other states clearly do not have lower capabilities today than they had previously. The crisis of the nation-state is rather located at the subjective level, in the fact that the gap between the promises of security and justice, and the observed capacities, has eroded its moral legitimacy (Dunn 1995). This loss of faith in the state leads directly to the erosion of the nation. The nation is in trouble when the state is in trouble.

The trouble occurs in three ways. First, to the extent that nationalism has been constructed by state élites so as to legitimate their claims to state sovereignty and governmental power, the spread of cynicism towards the capabilities and integrity of these élites has been manifested in the loss of faith in their claims, and the decline in the mobilising power of their legitimatory ideologies, including their visions of national identity. Most dramatically, the crisis of state legitimacy in the USSR involved the decline in the moral credibility of state élites and thence in the moral power of the assertion of Russian dominance which was, at least latterly, integral to their vision of Soviet identity (Hutchinson 1994). Elsewhere, claims by state élites that cultural disparities within the society were legitimated by processes of national assimilation, were similarly subjected to new critical challenges.

Second, the depiction of the nation as the social justice community has meant that the contemporary inequalities and inequities which have accompanied efforts at development, could easily be cited as evidence of the absence or incompleteness of nationhood. In the Burkean model of the nation, such inequalities provided the cement of mutual dependency and traditional obligation necessary for unity. But once the social justice model of the nation had been invoked, socio-economic disparities could be cited to disprove the 'one nation' claim, and those who felt disadvantaged could more easily assert countervailing claims. Thus, because of the inevitable unevenness of development processes, even those states which have been dramatically successful in delivering their development promises, like Singapore, have been vulnerable to claims that the impact has been inequitable. Meritocratic development benefited all Singaporeans, but not equally so, and it generated new socio-economic disparities between Malays and Chinese in the 1970s (Li 1988) (and then between English-educated and dialect-speaking Chinese in the 1980s). This prompted challenges to the ethnically-neutral depiction of the nation, and thence new efforts by state élites to reengineer a stronger national identity.[12]

Third, if indeed the power and resonance of national identity arose from its appeal as an imagined community able to fulfil the need of individuals for a sense of identity, emotional security and moral authority, then this appeal was directly undermined by the increasing perception of state élites as the cause of disruption, rather than the solution. Once the state had identified itself as the primary engine of development, it had to implement the policies necessary to promote economic, social and cultural change. Even where such policies have generated rapid development, the state came to be perceived, at least in part, as the instrument of the disruption and social dislocation associated with rapid modernisation. Where the policies failed, and came to be seen as the cause of socio-economic collapse, the identification of the disruptive culprits was even easier. In both situations, individuals who had looked to the nation-state as a source of protection against the insecurities of the contemporary world, began to see it as a source of insecurity against which they needed some protection. If the imagined community of the existing nation-state did not offer a sense of security, insecure individuals might well begin to look, and imagine, elsewhere.

This loss of faith in state élites, and in their developmental vision of the nation, has had the effect of exposing the tensions between the civic and ethnocultural aspects of nationalist ideologies, which had hitherto been hidden by the vision of development and social justice. So long as it was believed that all those residing in the state's territory were in the process both of integration into national citizenship and of assimilation into the ethnocultural nation, then the contemporary discontinuity between political integration and ethnocultural assimilation could be ignored. Those presently marginalised could hope that progress would mean that they or their children would be able to become both territorial citizens and ethnocultural members of the nation-state. But the erosion of developmental optimism has meant that it has suddenly become apparent that the vision of a convergence of political integration and ethnocultural assimilation was at best a naïve hope, and at worst a deliberate plot.

Ethnic minorities within modern states are now regularly depicted as being permanently marginalised, because their eventual full integration into the civic nation is vitiated by the barriers to their effective ethnocultural assimilation. Once this has been realised, then those who are marginalised begin to abandon their vain pursuit and begin to assert their minority rights, both to a political autonomy which challenges notions of political integration into the existing nation-state, and to a cultural self-determination which challenges notions of ethnocultural assimilation into the existing nation-state. The vision of the assimilating ethnocultural nation gives way to the recognition that society is presently divided between the high-status members of the core ethnic community, and the low-status members of the unassimilated minorities. The vision of the integrating civic nation, which seemed to promise equal status and social justice to all citizens irrespective of ethnic attributes and origin, gives way to the recognition that citizenship status is related to class position, and that class disparities are increasing. The two disillusionments come together in the growth of a new ideological formula: that the ethnic minorities in contemporary states are clustered in subordinate class positions, trapped in those positions by the ethnic domination policies of state élites, disguised as cultural assimilation policies. This ideological formula is powerful because it is partly true.

From the standpoint of ethnocultural nationalism, civic nationalism is revealed as the attempt to promote programmes aimed at subordinating minority ethnic cultures to majority ethnic cultures, by disguising them in the language of a culturally neutral political integration. Proponents of minority ethnocultural nationalisms therefore denounce as ethnocentric, racist or genocidal, the majoritarian claims of assimilationist nationalism. For their part, the proponents of civic nationalism proclaim the virtues of political integration, deny the accusations that civic nationalism is a cover for ethnic domination, demonise minority ethnic nationalisms as the ethnocentric assertion of group rights over individual rights, and seek to put the genie of minority rights back in its bottle.

Thus, instead of seeing nationalism as being either in decline, or as resurgent, the argument developed here is that the politics of nationalism becomes increasingly problematic and unstable as the two forms of nationalism, civic and ethnocultural, exchange their previous mutual embrace in the service of the modern state, for a mutual confrontation in the service of the dismemberment of the modern state.[13] The contemporary contentiousness of nationalist politics, which is evident not only in ethnic violence and separatist conflicts, but also in the endemic intolerance of confrontational 'debates' on multiculturalism and racism, can be understood therefore, in terms of a new realisation as to the lack of fit between these two conceptualisations of nationalism.

The new legitimacy of ethnicity and ethno-regionalism

> The problems of state-led development made individuals increasingly susceptible to the ideologies of counter-élites seeking to mobilise support by depicting ethnic minorities and regional peripheries as kinship communities suffering disadvantage, and thereby as potential nations with social justice rights.

The immediate reason for the failure of so many states to effectively deal with the tensions between civic and ethnocultural nationalisms, in the period since the late 1960s, seems to be that the culture of politics has shifted from, in Oakeshottean terms, practice to rationalism. Identity is no longer regarded as something which emerges in the practice of politics, but rather something which must be consciously engineered. As Tom Nairn says:

> 'Identity' has emerged from neutrality and become a positive term . . . Nationalities have always had identity. But now it seems they must have it. No

longer taken for granted, identity has to measure up to certain standards. The comfortable old clothes won't do: identity must toe a line of uniformed respectability. If defective, its shames call out for remedy, or at least a cover-up; if 'rediscovered', it must then be 'preserved' from further violation; and above all it has to be asserted ('proudly') and so get itself recognised by outsiders. Yes, it's time the world stopped smirking about *our* identity.

(1997: 183)

'Comfortable old clothes' can be eclectic without attracting attention, but 'proud assertions' deliberately attract such attention, so that any ambiguities are probed for inconsistencies. The distinction between the community denoted by territorial residence and civic pride, and the community denoted by ethnocultural attributes and belief in common ancestry, which might have been hidden in the old clothes, is now subject to close scrutiny. It thus becomes both more politically salient, and less amenable to resolution. The politics of national identity is now more difficult to resolve because it is conducted in the spotlight.

But this merely exacerbates more fundamental problems which have led to the confrontations between established state nationalisms and emergent minority and peripheral nationalisms. There are four main factors at work. First, so long as the myth of the nation-state was strong, any political assertion of ethnic autonomy claims could be convincingly portrayed by state élites as subversive tribalist, sectarian, communalist or racist threats to the nation; and regionalist claims could be similarly demonised as separatist or secessionist threats to the sovereignty of the state. Alternatively, in the liberal tradition, ethnic attachments could be marginalised and depoliticised by being portrayed as private interests, attributes and attach-ments. Any claims for special ethnic rights could be legitimately disregarded by the ethnically colour-blind state committed to universalistic procedures and norms of limited government. In the same way, regionalist claims could be politically defused and routinised by being treated as issues of administrative decentralisation. But once the myth of the assimilated nation had begun to lose its power, and its aura as a moral imperative, attempts by state élites to demonise, marginalise or depoliticise such minority ethnic and regionalist claims also lost their power. Ethnic and ethno-regional assertions became respectable and could indeed be portrayed as legitimate and politically central claims to communitarian empowerment, cultural justice, minority rights or ethno-national autonomy. Thus the crisis of state legitimacy, which is manifested as the erosion of the nation-state myth, in turn, generates the new awareness of, and receptivity to, new nationalist claims.

Second, the new depiction of minority or peripheral community claims as communitarian rights derives legitimacy from the previous depiction of the majority ethnic culture as the core of the assimilating nation. The counter-élites of disad-vantaged ethnic and regional groups thus are merely employing for themselves the language of communitarian ethnic and homeland rights which the state élites had previously employed in the service of the nation-state. Since ethnic minorities and peripheral regions have frequently been disproportionately disadvantaged in the development process, the socio-economic interests of the disadvantaged can then convincingly be portrayed as the cultural and political rights of the hitherto suppressed authentic nations.

Third, this tendency for ethnocultural minorities and peripheral regions to be disadvantaged in the development process was never entirely accidental. In some instances, it arose explicitly out of the discriminatory policies employed by the élites of those ethnic and regional communities who came to dominate state institutions, and who then used the language of national integration as the camouflage for ethnic and regional domination. This happened in Sri Lanka and Burma. But even where ethnic and ethno-regional discrimination did not become explicit state policy, commitment to policies of ethnocultural assimilation and political centralisation meant that some members of ethnic minority and peripheral groups remained disadvantaged by their lack of fluency in and access to the dominant culture. In the case of indigenous minorities, such as the Canadian Indians, the result of assimi-lationist nationalism was frequently the loss of viability of the minority ethnic culture, accompanied by the failure of access to the majority culture (Kymlicka 1989). The frequent location of ethnic minority groups in economically marginalised peripheral regions of the state, which sometimes arose from deliberate internal colonialist policies, has further exacerbated this tendency for ethnic and peripheral minorities to be disproportionately represented among the socio-economically disadvantaged, as well as the culturally disadvantaged. It is this marginalisation by the state of its ethnic minorities which Anthony Smith identifies as the core issue:

> What has brought the issue of the 'nation-state' to a head has been its predominantly plural ethnic character, the arousal of previously dormant and submerged minority *ethnies* by the social penetration and cultural regimentation of the 'scientific state' run by élites from the dominant *ethnie*, coupled with unfulfilled popular expectations, and the resulting growing pressure of discontented minorities on the political arena of the centre and its dominant ethnic community.
>
> (1995: 102)

Finally, the erosion of the imagined nation-state means that individuals experiencing social disruption and anomie begin to search for a new imagined community. The ethnic or regionalist community is the major beneficiary because of its ability (in some cases better than the state) to mimic the kinship group and kinship home, and thus provide the identity, security and authority epitomised in the family bond. Such a sense of ethnic and regional community can develop among individuals who neither share significant common cultural attributes nor who are particularly distinctive from their neighbours; and it can refer to recent commonalities of circumstance. Nevertheless, such groups can construct a national consciousness by combining myths of common ancestry, with claims to commitment to territorial institutions, so as to claim rights to an autonomous national destiny. If the established state claiming to be the ethnocultural and civic nation cannot offer the necessary protection, then it is the emergent ethnocultural and civic nation claiming to be the potential state which offers the next best bet.

Such minority or peripheral nationalisms develop, however, only when their marginalised or displaced élites seek to rebuild authority by mobilising grievances among their dislocated communities relating to the suppression of their regional institutions (civic nationalism), or the suppression of their ethnic language and culture (ethnocultural nationalism). Sometimes these minority or peripheral claims may appear not to pose a direct threat to the sovereignty of the existing state because they do not intertwine civic and ethnocultural nationalisms together, as with pre-dominantly cultural claims for support of migrant ethnic minority communities in Australia; or predominantly civil calls for regional devolution and reallocations, as with the muted calls for devolution to a northeastern region in the UK. But some emergent nationalisms have the capacity to become strong if their élites are able to bridge the gap between appeals to a pride in the distinctive civic or state institutions of the peripheral community, and appeals to a pride in its unique ethnic culture, by generating in their populace a sense of progress towards an ideal (national destiny) in which the two, civic nationalism and ethnocultural nationalism, can once more coincide. Though this time to oppose, rather than to support, the existing state.

The multicultural solution, or dilemma

Attempts by state élites to manage ethnic claims by strategies of multi-culturalism are problematic. It is unclear whether they promise to resolve the nationalist problem by finally disengaging the civic and ethnocultural visions, or by ensuring the continued ambiguity between the two.

The inability of state élites to sustain their earlier strategies of demonising and marginalising minority and peripheral claims has left them with the choice of either confronting the challenges head on, culminating in the numerous and widespread violent ethnic and ethno-regional conflicts, or searching for new strategies which seek to accommodate or manage such claims. The adoption of these latter strategies involves, however, the dismantling of the earlier myths of assimilation, and their replacement by new symbols of multicultural nationalism. Multiculturalism seems in some respects to offer a new vision of nationalism in which the links between civic and ethnocultural nationalism are finally broken. But the break is not always a clean one. Indeed multiculturalism may sometimes be a strategy which seeks to reintwine deliberately the civic and ethnocultural visions by creating new ambiguities between the two, thus returning us to that prior state of affairs where the tensions between civic and ethnocultural nationalisms were not widely understood, and were therefore not deeply politically salient. This is so because the term 'multiculturalism' is surrounded by an ambiguity which cannot easily distinguish between the (civic) call to celebrate the ethnic diversity of the societies which inhabit all contemporary states while being consciously 'colour-blind' in allocating power and status; or the (ethnocultural) call to restructure the institutions of the state so as to conduct politics specifically on 'ethnic arithmetic' lines. This confusion as to the significance of 'multiculturalism' is abetted by the fog surrounding the word 'equality'. It can be used to denote an ideal in which citizens are all subject to the same universalistic rules; and also an ideal in which each ethnic segment is subject to different rules which will compensate for existing inequities so as to generate equal outcomes. The politics of multiculturalism is thus potentially as problematical as is the politics of the tension between civic and ethnocultural nationalism which has been surveyed here. The character of multicultural politics no doubt depends partly on the ethnic composition of the society concerned, but the focal concern here will be on the impact of the character and strategies of the state. Subsequent discussions in Chapter 8 will examine a managerial (corporatist) strategy by the state, and an accommodationist (pluralist) strategy, in order to assess their relative merits in providing a 'God-appointed' process of transcending and transforming the nation-state; or in offering, instead, a quick road to misery and wretchedness. But if we wish to assess the politics of the disentwining of civic and ethnocultural nationalisms, and then also to assess the politics of multiculturalism which arises from that disentwining, we will need to begin by examining the ethical character of civic nationalism and ethnocultural nationalism.

3 Are there two nationalisms?

Good–civic and bad–ethnocultural

It has been suggested thus far that the contentious nature of nationalist politics may be related to tensions between civic nationalism and ethnocultural nationalism. Such contentions invariably involve proponents of each side asserting that their nationalism offers the authentic promise of liberation, whereas that of their opponents offers only a conception of nationhood which would bring oppression. The question arises, therefore, as to whether such claims might sometimes be true. Is nationalism, in the words of Dryden, a Janus who 'wears almost everywhere two faces; and you have scarce begun to admire the one, ere you despise the other'?

Numerous writers have endorsed the suggestion that there are two different types of nationalism, and have suggested by their choice of terminology that ethnocultural nationalism (labelled as 'integral', 'organic', 'ascriptive', 'exclusive' or 'radical')[1] is intrinsically authoritarian and collectivist; while civic nationalism, (denoted as 'liberal' nationalism, but also by terms like 'political', 'social' or 'voluntarist')[2] is predominantly or at least potentially democratic and individualistic.

The two variously denoted forms of nationalism are analytically distinct. However, the fact that they intertwine in particular nation-states and nationalist movements so that one form may appear more dominant, has engendered the frequent use of the two analytical models as explanatory categories for distinguishing between those nationalisms which promote individual liberty, and those which suppress it. The purpose of this chapter is first to explain how the distinction between civic and ethnocultural nationalisms has been employed in the literature. Second, to unpack this distinction so as to indicate problems with the way in which it has been linked to the liberal–illiberal dichotomy. Third, to derive from these discussions an approach which recognises that both ethnocultural and civic nationalisms have the capacity to emerge in liberal or illiberal forms. It might be true that some nationalisms, which are predominantly ethnocultural, are less liberal than other predominantly civic nationalisms. But it is not always or intrinsically so, and we need to look carefully at the nature of the argument, in order to assess why.

The distinction between ethnocultural and civic nationalisms

The widespread depiction of ethnocultural nationalism as illiberal and civic nationalism as liberal is based partly on the distinction between irrational and rational attachments, partly on the allegedly liberalising impact of the middle classes, and partly on a distinction between reactive and self-generated identities.

As has been noted, 'ethnocultural nationalism' refers to a sense of community which focuses on belief in myths of common ancestry; and on the perception that these myths are validated by contemporary similarities of, for example, physiognomy, language or religion. The myth of common ancestry, related myths of homeland origin and migration, and the pride in the contemporary linguistic, cultural or physical evidence of common kinship, provide the basis for claims to authenticity, and thence for claims to the right of collective national self-determination. Ethnocultural nationalism thus employs the same type of myths of common ancestry which are denoted by the term 'ethnicity'.[3] The term 'ethnocultural nationalism', is preferred to the term 'ethnic nationalism' however, simply because the term 'ethnicity' is hotly contested between those who use it to refer to such myths, and those who use it to refer to the biological *fact* of genetically fixed primordial racial attributes. The use of the term 'ethnic' to refer to ethnocultural nationalism, might thus be interpreted by some (as, for example, by Will Kymlicka)[4] to indicate precisely the definitional assumption which is critically examined here: that 'ethnic' nationalism is *necessarily* ascriptively closed, and thence illiberal. The term 'ethnocultural nationalism' is deliberately chosen here as a hybrid term which denotes no such assumption, and which therefore facilitates the examination of whether those nationalisms which are illiberal, are or are not so because of their belief in common ancestry.

Several writers have suggested recently that the concept of civic nationalism should be discarded (Kymlicka forthcoming, Yack 1999). They suggest that if the concept refers to a voluntaristic and ahistorical political community which is ethnically neutral, then such a community is not only unattainable, it is also not really a candidate for nationalist affiliation since it cannot provide the sense of belonging and rootedness which give nationalism its power. Such critics suggest, further, that 'civic nationalism' should be regarded simply as a myth employed by ethnic majorities to camouflage the fact that national institutions and values reflect and promote their own culture, while ensuring the subordination of ethnic minorities.

The problem lies with the initial definition. If civic nationalism were to be defined, as it is here, as the attachment to the public culture, way of life, land and civic institutions, shared by the community created through residence in a particular territory (rather than by the ethnic community created through common ancestry), then there seems no *a priori* reason for assuming that such an attachment need be weak, or that it cannot develop and promote a sense of its continuity through time, in a shared past and a shared destiny. The perceptions of ethnic minorities probably do frequently differ from those of ethnic majorities, concerning the civic nationalist claims to ethnic neutrality, but these differing perceptions do not indicate that the civic nationalist claim to ethnic neutrality is intrinsically impossible, or even empirically unlikely.

The civic ideal of complete ethnic blindness may indeed be as unattainable for the civic nation as is the ideal of a strictly racially based exclusivism for an ethnocultural nation, but this does not detract from the utility of either concept as an ideal type. It seems reasonable to suggest that members of dominant ethnic groups might sometimes be imbued with a conscious pride in their ethnic dominance (Chinese chauvinism in Singapore, English supremacism in Britain), might sometimes take their ethnicity and their nationality for granted, and might sometimes consciously seek public institutions, practices and values which disregard ethnic differences so as to mobilise a trans-ethnic civic community. If each of these is possible, then the assumption that all claims to civic nationalism are fraudulent seems unwaranted, and conceptually unhelpful.[5]

The term 'civic nationalism' refers, then, to a sense of community which is focused on the belief that residence in a common territorial homeland, and commitment to its state and civil society institutions, generate a distinctive national character and civic culture, such that all citizens, irrespective of their diverse ancestry, comprise a community in progress, with a common destiny. This commitment to a common destiny, tied into the idea of common loyalty to the territory and its institutions, means that civic nationalism implies the acquisition of ethical obligations, and should not be regarded simply as a voluntary association lacking emotive power. This emotive power is often identified as a sense of pride in the civic culture, which serves to raise the people from a rabble to a nation, so that 'every member of the "people" . . . partakes of its elite quality' (Greenfeld 1992: 7). It thus 'dignif[ies] a man's suffering and gives him a hopeful direction in which to work' (Minogue 1967: 32).

Civic nationalism is sometimes depicted as 'forward-looking' in the sense that the vision is of a community in the process of formation, while ethnocultural nationalism is seen as backward-looking, in that the vision of the community is located in myths of the past. But this should not be interpreted to imply that the former is in some *moral* sense 'progressive' and the latter 'regressive', since morality is clearly not dependent on chronology. Moreover, such a definition does not completely resolve the difficulty in distinguishing the two forms of nationalism, since it is evident that ethnocultural nationalisms built upon myths of common ancestry will seek to establish the authentic continuity of their community by proclaiming visions of common destiny – located in the future; and, by the same token, civic nationalisms which see the national community as one always in the process of becoming, might seek to promote a sense of evolutionary development by appealing to ideas of the inheritance of public institutions from the past.

Moreover, part of the reason why the distinction between the two is so difficult to apply to actual cases of nationalism, is not simply that the two ideal types combine in all particular cases, but more fundamentally because both forms of nationalism employ, in their mythology and symbolism, the language of the family. Civic nationalism is just as likely as ethnocultural nationalism to use the language of motherland and homeland, but uses it to refer to the home of residence or arrival, rather than to the home of origin.

The ideas of civic and ethnocultural nationalisms are clarified, and interwoven, in the work of classical theorists such as Johann Herder, Johann Fichte and Max Weber.[6] But the suggestion that this distinction might explain the difference between the good–liberal and bad–authoritarian forms of nationalism, probably originates with Karl Marx. Marx distinguished different conceptualisations of the nation in terms of the type of class interests they promoted. A liberal and democratic conception of the nation was therefore one which promoted the interests of the oppressed classes. By contrast, the ethnic and ethnocentric conception of the nation (symbolised in the German case in the language of *Volk* and *Vaterland*) was seen by him as a romantic myth of uniqueness and superiority which comprised an alienative reaction by insecure middle classes, and which could be 'readily . . . harnessed to the conservative purposes of absolutist and authoritarian states' (Benner 1995: 91). The connection between alienation and the promotion by the state of a nationalist myth of common ethnic attributes and common ancestry is indicated in the following passage:

> Out of [the] very contradiction between the interest of the individual and that of the community the latter takes an independent form as the state, divorced from the real interests of individual and community, and at the same time as an illusory communal life, always based, however, on the real ties existing in every family and tribal conglomeration (such as flesh and blood, language, division of labour on a larger scale, and other interests).
>
> (Marx, *The German Ideology*, in Feuer (1969: 295))

Marx's negative evaluation of ethnocultural nationalism was subsequently echoed by the early twentieth-century German historian Friedrich Meinecke, although they differed in their understanding of the role of the state. Meinecke distinguished between the *staatsnation*, which 'centres on the idea of individual and collective self-determination and derives from the individual's free will and subjective commitment to the nation', and the *kulturnation*, which:

> is founded upon seemingly objective criteria such as common heritage and language, a distinct area of settlement, religion, custom and history, and does not need to be mediated by a national state or other political form. Consciousness of unity, the sense of belonging together, develop independent of the state . . . It leaves individuals little scope to choose to which nation they belong.
>
> (Alter 1989: 14)

In Meinecke's formulation, as in Marx's, 'The voluntarist, liberal–democratic concept of nation is contrasted by a deterministic one that is frequently deemed undemocratic and irrational' (Alter 1989: 15).

Meinecke's distinction was subsequently reformulated by Hans Kohn (1944, 1962), who distinguished between a Western (particularly North Atlantic) nationalism and an East–Central European nationalism. Western nationalism was 'a predominantly political occurrence' (Kohn 1944: 329) following from the formation of the state. It 'was connected with the concepts of individual liberty and rational cosmopolitanism' (Kohn 1944: 330), which flourished in 'a new society' arising from the Reformation and characterised by the growth of 'middle classes and secular learning' (Kohn 1944: 331). By contrast, the 'Eastern' nationalism (which included German, Russian and Indian nationalisms) originated as a reaction to Western nationalism, was manifested in 'ethnographic demands', and developed in societies which were 'at a more backward stage of political and social development' (Kohn 1944: 329). This Eastern nationalism was 'excessive and militant' (Kohn 1962: 24), focused upon the peculiarities of the 'soul' of the 'natural' community, and relied on 'myths of the past and dreams of the future, an ideal fatherland, closely linked with the past, devoid of any immediate connection with the present' (Kohn 1944: 330–1). The model for this was German nationalism:

> held together, not by the will of its members nor by any obligations of contract, but by traditional ties of kinship and status . . . [and by] the infinitely vaguer concept of 'folk' which . . . lent itself more easily to the embroideries of imagination and the excitations of emotion. Its roots seemed to reach into the dark soil of primitive times and to have grown through thousands of hidden channels of unconscious development, not in the bright light of rational political ends, but in the mysterious womb of the people, deemed to be so much nearer to the forces of nature.
>
> (Kohn 1994: 331)

This argument as to the irrational and ascriptive basis of ethnocultural nationalism, contrasted with the rational and voluntaristic basis of civic nationalism, has been employed, with varying degrees of modification, by several modern theorists of nationalism; and it constitutes one of the most resilient themes in the literature. Thus, for example, Anthony Smith, after noting some criticisms of Kohn's distinction, concludes that it nevertheless 'remains valid and useful' (Smith 1991: 81). He then refers to the 'Western or civic model of the nation' as involving claims to 'historic territory, legal–political community, legal–political equality of members, and common civic culture and ideology'. In this model, 'an individual had to belong to some nation, but could choose to which he or she belonged' (Smith 1991: 11). He contrasts this with a 'non-Western or ethnic' concept whereby 'whether you stayed in your community or emigrated to another, you remained ineluctably, organically, a member of the community of your birth and were for ever stamped by it'. This latter nationalism is characterised by 'genealogy and presumed descent ties, popular mobilisation, vernacular languages, customs and traditions' (Smith

1991: 11–12).[7] Smith employs this distinction to discuss differences between the contemporary nationalisms in the West and those in the ex-Soviet sphere, and explains these partly in terms of differences in social structure; in particular, the presence or absence of a bourgeoisie which could mediate the mobilising activities of intellectuals (Smith 1995: 76–83).[8]

Liah Greenfeld offers a related distinction between 'individualistic–libertarian' and 'collectivist–authoritarian' models of nationalism. For her, the character of nationalism is related to the character of the particular class and status groups who were its architects, though she sees the responses of these architects, rather than the structure of the society, as the determining factor in the character of nationalism. Her schema nevertheless makes the general tendencies clear. Individualistic–libertarian nationalism, which interprets popular sovereignty as intrinsically linked with democratic ideas of equal individual status and liberty, 'is predicated on a transformation in the character of the relevant population' (Greenfeld 1992: 10), in that it can emerge only in 'civic' communities where membership is open and voluntaristic. By contrast, the collectivist and authoritarian form of nationalism 'result[s] from the application of the original idea to conditions which did not necessarily undergo such transformation' (Greenfeld 1992: 10), and is most likely to emerge where membership is on an ethnic basis, since such membership is 'inherent . . . [I]t has nothing to do with individual will, but constitutes a genetic characteristic'. In the ethnocultural nation, therefore, the idea of popular sovereignty is interpreted in unitary and inegalitarian terms: 'it tends to assume the character of a collective individual possessed of a single will, and someone is bound to be its interpreter' (Greenfeld 1992: 11). Michael Keating similarly distinguishes between ethnic and civic nationalisms: 'One presents membership of the national community as given, or ascriptive; the other sees individuals voluntarily constituting themselves as a collectivity' (1996: 3). Though he does note that 'civic nationalism can be violent and . . . civic values may be narrow and intolerantly applied' (Keating 1996: 7). James Kellas builds more directly on Kohn's typology in distinguishing between 'western' nationalism which was social and inclusive in form, was 'more liberal democratic, and did not engage in genocide, transfers of population etc.'; and eastern European nationalism which was ethnically exclusive, 'intolerant and often led to authoritarianism' (1991: 73–4).

David Miller has recently been critical of attempts to distinguish 'a desirable "Western" form of nationalism from an undesirable "Eastern" form' (1995). Nevertheless, he achieves something similar to this by contrasting what he calls 'nationality', which is liberal and tolerant, with 'nationalism' which refers to 'organic wholes' and is an 'illiberal and belligerent doctrine' (Miller 1995: 8). For Miller, this distinction is closely connected to the differences between ethnicity and nationality, with the former referring to 'a community formed by common descent and sharing cultural features' (1995: 19), and the latter referring to a community constituted by belief rather than by common attributes, and by 'a shared wish to continue their life in common' (1995: 23). Montserrat Guibernau repeats the argument that the civic nationalism of popular consent, associated with the rise of the bourgeoisie and the spread of Enlightenment ideas, has taken a liberal direction; while the ethnocultural nationalism of 'common language, blood and soil', reacting against the Enlightenment, has tended to an 'exclusivist, xenophobic, expansionist and oppressive character' (1996: 51–7). Tom Nairn sees civic nationalism as developing out of the institutions of an inherently liberal civil society, whereas ethnic nationalism is 'perceived as inherently . . . divisive, inward- and backward-looking, atavistic, aggressive and probably not too good for business either' (1997: 86).

The contributions of such theorists have done much to revive and refine the study of contemporary nationalism, and their variously formulated arguments undoubtedly have an intuitive appeal and a contemporary resonance, especially when one employs the imagery of the civic nationalisms of the USA or the UK on the one hand, and of Tamil, Kurdish or Serb ethnocultural nationalisms on the other. But correlation does not always indicate cause. Moreover, it would not need too much thought to generate apparent exceptions. Certainly, civic nationalism frequently takes an authoritarian form, as articulated by Suharto in Indonesia, or earlier by Jacobin nationalism in France (Hayes 1949: Ch. 3). Ethnocultural nationalism not only sometimes seems to take rather benign forms, as with the Welsh or Slovene cases, but is also often regarded as the carrier of minority rights and social justice. This is most noticeably so in its manifestation as contemporary claims by indigenous or minority ethnic communities for enhanced political autonomy and special rights. In this latter version, the moral evaluation of ethnocultural nationalism is often reversed, so that instead of being seen as intrinsically irrational and illiberal, it appears as intrinsic to individual development and true liberty. This is also suggested by Tzvetan Todorov in his discussion of French theorists such as Antonin Artaud and Montesquieu:

> Ethnocultural nationalism (that is, attachment to one's own culture) is a path towards universalism – by deepening the specificity of the particular within which one dwells. Civic nationalism . . . is a preferential choice in favor of one's own country over the others – thus, it is an antiuniversalist choice.
>
> (1993: 172)

Perhaps the main contemporary significance of the distinction between ethnocultural and civic nationalisms, and of this ambiguity regarding their moral evaluation, is in the debate as to the meaning and implications of 'multiculturalism'. Does this term refer simply to a civic nationalism whose public civic culture can accommodate the diversity of private ethnic cultures; or to an ethnocultural nationalist challenge to civic nationalism which threatens to divide the state into competing sovereignties? Is it to be applauded for challenging an existing ethnocultural nationalism which favours ethnic majorities, with new formulas which favour hitherto marginalised minorities? Or condemned for prioritising ascriptive and illiberal group rights over liberal individual rights?

The distinction needs examining for other reasons. As has already been noted, most nationalisms contain ingredients of both the civic and ethnocultural forms, so that there is disagreement, for example, among observers of Catalan nationalism in Spain, or East Timorese nationalism, or Scottish nationalism in the UK, as to how to characterise them. Should they be seen as minority ethnocultural nationalist movements, or as regionalist civic nationalisms?[9] There is clearly the danger that we characterise a nationalism as ethnocultural or civic in form, depending upon whether we wish to support or oppose it. Moreover, if we seek to explain the form which nationalism takes by reference to the fundamental character of the society, as is sometimes indicated by the civic–ethnocultural distinction, then how can this help to explain cases such as French, Quebec or Irish nationalisms, which seem to shift between authoritarian and liberal manifestations and to have both liberal and illiberal proponents?[10] Clarification as to the theoretical basis of the arguments is needed.

Conceptual ambiguity is likely when concepts offered as 'ideal-type' analytical models, turn out to contain clusters of arguments which might only be contingently connected. Thus, while the above distinctions between civic and ethnocultural nationalisms have facilitated some subtle discussions of particular cases, they have not really clarified the causes of their differences, because three distinct arguments have been interwoven, and need disentangling. First, there is the argument that the two nationalisms differ in that one is based on irrational primordial attachments, and the other on rational civil sentiments. Second, there is the argument that the differences depend upon whether or not there has been a social transformation, which has resulted in a strong middle class able to exert liberalising influences. Third, there is a suggestion, most explicitly made by Kohn, that the character of nationalism might be related to the issue of whether or not it develops as a reactive protest movement. Each of these arguments need examining. It will be argued that none of them are satisfactory, but that there are aspects of the middle-class argument, and of the reactivity argument, which can be reformulated so as to provide a useful starting point for explaining the liberalism or illiberalism of nationalism, once they have been disconnected from the civic–ethnocultural distinction.

The primordial–civil distinction

The dominant explanation for the alleged authoritarian nature of ethnocultural nationalism, offered in the above works, refers to the 'primordial' character of the community. In Clifford Geertz's formulation, primordial bonds are 'the "givens" – or, more precisely, as culture is inevitably involved in such matters, the assumed "givens" of social existence . . . These congruities of blood, speech, custom, and so on are seen to have an ineffable, and at times overpowering, coerciveness in and of themselves' (1963: 109). The resultant ethnocultural community is seen as illiberal in three respects, first, in the claim that membership of such a community is ascribed by birth and cannot be changed by individual free will; second, in the claim that such ethnocultural nationalism is inherently collectivist, so as to inhibit expressions of individual liberty; and third, in the claim that this ethnocultural nationalism constitutes an irrational and dominant attachment, from which individuals must free themselves before they can attain the status of rational beings. Further, such ethnocultural nationalism is frequently depicted as 'excessive' so as to signify claims to the superiority of one's own particular nation, rather than the acceptance of equal nationalisms.

These characterisations of ethnocultural nationalism as illiberal, derive from the idea that the belief in common ancestry (whether or not factually true), generates a particular type of emotional bond between the individual and the community of common kinship, which is one of blood rather than reason, variously described as primordial, instinctual, emotionally overwhelming and irrational. If this were the case, then all ethnocultural nationalisms would be intrinsically detrimental to the exercise of individual free will on the part of their members. Such a depiction of ethnicity, and thence of ethnocultural nationalism, has, however, come under increasing attack in recent years (Eller and Coughlan 1993). Even proponents of primordialism reduce the analytical rigour of their position by conceding that in all modern communities claiming common ancestry, this claim is not solely based on the objective cultural traits and the real facts of common ancestry, but rather on the power of the myths and symbols of kinship articulated by the modern poets, historians and politicians who seek to mobilise the people around the nationalist ideology. Some ethnocultural nationalisms claiming common ancestral roots are more invented than others, but all refer to the belief, rather than the fact, of common ancestry.

This means that membership of an ethnically defined cultural community is never completely ascriptive and immutable. Thus, Yael Tamir, arguing that ethnocultural nationalism can be liberal, has recently suggested, (using Sonia Ghandi as one of her examples) that, 'in reality individuals do assimilate, break cultural ties, and move from one national community to another' (1993: 25–32). The extent to which such assimilation into an ethnocultural nation is available to individuals, and the cost which it entails, clearly varies enormously from case to case, but religious conversion, migration, language change, in-marriage and cultural adoption are all possible entry routes, and may be accompanied by acquisition of the appropriate myths of common origin, ancestry, history and destiny.

It is frequently suggested, however, that ethnocultural nations which define themselves in terms of race, will be more closed to entry than will those which see language as the primary marker of common ancestry. This may in some cases be so, but it is instructive to remember that claims to distinct biological genealogy, and to clear population boundaries based on such genealogy are always necessarily 'dubious', so that 'it is an irony of our modern interpretation that such ['biosocial'] groups . . . readily appear more autochthonous, more embedded, and so more biologically integral, less mixed up with politics, movement, and modernity. The appearance is largely illusory, vanishing as it is grasped' (Chapman 1993: 24 and 29). Instead of postulating that it is racially based nationalisms which might be exclusivist and illiberal, it seems more likely to be those nationalisms which are confronted by threatening 'others' whom they seek to exclude, which might redefine their own nationality (and that of their enemies) in racial terms, on the initiative of their political or intellectual élites. Thus, for example, Chinese ethnocultural nationalism shifted from being one which was open to cultural assimilation, towards being defined in more closed terms as based on racial Han identity, in response to contact with distrusted Westerners (Dikotter 1990). Similarly, German ethnocultural nationalism, whose *Volk*-centred identity had been open to cultural assimilation, became closed and illiberal in response to perceived external threats, and accordingly had its identity redefined by political élites as a closed (but politically malleable) identity, based on myths of Aryan race, depicting its greatest enemies also in racial terms.[11]

The suggestion that ethnocultural nationalism is illiberal, because of the particularly strong emotional power of cultural identities based on common ancestry, is also open to doubt. There seems to be no *a priori* reason why the myth of common ethnic descent, which lies at the heart of ethnocultural nationalism, should constitute a bond which is any more emotionally powerful or hegemonic, than might be the bonds either to the family at one end of the scale, or to the state and its civic nation at the other. This is because the emotional power of the cultural or ethnic bond has a partially situational basis, and may vary between weak and strong, between being taken for granted or being conscious, depending in part on its utility for the pursuit of situational goals or for defence against situational threats (Ronen 1979). But, also, any claim that the bond of ethnocultural nationalism is stronger than that to the civic nation because the former can employ for itself the power of the 'family resemblance' (Horowitz 1985), must recognise that the civic nation similarly clothes itself in the myths and symbols of family.

Perhaps the strongest argument that ethnocultural nationalism is inherently illiberal, derives from the claim that the ethnic bond is necessarily collectivist. Liah Greenfeld explains this by saying that, whereas civic nationalism may refer simply to the idea of a sovereign people (those occupying a denoted territory) without any connotations of collective uniqueness, ethnocultural nationalism necessarily refers to the uniqueness of each community, since it defines them in terms of their particular cultural attributes, and of descent. She argues, then, that it is this shift of nationalism, from the idea of sovereignty to the idea of uniqueness, which prioritises the collectivity over the individual, and thus facilitates authoritarian assertions of a collective will (Greenfeld 1992).

This argument has been challenged by recent communitarian and liberal arguments, which see individual self-fulfilment as necessarily dependent upon membership of the ethnocultural community, arguments popularised in the language of minority rights and multiculturalism. Such arguments can be traced back to Herder and Fichte who had both seen the political autonomy of the ethnocultural nation as the necessary engine for individual freedom. Thus, 'in Fichte's hands . . . full self-determination for the individual came to require national self-determination' (Kedourie 1993: 137).[12] In contemporary theories, the argument that individual well-being and dignity depend upon the respect given to the ethnocultural nation, has generated both communitarian claims to group rights of cultural self-preservation and liberal claims to individual rights of access to cultural resources. But the link between the well-being of the individual and that of the ethnocultural community needs to be treated carefully, since it cannot simply be assumed that individual self-determination and national self-determination are equivalent, parallel or analogous concepts. The work of Will Kymlicka is important here

(Kymlicka 1989, 1995a). Kymlicka argues that individual liberty can only be attained by individuals who have access to full membership of a vibrant cultural community, and thence that ethnocultural communities which find themselves under threat, have the right to national self-determination so as to protect their cultural resources. Kymlicka does, however, seek to recognise the problem that some cultures are more oppressive of individual liberty than others, and that some group rights might suppress some individual rights. But it is clear from the communitarian–liberal debate on multiculturalism, that ethnocultural nationalism should not be seen as inherently inimical to individual liberty, and might in some cases and in some respects be conducive and indeed essential for it.[13]

Ethnicity derives its power from the belief on the part of individuals that they can fulfil themselves through identification with the mythical kinship community, so that ethnocultural nationalism always portrays itself as the engine of individual liberation and self-determination, and may at least in some cases actually function in this way. Thus, ethnocultural nationalism does not in any sense support the idea of an ethnic majority suppressing an ethnic minority. Indeed, the ethnocultural nationalist vision is specifically one which envisions each ethnic community as having its own political autonomy. Where suppression of ethnic minorities within an ethnocultural nation does occur, then, we might wish to blame it on the failure to implement the tenets of ethnocultural nationalism, rather than on those tenets themselves. This is not to say that some ethnocultural nationalisms may not portray other ethnocultural nations or ethnic communities as their enemies, and act illiberally towards them. But in this respect they are perhaps no different from some civic nationalisms.

The aspect of civic nationalism which is stressed in the formulations of the civic–ethnocultural dichotomy, is as a 'rational' and voluntaristic community of equal sovereign citizens. In Alter's words, 'the existence or otherwise of the nation depend[s] on the will of the individual . . . [and comprises] a community of politically aware citizens equal before the law irrespective of their social and economic status, ethnic origin and political beliefs' (1989: 14–15). Such a civic community is, then, depicted as intrinsically liberal in that it derives from, and exists to promote, the rational will of its individual citizens. But as Bernard Yack has noted in his discussion of 'the myth of the civic nation':

> It may be reasonable to contrast nations whose distinctive cultural inheritance centers on political symbols and political stories with nations whose cultural inheritance centers on language and stories about ethnic origins. But it is unreasonable and unrealistic to interpet this contrast as a distinction between the rational attachment to principle and the emotional celebration of inherited culture.
>
> (1999: 106)

The rational, voluntaristic basis of civic nationalism needs, therefore, to be questioned. Civic nationalisms are indeed voluntaristic in that they comprise 'the conscious creations of bodies of people who have elaborated and revised them in order to make sense of their social and political surroundings' (Miller 1995: 6). But civic nations are communities of obligation which demand allegiance, and which must therefore resist voluntaristic renunciations by present members, who are obliged to inherit decisions made by past generations. This demand of civic allegiance might be perceived as illiberal and ethnically biased, as Anthony Smith notes:

> civic nationalisms often demand, as the price of receiving citizenship, the surrender of ethnic community and individuality, the privatization of ethnic religion, and the marginalization of the ethnic culture and heritage of minorities within the borders of the national state. That was how Black elites and Jews were treated by French civic nationalism.
>
> (1995: 101)

The present generation can only be tied into the 'voluntaristic' nation if the nation depicts itself as 'a community that . . . stretches back and forward across the generations' (Miller 1995: 24). Thus, voluntaristic civic nationalisms embed their citizens within myths of historical continuity, and thereby become less voluntaristic.

Moreover, as noted above, Liah Greenfeld explains that liberal nationalism gives way to illiberal nationalism when the idea of popular sovereignty is distorted by political élites, so that instead of referring to the actual sovereignty of individuals, it becomes reinterpreted to refer only to the theoretical sovereignty of a collective will, so that 'the select few dictate to the masses who must obey'. But Greenfeld recognises that both civic and ethnocultural nationalisms may be collectivist in this way (1992: 11).[14] Further, the fragility of this particular civic–cultural distinction is reinforced once it is recognised that for the large majority of citizens of the predominantly civic nation, there is no choice as to national identity. They are born into their nation, rather than choosing it; and the extent to which they can choose entry into another predominantly civic nation may be just as limited by legal citizenship restrictions (even for entry into liberal UK, USA or Australia), as it might be by variable barriers to (and costs of) cultural assimilation in the case of predominantly ethnocultural nations.

It is indeed intrinsic to civic nationalism that it projects itself forward, since it is, in Greenfeld's words, an 'emergent phenomenon' (1992: 7) defined in terms of the possibilities of its development, which relate to pride in the public culture denoted by territorial statehood and citizenship, and to visions of common destiny. Backward projection is not intrinsic, and the emergent civic nationalism may seek to reject tradition and make a break with the past. Nevertheless, it is likely that, 'various stories [will be] concocted [such that] personal characteristics presently seen as constitutive of national identity are projected back on to . . . distant forbears', and 'the nation is conceived as a community extended in history and with a distinct character that is natural to its members' (Miller 1995: 34–5). Thus, even the predominantly civic nationalism of the USA was clothed in the language of common ancestry. Americans were thus depicted, by the authors of the 1787–8 Federalist

Papers, as 'descended from the same ancestors, speaking the same language, professing the same religion, attached to the same principles of government, very similar in their manners and customs . . . a band of brethren' (quoted in Walzer 1995: 139).

But it is at this point, when civic nations begin to employ the language of common ancestry and nature ('distant forbears' and 'natural' character) to refer to their pasts, and not just to their futures, that the ideal-type civic nationalism begins to intertwine with the ideal-type ethnocultural nationalism. It is intrinsic to civic nationalism that ideas of common ancestry refer not to the community, who are depicted rather as non-sanguine kin, but rather to the homeland which they inhabit. So long as the historical myths of the nation celebrate the diversity of the 'concocted stories' and the distinctiveness of their multiple 'forbears' who came together in the nationalist enterprise, then civic nationalism is maintained; but once the stories begin to employ the language of *common* descent – to refer to the national community, albeit colloquially, as a national 'race' descended from founding 'fathers' 'inheriting' common attributes – then the civil culture of civic nationalism is being intertwined with the ethnic culture of ethnocultural nationalism. Miller's attempt to see a clear distinction between a civic nationalism, which refers to a historical community comprising 'our forbears [who] have toiled and spilled their blood . . . [W]e who are born into it inherit an obligation [to] a community that stretches back and forth across the generations' (1995: 23) and an ethnocultural nationalism which 'claims that our fellow nationals must be our "kith and kin", a view that leads directly to racism' (1995: 25), seems, as Andrew Vincent notes, 'highly dubious' (1997: 23). All such claims to common ancestry denote ethnocultural nationalism, not civic nationalism; and when predominantly or avowedly civic nationalisms make such claims, we need to recognise that civic nationalism is once again eliding with ethnocultural nationalism. Max Weber suggested that this merging is likely, since 'the concept of "nationality" shares with that of "the people" (*Volk*) – in the ethnic sense – the vague connotation that whatever is felt to be distinctively common must derive from common descent' (Weber, in Guibernau 1996: 32). This is the significance of much of Anthony Smith's work. He accepts the distinction between civic and ethnocultural nationalisms, but then shows how the two intertwine in modern nationalisms which seek legitimacy through 'ethnic historicism', the process whereby intellectuals seek to reconcile the need for both legal–rational and religious legitimation, by promoting cultural regeneration movements. Smith shows that the outcome – the character of modern nationalism including its liberalism or illiberalism – may vary enormously, depending upon whether the intellectuals are secular or traditional; whether they are allied with or opposed to the state; whether the assimilationists, reformers or neo-traditionalists are dominant; and how the myths and symbols of community are employed. But these variations do not accord with the civic–ethnocultural distinction, and indeed cut across it.

It has been suggested, thus far, that the distinction between civic and ethnocultural nationalism cannot adequately be explained in terms of any difference between two types of society, the primordial organic community and the voluntaristic civil association. Actual modern nationalisms intertwine the two. But predominantly civic nationalisms which stress common destiny rather than common past (Suharto's Indonesia or Nkrumah's Ghana) can be in various respects illiberal or morally regressive, just as predominantly ethnocultural nationalisms stressing common kinship roots might be progressive 'moral innovators', as John Hutchinson has stressed (1994).

The middle-class argument

Kohn related the distinction between civic and ethnocultural nationalisms to the issue of whether social transformation had engendered a strong middle-class and civil society which could articulate nationalism, or whether these were absent or weak, in which case nationalism could be articulated only by 'scholars and poets, unsupported by public opinion – which did not exist' (1944: 330–1). The presence of such a strong middle class has frequently been seen as the key factor in the development of liberalism and democracy, as by Lipset (1960), Almond and Verba (1963), and Barrington Moore (1966). But the anti-liberal potentialities of the middle classes have also been recognised, by among others, J.S. Mill ([1859–61] 1970) and Alexis de Tocqueville (1840), and this potentiality is manifested, for example, in the rise of 'illiberal democracy' in contemporary Asia (Bell *et al.* 1995: Ch. 4). If, as Anthony Smith recognises, 'the commitment of the bourgeoisie to rational versions of nationalism is a dubious assumption' and if, as both he and John Hutchinson point out, ethnocultural nationalism seems to occur in countries with significant bourgeoisies as well as those without (Smith 1991: 81, Hutchinson 1987: 7 n. 1), then the argument begins to look distinctly fragile.

The ambiguities are particularly evident in the case of German nationalism, which plays a pivotal role in the development of the models under consideration, both as the home of the major theorists,[15] and as their classic case of central European ethnocultural nationalism. The problem is that this key case does not conform to the argument that ethnocultural nationalism is most likely to arise in communities with a weak civil society and a weak middle class. Meinecke recognised that German nationalism had begun as a liberal movement of the educated middle class, but had then taken a new authoritarian direction because of a 'sinister development in the German bourgeoisie' (1963: 2), which 'closed its mind more and more against the democratic idea' (1963: 31), and thus became vulnerable to statist manipulation of romantic ideas of a German folk-community (1963: 73–4). Erica Benner, in her recent elucidation of Karl Marx's analysis of German nationalism, shows that Marx also rejected the view that it was the weakness of the German middle classes which explained the rise of illiberal nationalism:

> It is important to stress that Marx and Engels regarded the bourgeoisie's prudential interests *vis-à-vis* the lower classes – and not bourgeois weakness in the face of intra-class divisions, international conflicts, and traditional ruling authorities – as the decisive factor explaining the collapse of the liberal–nationalist movement.
>
> (1995: 112)

Max Weber blamed 'the wretched countenence' of German nationalism on the 'immaturity' of the bourgeoisie, but by this he meant not their size or economic power, but rather their 'political philistinism' (Weber, in Dahbour and Ishay 1995: 121). Liah Greenfeld's work similarly challenges the theory that it is the middle classes who are the architects of a liberal civic nationalism. Indeed, as she notes, it is only the German case, among her European cases, which 'lends support to the view that nationalism is a middle-class phenomenon'.[16] But it is also the German case which is most illiberal. Greenfeld seeks to explain this as an exception in that the architects of German nationalism were middle-class intellectuals who were 'a group apart' (1992: 293), suspended between the wider middle class and the nobility, so that their commitment to enlightenment rationality was transformed into a romantic longing for collectivism by their 'dissatisfaction with their personal situation' (1992: 351) of 'isolation and exclusion' (1992: 346), as 'unsuccessful intellectuals' (1992: 345) imbued with an 'oppressive sense of status-inconsistency' (1992: 277). But her analysis does not support any claim that it is the weakness of the middle classes or of civil society which were the primary influences on the character of nationalism. The hypothesis which emerges, rather, is perhaps that nationalism will tend to take a liberal form where its major interpeters and articulators are from upwardly mobile class or status groups who no longer feel under threat, but who seek to 'preserv[e] and guarantee . . . their newly acquired status, human dignity and unhindered ability to be and do what they believed they were entitled to' (Greenfeld 1992: 56). By the same token, where nationalism is articulated by class or status groups which feel marginalised and insecure, it would take a more collectivist and illiberal form. But such a hypothesis does not quite work, since it leaves unexplained why the nationalist ideologies of one particular class – whether imbued with self-confidence or an inferiority complex, should resonate with the wider populace, so as to influence the complexion of the national identity. This seems to need further examination.

The reactivity argument

Kohn noted that his 'Central and Eastern European' ethnocultural nationalism 'grew in protest against and in conflict with the existing state pattern', with the aim 'to redraw the political boundaries'. This contrasted with Western civic nationalisms which were 'preceded by the formation of the future national state, or as in the case of the United States, coincided with it' (Kohn 1944: 329). He was not suggesting that nationalism would change its character, from ethnocultural to civic, the moment that autonomous territorial statehood was achieved; but rather that the difference between English and French nationalisms on the one hand, which he regarded as having had a liberal history, and German nationalism on the other, which he saw as having generated authoritarianism, arose from the latter's 'dependence on the West [which] often wounded the pride of the native educated class, as soon as it began to develop its own nationalism, and ended in an opposition to the "alien" example, and its liberal and rational outlook' (Kohn 1944: 330).

The suggestion seems to be, then, that ethnocultural nationalisms might be illiberal because they develop as reactions against threatening others, and seek to change the existing structure of states. In Kohn's words, ethnocultural nationalism 'looked for its justification and its differentiation to the heritage of its own past, and extolled the primitive and ancient depth and peculiarities of its traditions in contrast to Western rationalism and to universal standards. . . . [It was] dependent upon, and opposed to, influences from without . . . [It] lacked self-assurance; its inferiority complex was often compensated by overemphasis and overconfidence' (1994: 330).

Civic nationalisms, on the other hand, are depicted as liberal in that they are not reactive, but emerge rather out of an internally generated process, and function so as to legitimate, rather than to change, existing state structures. In the case of the English model ('God's firstborn'), 'national consciousness was first and foremost the consciousness of one's dignity as an individual . . . Thus English nationalism had time to gestate . . . and became a powerful force which no longer needed buttresses to exist. It acquired its own momentum. It existed in its own right' (Greenfeld 1992: 87). In the American model, nationalism grew out of its European 'other', 'not a movement of romantic protest against the Western equalitarian and rational attitude . . . but the consummation of this western attitude' (Kohn 1944: 291–2). 'Americans could unite men of different pasts, because on the basis of rationalism and individualism they rejected the foundations of the past . . . [relying instead on] the suggestions of their own good sense, the knowledge of their own situation, and the lessons of their own experience' (Kohn 1944: 324).

But this argument immediately faces the problem that there is a sense in which all nationalisms, whether civic or ethnocultural, are necessarily reactive in that their origin is in assertions of an identity demarcating the us from the them; the them being either the authoritarian ruler suppressing civil society, or the external enemy threatening societal unity. This applies just as much to nationalisms which are both predominantly civic and predominantly liberal – such as American nationalism which grew out of reactive rebellion against British rule; as it does to predominantly ethnocultural and predominantly illiberal nationalisms, as with the German case.

Nevertheless, it might be that there is a useful insight here. The greater the perception of a threatening other, the more likely it is that the society will need to mobilise itself as a collective entity against that threat, and thence to suppress individual liberties so as to promote that mobilisation. Greenfeld makes this point. She uses the term *ressentiment* primarily to refer to feelings of inferiority, and thence of envy and hatred, in reaction to other nationalisms, and explains that '*Ressentiment* not only makes a nation more aggressive, but represents an unusually powerful stimulant of national sentiment and collective action' (Greenfeld 1992: 488).

Granting this for the moment, it remains unclear as to whether ethnocultural nationalism is necessarily any more reactive in origin than is civic nationalism. It is also not clear that the reactive origin of nationalism necessarily determines its subsequent development, which may become either internally generated or may remain focused on *ressentiment*. In the case of ethnocultural nationalism, there does not seem to be anything intrinsically reactive about the process of building a modern nation on the basis of strong ethnic myths of common origin. Illiberalism might indeed be implied when the reaction to other nationalisms takes the form of ethnocentric assertions of superiority, in that a collectivist closure may be needed so as to maintain the demarcation. But ethnocultural nationalisms with reactive origins might well, as in Herder's vision, recognise the equal right of all ethnocultural communities to similar political autonomy in a brotherhood of nations. Such polycentric nationalisms are likely to develop, as Yael Tamir argues, in liberal directions (Tamir 1993: Ch. 4).

The suggestion that civic nationalism will be non-reactive and therefore liberal, similarly seems problematic. Indeed, since civic nationalism is portrayed as following from the achievement of statehood, rather than preceeding it, it seems vulnerable to illiberalism, in that the period between the acquisition of territorial statehood, and the subsequent mature development of national consciousness might well be conducive to the type of 'authoritarian–collectivist' shortcut to nationalism noted by Greenfeld, in which the sense of 'us' is generated by political élites, precisely against the 'them'. In this way, many of the anti-colonial nationalisms directed against European colonialism, have been predominantly civic in character, reactive in origin, and illiberal in politics.

A reformulation

Nationalism which is reactive in origin, and which is articulated by a marginalised group, is more likely to emerge in an illiberal form; but such illiberalism is not fixed, since it depends upon how nationalist élites portray the nation's enemies.

It might be possible to explain more effectively the difference between the good–liberal and bad–illiberal versions of nationalism if we make a connection between Kohn's distinction between nationalisms which arise out of an 'inferiority complex' in relation to an 'alien' other (1944: 330) and those which arise out of optimistic 'faith . . . in the virtues of life and liberty in the new and unfettered world' (1944: 293); and Greenfeld's distinction between those nationalisms which are articulated by classes or status groups feeling marginalised, and those articulated by an upwardly mobile class or status group imbued with self-confidence and pride. Such a connection is sometimes implied by Greenfeld,[17] but is more clearly indicated by Peter Alter in his distinction between what he termed 'Risorgimento' nationalism, and 'Integral' nationalism. Alter explains the rise of Fascist (integral) nationalism in Germany as being based both on the insecurities of the 'old and the new middle classes . . . [who] felt their material existence and social status to be under threat' (1989: 46); and also on the 'crisis of national self-confidence, the putative looming of extraordinary perils from outside, real or perceived threats to the continued existence of the nation' (1989: 46). Liberal (Risorgimento) nationalism similarly began as a 'protest movement' (1989: 29) but developed in a liberal direction first, because it 'accompanie[d] the liberation . . . of a new social strata' (1989: 28), and, second, because it articulated an intrinsically self-confident mood of awakening and resurrection which saw a process of emancipation from oppression as already underway or imminent.

Thus, instead of arguing, as hitherto, that ethnocultural nationalisms are intrinsically illiberal, it may be useful to reformulate the argument. Perhaps it is those nationalisms, whether civic or ethnocultural, which are articulated by insecure élites and which constitute *ressentiment*-based reactions against others who are perceived as threatening, which consequently become illiberal. By the same token, perhaps civic and ethnocultural nationalisms which begin as protest movements but do not develop their identity primarily in relation to threatening others, and which are articulated by self-confident élites, are most likely to take a liberal form. Feelings of insecurity on the part both of the articulators of nationalist ideologies, and of their mass audiences, have the potentiality to transform all nationalisms in collectivist and illiberal directions, irrespective of their civic and ethnocultural mix, depending upon how the other and thence the self are depicted.

This reformulation of the argument builds upon the insights of Kohn and Meinecke, but involves a shift of focus. Instead of looking to the character of the community or the incidence of middle classes for the explanation of whether nationalism is liberal or authoritarian, we are led to look both at the ways in which political élites depict the nationalist goals, and the insecurities, threats or enemies which inhibit their attainment; and also at the receptivity of the wider populace to these nationalist visions and threats.

Illiberal nationalism is thus most likely when it is articulated by an insecure class or strata, and where the wider populace is also experiencing insecurities which make it receptive to the collectivist solutions offered by propagators of nationalism. Political leaders may, in differing circumstances, portray contemporary threats as coming from oppositionist activists or from class unrest, and may thereby be led, as in the case of Singapore, in the direction of depicting ideas of individual rights and liberties as the primary threat to the nationalist vision. They can then assert that the survival and development of the predominantly civic nation depends upon ensuring that the national 'general will' is not weakened or subverted by the partial vested interests of dissident individuals. In those cases where opposition is clustered in particular regions of the country, or among particular linguistic groups, then political élites may choose to demonise such opposition, as in contemporary Kenya, by depicting it as ethnic in origin, and denigrating it as sectarianism, communalism, or racism. Elsewhere, it may be that political leaders can convince the populace that the threat comes from outside – from other nation-states whose territorial, economic or political claims can be shown to impinge on the national destiny. Such nationalisms will be 'illiberal' in the sense that they assert the superiority of the national 'us', over the alien other, either in xenophobic attacks on specific nation-states, or in more generalised denigrations of foreign influences as Communist, Western values, Asian menace, etc. Political élites who wish to close off their society against external influences or employ scapegoat strategies against minorities, might, as previously noted, find it useful to depict the threats in racial terms, and might also choose to reformulate myths of common history in racial terms. The influence of such depictions upon national consciousness partly depends, no doubt, both on the culture of the society, and on the actual situational challenges, and thence the types of insecurities facing the society; but political élites do have flexibility in the portrayal of enemies, and this gives a fluidity to the character of nationalism, and in particular to the liberalism or illiberalism of nationalist politics.

Thus, civic nationalism may develop in either liberal or illiberal directions depending upon how effectively its visions of civic community are employed by the mobilising élites to resolve societal aspirations or fears. And ethnocultural nationalism should be seen as neither intrinsically the 'progressive' engine of minority and indigenous ethnic rights, nor intrinsically 'regressive' and oppressive of the individual, as its recent manifestations in the Balkans might seem to indicate. As John Hutchinson showed in his study of ethnocultural nationalism, the character of Irish nationalism changed remarkably in three different 'revivals', from Anglo-Irish and liberal to Gaelic and populist, depending upon which intellectuals were mobilising it; which threats and dangers they stressed; and which symbols – religious or secular – they employed (1987).

The distinction between the two ideal-type models of nationalism, civic and ethnocultural, is indeed a significant one, distinguishing visions of community which are rooted in perceptions of common ancestry, from those which focus on perceptions of the continuous integration of individuals of diverse backgrounds into one new family home, with its distinctive institutions and common destiny. This distinction is central to an understanding of the political tensions and dynamics of modern nationalisms, and in particular to the debate as to how states should be managing their ethnic minorities. But the focus here has been upon unpacking the sets of assumptions which have been associated with the two terms in relation to their allegedly intrinsic liberalism or illiberalism. The view that civic nationalism is liberal because it refers to a voluntaristic society, while ethnocultural nationalism is illiberal because it refers to an ascriptive community, has been criticised here, since both forms of nationalism seek to tie the component individuals into communities of obligation which are depicted as persisting through time, and both have the capacity to prioritise either the collectivity or the individual. The view that civic nationalism is liberal because of the presence of a strong middle class was also criticised, on the ground that illiberal middle classes are not unusual. Finally, the view that ethnocultural nationalism tends to be illiberal because its origins are reactive, was criticised on the grounds that the link between ethnocultural nationalism and reactive nationalism seems more likely to be a contingent one. It was then argued, however, that nationalisms which are both articulated by a marginalised or insecure class or status group, and which appeal to a widespread *ressentiment*-based reaction to a threatening other, are indeed more likely to be illiberal than are nationalisms which are internally generated and articulated by secure élites. But the nature and extent of this illiberalism should be seen as a political variable.

The conclusion is that the difference between liberal and illiberal manifestations of nationalism cannot be explained by reference to the distinction between its civic and ethnocultural forms. Nationalism does have two ideological faces, civic and ethnocultural, but the political character of both is surely protean rather than Janus-faced.

4 Constructing nationalism

The case of the Basques

Disagreements as to how to explain nationalist conflicts sometimes focus on which of the three conceptual languages outlined in Chapter 1 to employ, and thence on which facts to isolate as key causal factors. Does explanation begin with the facts of racial or tribal difference, or with those of competing class interests, or with the construction of new myths of identity? Sophisticated observers might respond by saying that complex events surely require all perspectives to be taken into account, but this balanced judgement faces the problem of explaining how the behaviour of those involved can be depicted as being based on primordial instinct and rational choice and ideological prejudice, when these are usually regarded as incompatible mental processes. If good explanation must be clear and consistent, then the task becomes not that of combining the three approaches, but rather that of examining each one so as to show why and how one of them might offer deeper insights than the others.

In order to see how the different perspectives may be applied in practice, and why the constructivist approach might be preferred, the case of Basque nationalism has been selected. The reasons for the selection of this particular case are that the literature on the Basques provides rich evidence of the use of all three conceptual approaches, and that the Basque issue is one which fits the dominant themes of this book; the tension between the claims of an established nation-state and the claims of an emergent peripheral nationalism; and the tension between civic nationalism and ethnocultural nationalism.

A primordialist approach

> From this perspective, it is the genetic and linguistic distinctiveness of the Basque community, and the Spanish invasions of Basque autonomy, which explain the intensity of Basque commitment to independence from Spain.

The primordialist approach is usually employed as one thread of argument in attempts to explain ethnicity and nationalism, rather than as the sole basis for analysis. It emerges in suggestions that nationalist movements are the expression of a group solidarity based on linguistic, racial and cultural affinities; and that claims by such a group to common descent should not be regarded simply as imaginings or inventions, but should be taken seriously as indicators that it is the authentic histories of common ancestry and homeland origin which provide the roots of modern nationalism. This primordialist line of argument leads directly to the suggestion that it is the lack of such authenticity which undermines the claims to nationhood of many contemporary states, and makes them vulnerable to minority nationalisms which have hitherto been suppressed by authoritarian regimes, but have now re-emerged as these states either weaken or are democratised.

If the first test of a theory is whether it seems to fit the main facts, then the primordialist approach appears to pass this test in the case of Spain and the Basques, at least in two respects. First, it seems sensible to see Spanish history after 1479 in 'plural society' terms, with the attempts by Castile to exert centralised state control sometimes containing, but sometimes stimulating, peripheral ethnic nationalisms. Castile's attempt to unify and dominate the Iberian peninsular, which comprised a patchwork of distinct political and cultural communities, developed into the attempt to build a modern nation-state. But dynastic struggles inhibited this attempt, and the various moves to integrate peripheral regions by force, most notably the Basque and Catalan regions, served only to stimulate the national consciousness of these distinct communities. Eventually, in the twentieth century, the state did achieve more effective political control 'from above', through the centralising dictatorships of Primo de Rivera (1923–30) and then Franco (1939–75), but the intervening and subsequent periods of democratisation saw the re-emergence of peripheral nationalisms. This has resulted in the new Spanish Constitution (1979) attempting to reconcile the earlier claim that Spain was a monolithic nation-state, with the recognition that it is a federation of nationalities.

Second, the primordialist approach seems to also offer an explanation as to why it is the Basques who have been the most strident and violent of Spain's minority nationalists. The explanation is that their location at the western end of the Pyrenees facilitated their relative isolation from neighbours since pre-Roman times so as to protect in some degree, their genetic distinctiveness, cultural cohesion and political autonomy. The Basques claim biological distinctiveness, manifested in a distinctive physiognomy and indicated in a distinctive haematology (MacClancy 1993).[1] Their linguistic distinctiveness lies in the fact that their Euskara language is the only non-Indo-European language spoken in western Europe. The ability of the Basques to remain so clearly demarcated from their immediate neighbours in terms of both biology and language, derives from the high level of endogamy relating to their geographical isolation, and also from their success in combining economic integration with Spain with some political autonomy until the middle of the nineteenth century. In some formulations, this indicates that a Basque cultural and political consciousness must have existed 'for many centuries' (Conversi 1997: 44).[2] But it seems more likely that it was the threats to Basque distinctiveness and autonomy in the nineteenth century, from the Spanish state, the spread of Castilian culture and the rapid growth of urban industrialisation, which changed an inchoate and unconscious Basque sense of identity, hitherto experienced at the instinctual, unconscious, taken-for-granted level, into a conscious mass sentiment. This sense of collective identity was subsequently mobilised by political élites into an organised nationalist movement. It was the seriousness of these threats to Basque distinctiveness and identity, and of the subsequent threats posed by Franco's attempts to wipe out Basque culture and language in the twentieth century, which gave Basque nationalism its intensity. This intensity has been manifested in the fact that the native Basques are the only community within Spain with a significant proportion identifying themselves in exclusivist terms, rather than identifying themselves concurrently as Spanish; and in their support for a radical nationalism which has advocated violence in pursuit of its self-determination goal.[3]

The primordialist approach thus seems initially to offer a useful first overview. But it might not stand up to closer scrutiny and might indeed in some respects be misleading. The problem can be stated in simple terms. If primordialism explains the strength of the nationalist movement as arising out of the authenticity of the community's roots in common ancestry, and the distinctiveness of their ethnocultural attributes, then it is clear that, in the short term, nationalist assertions will be stimulated by any invasions of the community's autonomy and any threats to its biological and cultural distinctiveness. But, in the longer term, one would expect political support for nationalism to erode in line with the progressive erosion of the genetic, linguistic and ethnocultural distinctiveness of the community. By the nineteenth century, the Basques were politically divided, and the relative isolation of their various mountain and valley settlements had generated the development of numerous different dialect groups. By the early part of this century their genetic distinctiveness was probably already eroding significantly (MacClancy 1993: 103), and Basque culture was also being eroded by the processes of urbanisation and industrialisation. Use of the Euskara language continued to decline in relation to the use of Castilian, so that by the middle of the nineteenth century its use was mainly confined to the fishing communities and rural peasantry, and was being further eroded from the 1880s by the use of Castilian in the new primary schools (MacClancy 1996: 210). By the 1970s, it was spoken by only about 30 per cent of native Basques and about 19 per cent of residents of the Basque Country.[4] However, support for the Basque Nationalist Party (PNV) has been strongest in the most urbanised and industrialised areas, where the Basque language has been least spoken. Overall, support for Basque nationalism has increased from slightly over 35 per cent of votes in the elections of the 1930s, to 43 per cent in the two general elections of the 1970s, and 56.5 per cent in the general elections of the 1980s. In the regional elections, since 1980, support for the nationalist parties has remained stable, averaging 64 per cent.[5] If the political defence of Basque culture and political autonomy were to be explained simply as the articulation of an instinctual bond to race and culture, then one would expect that Basque nationalism would not have increased in strength throughout the twentieth century.

The immediate implication is that something else is going on. The socio-biology literature, which is often cited in support of the primordialist argument, suggests that political behaviour might indeed be influenced by some form of ethnocentric instinct, to favour the 'us' over the 'them', and it seems feasible that nationalist movements might be able to tap into this tendency. But (assuming such an instinct) it does not follow that the 'us' with which we identify, is necessarily a biological 'us'- an organic genetic community. We may indeed identify with the genetic family for some purposes and in some situations, but we may equally easily identify with great emotional intensity with groups which are obviously not genetically based and which are quite obviously 'invented' (as in allegiances to football clubs, or more pertinently here, with administrative regions, political parties or states). This seems to imply the need to examine more carefully the relationship between the emotional intensity of a nationalist movement and its cultural claim to common ancestry.

Of course, no serious analyst of this or any other nationalist movement would wish to explain politics solely as the manifestation of instinct. The basic primordialist argument clearly needs modifying by other arguments, and the most widespread of such argument is to suggest that nationalism develops when the instincts of the masses are tapped by the entrepreneurial élites who mobilise the nationalist movements, and when these élites appeal not only to instincts, but also to the interests of the community. This involves a shift to the language of situationalism.

A situationalist approach

This approach focuses on the fact that support for Basque nationalism has come from those classes and sections of society whose interests have been most threatened by economic change and Spanish political oppression.

The situationalist approach tends to be employed most overtly by those who depict nationalist movements as resources employed for the promotion of material interests. In one formulation it focuses upon how specific class or status groups within a society may vary in their support for nationalism, depending upon whether or not it appears politically or economically useful to them in a particular situation. In another formulation, it suggests that whole regional or ethnocultural societies might develop a sense of national identity in order to defend their common interests against externally generated economic or political threats. Differing aspects of Basque nationalist politics are illuminated by each of these perspectives. The purpose here is to indicate these insights, but then, as with the previous discussion of primordialism, to point to the particular limitations which are inherent in the insights. Situationalism is quite clearly useful in explaining the rational-choice elements in nationalist politics, but this is the politics of bounded rationality. The ways in which preferences are formed, and the ways in which rational interests come to be perceived as inherent rights, will need examining from a different perspective.

Basque nationalism began as an argument developed in the mid-nineteenth century by jurists, Catholic priests, and the rural gentry who comprised the Basque political élites and the governing juntas. Their authority and administrative positions were directly threatened by the efforts of the Spanish state to remove the institutions of provincial self-government, the *Fueros*, which had hitherto ensured a degree of political and financial autonomy for the Basques.[6] The élites initially sought to defend their status and interests by mobilising support for the ultra-Conservative and pro-Catholic Carlist rebellions against the Spanish monarchy.[7] But with the Carlist defeat of 1841, they needed a new defence, and focused upon the claim that the *Fueros* were created not by negotiations with Spanish monarchs, but were indigenous Basque attributes. It was this argument which was picked up by other marginalised groups in Basque society in the 1890s, so as to provide a basis for Basque nationalism.

It was, however, the rapid industrialisation of the Basque region, and the new class tensions this generated, which gave birth to this Basque nationalism. Between about 1875 and 1920 iron mining, iron and steel manufacturing and shipbuilding expanded rapidly, particularly in the Vizcayan province. This involved the rapid influx of migrant workers from the poorer regions of Spain,[8] and also the emergence of a Basque industrial bourgeoisie with major financial interests in Spain.[9] Squeezed in between these two classes were the Basque lower-middle-class groups, mainly artisans and white-collar workers. This 'petty bourgeoisie' provided a major support base for the new Basque Nationalist Party (PNV) formed in 1894, seeking to defend their interests against the rapidly rising tide of immigrants, and against the oligopolistic activities of the major industrialists. The fact that the class division between the petty bourgeoisie and the new industrial workers largely coincided with a division of labour between native Basques and Spanish migrants,[10] meant that the class tension was perceived as a clash of cultures, with Basque nationalism asserting the superiority of Basque culture over that of the Spanish workers. For their part, the migrant Spanish workers defended their own class interests through involvement in the Spanish Socialist Workers' Party (PSOE), advocating a proletarian Spanish nation; while most of the industrial oligopoly opposed Basque nationalism because of their concern to ensure Spanish protectionism for their Vizcayan industries (Letamendia 1995: 180–1).

This class basis of Basque nationalism changed somewhat as the industrialisation of the Basque region developed. From 1898 onwards, the PNV was supported by wealthy industrialists and businessmen who felt excluded from the oligopolistic 'inner circle', and also by the growing *Euskalerriacos* middle class (shopkeepers, professionals as well as businessmen) (Smith and Mar-Molinero 1996: 13). The middle class grew most dramatically during the 1960s when the Basque economy experienced its second major boom period. Some of these were indeed pro-Spanish because of their involvement in the Franco regime and its capitalist economy. But others actively opposed Franco through support for the PNV and ETA (*Euskadi Ta Azkatasuna*: Freedom for the Basque Country), at least partly because of the fact that they were being taxed in order to subsidise the Spanish state and the poorer Spanish regions.[11] While most radical ETA activists were lower middle class, its founders, some of its factions, and many of its supporters, included members of the bourgeois intelligentsia.[12]

From the mid-1970s up to the mid-1980s, during the period of economic downturn and restructuring, support for Basque nationalist parties increased in line with the rise in unemployment.[13] This was because Basque workers blamed the new unemployment on Spain's economic mismanagement, and saw Basque independence as the solution. But the boom of the 1960s had brought a new influx of migrant workers, and this brought renewed tension to Basque nationalist politics. In 1959, middle-class intellectuals and students, impatient with the PNV's lack of success against Franco, and its compromises with Spanish republicanism, had broken away to form ETA, which, from 1963 onwards, became increasingly imbued with Marxist ideas of socialist revolution and Fanonist ideas of armed struggle. In the 1970s therefore, the socialist wing of ETA, several of whose leaders were migrants, sought to mobilise the support of all workers in the Basque Country, including migrants. But many native Basque workers now saw the migrant workers as their economic rivals for scarce jobs, rather than as fellow victims of economic hardship and political repression. The result was that, while the migrant workers split between those who identified with socialist parties and those who supported Basque nationalism, some native Basque workers increased their support for Basque nationalism at least in part in order to defend their interests against these migrant workers.

This type of situationalist explanation, in terms of the primarily economic interests of different groups, is important in illuminating variations in support for Basque nationalism.[14] Indeed, once it has been recognised that nationalism is one possible resource for the defence of individual and group interests, it becomes clear that there might be numerous such interests involved, and that these 'interests' might carry with them a variety of fears, anxieties and insecurities. Thus, in the 1890s, it had been the fear of 'godless, immigrant proletarian socialism' (Hobsbawm 1990: 119) which terrified the native Basque population and 'broke the stability of traditional forms of social life' (Romanones, in Shubert 1990: 128). During the Franco period, it is likely that 'almost every family ha[d] one of its members or friends in prison or suffering the effects of brutal repression' (Perez-Agote, in Guibernau 1996: 62). In the 1970s and 1980s, the collapse of the Basque economy (from 7.6 per cent growth per year prior to 1973, to 0.7 per cent thereafter) pushed youth unemployment up dramatically from 12 per cent in 1976 to 59.2 per cent in 1986. The problem, then, is that the range of interests which might underlie support for nationalism is so diverse, and in some periods the interests are so intense, that nationalism begins to be seen as a resource for the defence of a whole 'way of life', rather than for the defence of a specific interest. But the more pervasive and acute the perceived threat, the more likely it is that people will respond 'not through appeals to reason, but through appeals to emotions' (Connor 1994: 204). Given that the Basque economy is highly dependent on integration with the Spanish economy, there is, as Medrano has noted, no clear economic rationality behind Basque demands for independence.[15] Reason and emotion are not necessarily antithetical, however, and we will need to examine further how they intertwine so as to change people's sense of identity and engender nationalism.

The situationalist approach does offer a further insight into the development of Basque nationalism, in its explanation for the continuation of significant Basque support for a radical 'nationalism of resistance', including terrorist violence, during and after the period of transition to Spanish democracy. The logic behind ETA's terrorist violence was that it would force concessions during the 'window of opportunity' created by the transition from military dictatorship to parliamentary democracy. Thus, support for ETA violence continued after the death of Franco (1975), after the proclamation of a democratic constitution (1978), and after the election of an autonomous Basque (PNV) regional government (1980).[16] Throughout this period, 'ETA continued to act as if nothing had changed [and] . . . did not end terrorism . . . (T)he radical nationalist option continued to enjoy widespread support' (Shubert 1990: 248).

This might be explainable as a rational strategy of using violence to try to gain further concessions, were it not for the fact that it served to exacerbate the Spanish antagonism against which the Basques claimed to be reacting. The Spanish government saw Basque violence as the cause of Spanish repression: the Basques saw Spanish repression as the cause for Basque 'retaliation'.[17] This was indeed the logic of the ETA-M strategy, but that logic assumed rather than explained the mutual antagonism. The problem is that, in any situation where each side depicts the other as the instigator of violence and of confrontation, we cannot rely on the logic used by each side to understand the preconceptions of confrontation which underpin that logic. The Basque response to Spanish democratisation is only comprehensible once we understand how Basque identity had come to be constructed so as to exclude, distrust and denigrate the Spanish. If this antagonism to Spain were only a rational response to the repression of the Franco regime, then we would still need to explain the lack of situational fluidity in Basque identity which ensured the retention of this antagonism in the context of post-Franco democratic Spain. But in fact it pre-dated Franco, and remained intact through differing situations. The situationalist stress on the rational and fluid basis of national identities and programmes, does little to explain the persistence and resilience of nationalist preconceptions in the face of changing contexts and circumstances.

Various studies have confirmed that most Spaniards presently regard themselves as having dual nationality – that of their ethnic or regional community, and that of Spain. This is true, for example, of Catalans, who were subject to similar political and cultural repression from successive Spanish monarchs and from Franco, as were the Basques. According to Michael Keating, less than 10 per cent of those in Catalonia identify themselves as solely Catalan, despite the fact that 96 per cent of them understand the Catalan language and 74 per cent of them speak it (Keating 1996: 140). The only significant exception to the tendency of Spaniards to dual nationality is in the Basque Country, where about 45 per cent of native Basques, and about 30 per cent of Basque Country residents, identify themselves as solely Basque, despite the fact that only about 25 per cent of the population speak the Euskara language fluently.[18] The contrast between the dual identity of Catalans and other Spaniards, and the exclusive identity of these Basques might not simply be a situational response to contemporary realities. Indeed, it seems likely that it can be explained as an ideological preconception which has roots in the beginnings of nationalist politics.

The constructivist approach

From this perspective, Basque nationalism is depicted as an ideological myth invented in the nineteenth century by marginalised classes to try to make sense of the frightening social disruptions associated with Spanish integration and rapid industrialisation. The reactive construction of Basque virtue counterposed to Castilian and Spanish inferiority then acts as an ideological preconception generating subsequent reactions to, and perceptions of, the Spanish state.

The constructivist approach employed here begins with the suggestion that even if some class or status groups employ nationalism as a resource for the pursuit of their specific material interests, the process whereby calls for less unemployment, higher wages, higher profits, etc., get translated into a belief in common ancestry or in the right of homeland autonomy, needs more explanation. The explanation offered, is that it is not specific interests which generate nationalism, so much as diffuse feelings of insecurity and uncertainty, which arise when a society's authority structure and social hierarchy are disrupted by rapid social changes such as those related to colonisation, modernisation and industrialisation. The argument is that the complexities of these processes, and the anxieties they generate, have the effect of inhibiting or modifying rational-choice calculations, so that those involved search for simple ideological formulas which can offer a new sense of certainty. The nationalist myth offers one such formula, since it provides individuals with a sense of identity as members of a perceived kinship and homeland community, diagnoses contemporary dislocations as arising from the transgression of the rights of that community and offers a political movement to restore those rights so as to resolve the dislocations. This nationalist myth provides a basis for national identity when it is employed by displaced élites in search of authority, to mobilise dislocated masses in search of security.

From this perspective, it was the combined impact of pressures of Castilian assimilation, the centralising expansion of the Spanish state, and the experience of rapid industrialisation and urbanisation, which, during the latter half of the nineteenth century, led the displaced élites and marginalised classes in the Basque Country to construct new myths of Basque 'medieval' political rights, racial purity and cultural identity. These myths served to make simplistic sense of contemporary problems by counterposing the vision of a harmonious, egalitarian and virtuous Basque 'us'; with a culturally inferior and politically threatening Spanish 'other'. This reactive construction of identity provided the main ideological basis for Basque nationalism for most of the twentieth century. By the end of the 1980s, however, there were signs that this reactive identity was being supplemented by a different form of constructed identity with a more internally generated institutional basis, deriving from the post-1978 experience of institutional Basque autonomy.

The reactive and *ressentiment*-based Basque identity which was mobilised into nationalism from the 1890s onwards, involved the construction of two distinct myths of Basque identity: the civic myth, which emerged initially so as to define the Basque community in territorial terms as claimants of the right to *Fueros* self-government; and the ethnocultural myth, which defined the Basque community initially in terms of the assertion of racial purity. The changing relationships between these two visions of community have been manifested in the changing politics of Basque nationalism, from periods of stable coalition, to periods of factional and fractious disunity. The following discussion seeks first to explain the reactive origins of Basque nationalism, which generated the exclusivist tendencies. Second, it outlines the civic and ethnocultural strands of Basque nationalism so as to show the intertwining of the two which culminated in the Basque solidarity generated at the time of the Burgos trial in 1970. Third, it explains the deep factional contentions of Basque politics in the 1970s and 1980s in the context of the unravelling of the civic and ethnocultural strands of Basque nationalism. Finally, it indicates the factors which have led to a new overlapping of the civic and ethnocultural visions so as to generate a degree of nationalist convergence among the Basques.

It has been suggested that

> by far the most plausible origin [of the psychological and emotive power of nationalism] lies in the . . . multi-generational struggle between the rural past and the urban–industrial future . . . where peasant rurality has been close, recent, still accessible to the people undergoing 'nationalisation', and therefore still capable of infusing violent personal or familial emotions into its language and rhetoric.
>
> (Nairn 1997: 104–6)

This indicates that it was the rapidity of the industrialisation and urbanisation of parts of Basque society in the late nineteenth century, which on the one hand disrupted the existing rural social structure and engendered a sense of insecurity; and on the other hand gave emotional power to the construction of new visions of security. But which visions of security?

Most accounts of Basque nationalism, whatever their dominant mode of analysis, identify Sabino Arana (1865–1903) as its founder. In 1894, he founded a new political organisation, *Euzkeldun Batzokija* (the Basque Club), and followed this in 1895 with the initially clandestine *Eusko Alderdi Jeltzalea* (Basque followers of God and the Old Laws, otherwise known as the *Partido Nacionalista Vasco*, the Basque Nationalist Party). He invented a flag, an anthem, a newspaper, a name (Euzkadi) for the Basque homeland, and an annual 'Basque Fatherland Day'. He also presented a new political programme for Basque independence, which was legitimated by a nationalist interpretation of Basque identity, history and destiny.[19] A primordialist attempt to depict Arana as simply articulating a previously inchoate or unconscious identity faces the problem that his idea of a link between myths of Basque racial purity and claims to Basque political independence, was a new one. Similarly, a situationalist depiction of his role as that of articulating the rational, economic interests of a native working class against immigrant competition faces the problem that Arana sought to appeal primarily to the cultural concerns of the petty bourgeoisie. It seems difficult to avoid the conclusion that Arana's employment of religious language, which linked ideas of racial purity with a reinterpretation of the *Fueros* as symbols of moral superiority and political unity, was not just an articulation of either pre-existing instincts or pre-existing interests, but rather involved a major reconstruction of ideas of identity, history and destiny. It created a new ideology employing powerful myths of grievance and destiny, to mobilise a new pan-Basque community towards a new goal of political independence from Spain. The language is that of constructivism.

Arana was the son of a member of the Basque rural gentry, and his construction of Basque nationalism was motivated by a concern to prevent his family's social decline.[20] The explanation of Basque nationalism must therefore begin with an understanding of the displacement of this rural élite, and their consequent concern to find new ideologies with which to re-establish authority in their community. The problems facing the traditional Basque élites (and the petty bourgeoisie and peasantry) derived from the pressures of centralisation, assimilation and industrial-isation, which were more disruptive and threatening for the Basques than, for example, for the Catalans.

During the fifteenth and sixteenth centuries, the Basque Country's incorporation into Castile meant that the Basque élite had a more pro-Spanish orientation than that of Catalonia which was administered as part of Aragon (Medrano 1995: Ch. 2). But Catalonia had become fully integrated into Spain after the Spanish War of Succession (1716), so that by the nineteenth century, when the Spanish state became more effectively centralised, the traditional Catalan élites, and also the new Catalan middle classes, were able to move into new economic and élite positions, since they could 'play in several political and economic arenas; the domestic, the Spanish, the Mediterranean, and for a time the imperial' (Keating 1996: 115). This mobility was reflected in their constructions of Catalan identity, which was depicted as linked with, rather than antithetical to, Spanish identity. By contrast, the Basque rural gentry, who had favoured the absolutist monarchy which granted them the *Fueros*, were displaced as a result of the defeat of the Carlist cause and the new political centralisation which followed it, and lacked allies at the centre to give them access to the *Caciquismo* (patrimonial factions), which dominated Spanish political life after 1875. Moreover, the displacement of this traditional Basque élite coincided with the onset of a rapid industrialisation process which, unlike that of Catalonia, eroded the living standards of the rural peasantry and increasingly marginalised the lower and middle bourgeoisies, unable to compete with the small Basque capitalist oligarchy and the foreign capitalists who had the capital to dominate the new mining and iron and steel industries (Medrano 1995). Thus the marginalisation of the old élites occurred in the context of the uprooting of the traditional social structure and the rapid emergence of new capitalist tensions. The displaced Basque élites responded reactively rather than rationally, resorting to a simple ideological formula of the good 'us' versus the bad 'them'. They constructed a new vision of an idealised Basque national identity counterposed to a demonised Spanish identity.

During the first half of the nineteenth century, Basque political élites had portrayed the relationship between the Basques and Spain in Carlist terms – as a conservative crusade to uphold traditional rural Catholic values in the face of the spectre of an urban liberal 'Gomorrah' promoted by the 'traitorous crowd of crooks' controlling the Spanish monarchy (Carr 1966: 184, 187). This Carlist language of opposition to Spanish centralisation received the support of the bulk of the Basque peasantry, not because of their Catholicism, but rather because of the collapse of the agricultural economy which sustained their way of life (Medrano 1995: Ch. 4).

As Carlism declined, the construction of enemy, identity and destiny was reformulated. The religious symbolism of Carlism gave way to more overtly anti-Spanish symbolism. The *Fueros* were portrayed, not as concessionary privileges negotiated with Spanish monarchs, but rather as inherent rights of political autonomy which pre-dated the Spanish monarchy and derived from 'the purity of the (Basque) bloodlines that connected them directly to the descendants of Noah'. This *Fuerista* ('foralist') view of the issue was mainly 'an educated elite's view of Basque history and rights' (Greenwood 1985: 210), but, by the 1860s, it had been propagated among the rural peasantry as a kind of pre-nationalism, made popular in 'the ballads of Iparraguirre' (Carr 1966: 557). When the *Fueros* were finally abolished in 1876, *Fuerista* became a rallying cry which united the rural nobility, the new bourgeoisie and the general populace. This was initially so because the abolition of the *Fueros* in 1876 did directly threaten their respective material interests. But foralism also became a symbol for ideas of Basque cultural regeneration (Medrano 1995: 69–74).

When Sabino Arana was persuaded (by his brother) that Carlism was no longer a useful way to 'prevent Spanish influence' (Medrano 1995: 79), he built directly on these foralist myths, employing a morally absolutist religious language to contrast the virtuous Basques with the degenerate *Maketos* Spanish. The latter were depicted as an inferior mix of races, such that:

> the rubbing together of our people with the Spanish . . . immediately and necessarily leads to ignorance and a drop in intelligence, to weakness and corruption of the heart, and to a total estrangement: in a word, to the end of all human society.
>
> (Arana, in MacClancy 1993: 105)

Arana depicted the Vizcayans (and subsequently all Basques) contrastingly as an 'extremely original race . . . an isolate in the universe . . . not racially Spanish (and) . . . intelligent and clever at all kinds of jobs' (Arana, in MacClancy 1993: 105). Once this formula had been articulated, it resonated with a Basque society undergoing the strains of urbanisation, and its depiction of Spain as both inferior and threatening could then be validated by subsequent events, including the repressive, centralising dictatorships of Primo de Rivera and Franco.

Basque nationalism emerges, then, as a classic case of a reactive nationalism, articulated by marginalised social groups and resonating with a society imbued with a *ressentiment* (envy and hatred) towards a Spanish 'other' which was portrayed in ethnocultural nationalist terms as the threat of Castilian domination or as the threat of contamination by an 'inferior' Spanish race. But this portrayal of Spain was itself a constructed one. Junco has shown how the 'weak and insufficient' nature of Spanish nationalism during the nineteenth century was related to the different 'mythical constructions' of Spain – as a civic–patriotic 'war of independence' identity, as a Romantic Spanish soul, as a Liberal emancipatory integration process, and as a conservative Catholic nationalism (Junco 1996). The tensions between these different constructions engendered a weakness of national identity which meant that by the end of the nineteenth century, in Junco's analysis, 'the most significant role left to Spanish nationalism was the purely reactionary one of serving as a unifying ideology of all those opposed to (liberal or social) revolution and, in the twentieth century, to Catalan and Basque autonomy' (Junco 1996: 103). Thus, on the one hand it is clear that the nineteenth-century Basque depiction of Spain in primarily ethnocultural nationalist terms of linguistic or racial domination, was only one of several possible ideological depictions of Spain, which could alternatively have been depicted in civic terms. On the other hand it is evident that it was this 'ethnocultural domination' vision of Spain, employed by the Basques, which helped to engender the twentieth-century development of a Spanish 'garrison mentality' nationalism against the Basque and Catalan threats. These constructed visions of nationalism employed in the nineteenth century promoted the confrontationalism of the twentieth century.

Once constructed in this way, these visions of Basque and Spanish identity acted as ideological sieves through which subsequent experiences were filtered. The Basque nationalism constructed in the late nineteenth century has generated the exclusivist construction of Basque identity, and the commitment to self-determination, which have persisted. But the politics of this nationalism has nevertheless varied, and the variations can be illuminated by examining the other, internal, aspect of Basque nationalism – the relationship between its civic and its ethnocultural facets.

The interweaving of the civic and ethnocultural strands of Basque nationalism

Basque civic nationalism focused upon the myth of Fueral autonomy, while Basque ethnocultural nationalism focused upon the myth of common ancestry. The initial symbolising of Basque identity in racial terms failed to interweave the two strands of nationalism, but this was facilitated by the shift to a focus on the symbolism of language.

It has previously been suggested (Chapter 2) that nationalism provides a stable framework for politics when the belief in common ancestry, which characterises ethnocultural nationalism, is intertwined with the pride in the state and civil society institutions of the territorial homeland which characterises civic nationalism. This intertwining means that political integration and cultural assimilation can proceed together so as to promote the development of the nation-state, rather than being in tension with each other. In the case of Spain, such progress was inhibited, as has been noted, by the weaknesses of the state and by the peripheral focus of economic development. This meant that the Basques experienced Spanish political integration as a disruptive process of centralisation, and Spanish cultural assimilation as an assertion of Castilian domination. But their reaction to this, in the construction of Basque nationalism, was such as to interweave the civic and ethnocultural elements, so as to provide a stable and unifying basis for Basque politics; so long as, and to the extent that, this interweaving remained intact.

As Marianne Heiberg has noted, Arana's ideology was built around two sets of related symbols. The ethnocultural symbols of language, religion, custom and character, which 'defined the Basque mode of being in opposition to the Spanish one'; and the civic symbols, referring to the *Fueros* and historical sovereignty, which 'served to separate the Basque Country . . . from the process of state unification' (Heiberg 1989: 51).[21] The subsequent effectiveness of these two aspects of Basque nationalism in unifying, and mobilising support from, all sections of Basque society, has depended primarily on the different ways in which the common ancestry claim of ethnocultural nationalism, and the territorial identity claim of civic nationalism, have been denoted. The initial formulation, in which a civic pride focusing upon the call for restoration of the *Fueros* was intertwined with a call for the defence of Basque racial purity, proved of limited utility in unifying the Basques against the Spanish workers, and this was reflected in the factional disunity of Basque nationalist politics which was evident until the 1930s.

So long as Basque ethnocultural identity was defined in racial terms, support for the nationalist movement was in danger of being restricted by the very erosion of racial purity against which it sought to fight (MacClancy 1993: 106). In 1894, membership of Arana's 'Basque Club', which preceded the PNV, had required the ability to show by surname the possession of four male Basque grandparents, but by 1908 the resultant low membership meant that this had to be relaxed to one grandparent. Moreover, the issue of race began to be seen as demarcating, rather than unifying, the rivalries between radicals and moderates over whether to aim for political autonomy or full secession, and whether to oppose or promote industrialisation. These rivalries were eased somewhat, therefore, as the marker of Basque cultural virtue began to shift from a racial criterion towards commitment to the Euskara language, since this change of emphasis facilitated a compromise between radicals seeking to maximise the purity of the movement, and moderates seeking to maximise political support for it. This shift from race to language as the symbolic focus of Basque nationalism happened slowly, gaining impetus from about 1918 onwards (Conversi 1997: 70–2). Its role as a focus for Basque nationalism was not based on its utility as a boundary marker, however, since its limited currency deprived it of any such utility (Conversi 1990). Its effectiveness in facilitating the unifying and mobilising of Basque society arose instead from its symbolic role in bridging the gap between those whose primary concern was the restoration of foral autonomy, and those more concerned with ethnocultural revival. The Euskara language came to function both as a symbol of pride in Basque cultural virtue and also as a symbol of Basque civil autonomy. Basque identity, in both versions, did not demand fluency in the Euskara language, but rather the display of commitment to its preservation, and pride in its existence. This symbolic role of the language, as the unifying symbol of Basque nationalism, is indicated by the statistics showing that while only a small minority of residents of the Basque Country read, write or speak the language, the large majority, nevertheless, wish it to be institutionalised in the education system, and would like their children to be taught it.[22]

This overlapping of the ethnocultural nationalist concern with cultural regeneration and the civic nationalist concern with territorial autonomy, facilitated the growth in support for Basque nationalism. Factional rivalries within Basque nationalism, concerning the degree of radicalism and attitudes to capitalism continued, but, by the 1930s, these rivalries were becoming muted, in part because of the experience of suppression under Primo de Rivera's dictatorship, but in part also because of the new role of Euskara. Basque nationalism's initial support came from urban Vizcaya, and in 1917 and 1918 it won the municipal elections so as to control the Vizcayan *Diputacion Provincial*. The split between the more radical PNV and the less radical CNV (Basque Nationalist Communion) inhibited subsequent electoral successes, but, by the 1930s, the ideological and factional rivalries were sufficiently resolved to bring together those from the different Basque provinces, from rural and urban areas, and from various class positions. In the 1933 general elections, this linguistically (and religiously) focused Basque nationalism was able to mobilise 41 per cent of the vote in Bilbao, 57 per cent in the rest of Vizcaya, 46 per cent in Guipuzcoa and 29 per cent in Alava (Medrano 1995: 80–9). Its parallel success in the 1936 elections paved the way for the eventual passing of the 1936 Statute of Autonomy, a step which had been supported in a plebiscite by 84 per cent of voters in the three Basque provinces, with a turnout of 87 per cent (Conversi 1997: 75). This autonomy was undermined after nine months by the Civil War and Franco's victory, but the PNV's nationalist victory briefly brought a Basque government to power, which mobilised the Basque Country on the Republican side. 'Strongly Catholic, socially conservative, but based on strong popular support democratically expressed, the Basques fought bravely, and more humanely than most of their fellow Republicans' (Seton-Watson 1977: 58).

The unifying potentiality of Basque nationalism, evident for example in the 1933 plebiscite, the workers' protests of 1947 and 1951, and the 1970 Burgos trial, has coexisted with its fissiparous tendencies, which became most evident during the 1970s. Prior to that, the divisive impact of élite rivalries was inhibited by the fact that both the more conservative ethnocultural nationalists and the more radical civic nationalists, shared a common symbolism, in pride in the Basque language. This owed much to the suppression of the language, which began with the 1902 government decree forbidding religious instruction in languages other than Spanish, but took dramatic form with Franco's campaign to prohibit the use of Euskara. This was central to Franco's vision of a Spanish national regeneration based on Castilian culture, and the eradication of regionalist threats to unity. Commitment to the Euskara language thus became a rallying cry for Basque nationalism. Indeed, much of the Basque resistance to Franco had to focus upon the promotion of Basque symbolism relating to the language, the flag or the national day (Medrano 1995: 136). Then when Franco began to ease the repression from 1960 onwards, by allowing private Basque-language schools (*Ikastolas*), it played a major role in raising Basque expectations for change. By the early 1970s, therefore, when Basque solidarity against Francoist persecution was displayed most dramatically in response to the Burgos trial,[23] Basque nationalism was almost universally defined in 'linguistic pride' and cultural regeneration terms. It is not being suggested here that the linguistic focus of Basque nationalism caused this unifying mobilisation, merely that it enabled it. Franco's repression was able to unite migrants and native Basques behind support for radical Basque nationalism, because its ideological focus was such as to facilitate the coming together of those primarily concerned with ethnocultural regeneration, and those primarily concerned with political autonomy.

Basque nationalism had originally united the native Basques against the Spanish migrant workers who had flooded into the region between 1875 and 1920, and who mostly supported the socialist parties.[24] During the Franco era, this in-migration to the Basque Country continued, but the experience of Franco's repression, which subjected all residents to political persecution, probably facilitated the process whereby some of these migrants or their children, began to identify with the Basque cause, vote for Basque parties, intermarry, assimilate or learn the language. Migrant workers and native Basques thus joined together in the general strikes against Franco in 1947 and 1951.

ETA had initially developed out of the 'Ekin' group within the PNV in the 1950s, as a 'politically impatient' ethnocultural nationalist movement, defining Basque nationalism in linguistic terms (Conversi 1997: 87–93). However, after the post-1960 economic boom brought a new influx of Spanish workers, ETA increasingly took a socialist direction, and moved, albeit hesitantly, towards a civic nationalism which was made explicit in its 1967 commitment to *Pueblo Trabajador Vasco* (Basque working people), allowing ETA to mobilise support from 'all the workers who today live in our soil, without distinction of origin' (ETA, 1979, in MacClancy 1993: 107. See also Conversi 1997: 203–5).[25]

ETA's radical mobilisation activities generated unprecedented popular support for Basque nationalism, most dramatically at the Burgos trial. But this was a display of sympathy for ETA and opposition to Spanish oppression, rather than a new consensus as to the methods and goals of radical nationalism; and the interweaving of ethnocultural nationalism and civic nationalism was always a fragile one. The 1970 Burgos trial heralded, not a new political unity within Basque nationalism, but rather an upsurge of political and ideological disunity.

The disentwining of the civic and ethnocultural strands of Basque nationalism

> The increased factionalism of Basque nationalism, from the mid-1970s to the early 1990s, is explained in terms of the failure of its ideology to offer one clear diagnosis of the economic downturn and of the implications of the transition from the Franco era. When Basque nationalism offered competing civic and ethnocultural depictions of Basque identity and of the Spanish 'other', disagreements as to nationalist strategies escalated into ideological cleavages.

Prior to the Burgos trial, 'most people in Euskadi were unaware of the internal conflicts [within ETA] and saw ETA as a homogeneous body. Holding a belief in ETA's ideological continuity, its external supporters and sympathisers understood these conflicts as nothing but detail' (Conversi 1997: 98). Soon after the Burgos trial however, and until the early 1990s, ETA's internal factionalism 'hopelessly divide[d] Basque society' (Letamendia 1995: 195). This shift towards nationalist disunity was precipitated by the post-1973 economic collapse.

This economic slump hit the Basque Country particularly hard.[26] The crisis had various causes related to the international economy and to Spanish government policies, but the Basques already had in place two simple ideological diagnoses for the collapse. Both depicted Spain as the culprit, but while the socialist and civic-oriented Basque nationalism espoused by ETA depicted the enemy as Spanish capitalism, the more ethnocultural nationalist diagnosis saw 'excessive' Spanish immigration into the Basque Country as the cause. Basque nationalism thus now offered two competing visions of the Basque 'us': one which included the migrant workers in the region as fellow victims; and one which depicted them as the Spanish enemy. This ideological dilemma was exacerbated after Franco's death by a new dilemma as to how the Spanish 'enemy' should be portrayed. Franco's policies of the repression of Basque language and culture had facilitated the depiction of Spanish nationalism, by most Basques, as a predominantly ethnocultural nation-alism, continuing the threat of Castilian domination which had faced the Basques since the early nineteenth century. But Basques were faced with a new ideological choice with the proposals for a new democratic constitution which would recognise the Basques as a distinct ethnic nationality with their own autonomous government and with Euskara as their official language alongside Castilian.[27] They could continue depicting Spain as an ethnocultural nationalist threat to Basque nation-alism, or Spain could now be portrayed as a predominantly civic nationalism which could be viewed as potentially able to accommodate further Basque autonomy, and thus be negotiated with.

It was these two sets of competing ideological diagnoses, offering a choice between a civic and an ethnocultural vision of the Basque community, and a choice between a civic and an ethnocultural vision of Spain, which underlay the intense political factionalism and fractiousness which split ETA ideologically into its various culturalist and civic splinters, and divided Basque society.[28] Instead of offering ideological certainty, Basque nationalism now seemed to offer ideological equivocation. The tensions erupted between the various conservative and socialist wings of Basque nationalism and primarily took the form of disagreements about the strategy of armed struggle, but their origin lay in these new ideological dilemmas of Basque nationalism which gave new political salience to ambiguities as to the Basque community; whether it referred to *la raza vasca* (the Basque race), to *abertzale* (Basque patriots, irrespective of birth), or to *el pueblo trabajador vasco* (the Basque working people).

Towards a civic–ethnocultural convergence

During the 1990s, the different strands of Basque nationalism began to converge, as the Basque Autonomous Region provided an institutional framework which promoted progress towards both cultural renewal and civic autonomy, so that the visions of civic nationalism and ethnocultural nationalism once more began to overlap. This institutional basis for identity thus began to replace the earlier reactive basis of Basque nationalism.

Contemporary Basque politics still involves significant divisions, most importantly relating to the exclusion of Navarre and the French Basque areas from the Basque Autonomous Community, and to the division within the latter Community between supporters of the Basque nationalist parties seeking independence, and those of the Spanish political parties favouring the present constitutional autonomy. Nevertheless, there are clear signs that the previous intensity both of the splits within Basque nationalism, and of the disagreement between nationalists and constitutionalists, has begun to move, albeit hesitantly, towards a new politics of pluralist accommodation in which the proponents of violence have been increasingly marginalised.

The process began in January 1988, when a 'front for peace' emerged in which the leaders of all parties in the Basque Country other than *Herri Batasuna*, signed the Pact of Ajuria-Enea, an 'Agreement for the Normalisation and Pacification of Euskadi' to work together to oppose violence. In 1990, *Herri Batasuna*'s explicit commitment to self-determination was adopted by the PNV, EE and EA and was approved by an absolute majority of the Basque Autonomous parliament. In 1997 this process of nationalist convergence was interrupted dramatically by the ETA murder of a PP (People's Party) municipal councillor, but revulsion against this act propelled the process, and pressure from the nationalist parties pushed ETA to sign the September 1998 Declaration of Lizarra, renouncing violence, and calling, with all other nationalist parties, for a referendum on independence from Spain.[29] In the October 1998 Basque regional election, which was regarded by all sides as such a referendum, there was a record turnout of 70 per cent, and a 54.68 per cent vote for the nationalist parties, who were thus able to form, for the first time, a wholly nationalist coalition government.[30] The region is indeed still divided between supporters of the Basque nationalist parties favouring independence, and supporters of the Spanish parties favouring the present form of autonomy, but this disagreement is ameliorated by the emergent consensus against ETA's violence, so that the political disagreement no longer marks a deep social divide within Basque society, as it did in the past.[31] The reduced polarisation is possibly related to the fact that the largest non-nationalist vote has been for the conservative People's Party (the present governing party in Spain), which until recently relied on the PNV for its survival. The PNV meanwhile dominated the government of the Basque Country from 1985 to 1998 only with the support of the Madrid-based Socialist Party. These elements of convergence and alliance do not end the factional rivalries for power in Basque politics, but they do begin to obscure and ameliorate the old cleavages so as to open the door to pluralistic politics.

Various developments have combined to produce this trend towards accommodation, but the core factor appears to be that the experience of living within the institutional framework provided by the Basque Autonomous Community, has provided a focal point for a modified and more self-confident Basque identity, in which the cleavage between native Basques and migrants has ceased to be politically salient.[32] This is partly because the achievement of the most far-reaching regional autonomy in Western Europe, and then the relative effectiveness of the nationalist-led Basque governments, has reduced the kind of disillusionment with nationalist élites which had stimulated the factional split of 1959, when ETA broke with the PNV.[33] In particular, the government's effective promotion of Euskara, in schools, the media and in the selection of senior public officials, has helped to bring the various nationalist parties together, and has meant that migrants and natives alike are choosing to educate their children in the language.[34] There is indeed the possibility that the development of consensus among the Basque nationalist *abertzale*, will provoke increasing resentment among non-nationalist *espanolistas* who feel marginalised in the institutions of the Basque Community.[35] But such social tensions do not presently seem high, and are ameliorated by the fact that almost all the Basque nationalist parties (who depend upon non-natives for most of their political support) explicitly recognise that Basque self-determination should be by all residents of the territory, irrespective of ethnic origin;[36] as well as by the fact that while only about 21 per cent of those in the Basque Country are native Basques, about 75 per cent of the population now self-identify as Basques.[37]

Contemporary Basque nationalism is thus able to offer a home to those of both civic and ethnocultural orientations, such that there is increasing overlap between those who identify Basqueness primarily in terms of pride in the language, and those who identify it primarily in territorial terms.[38] Nationalism does not of itself produce agreement on political issues, particularly on the question of autonomy versus independence, but the increased interweaving of civic and ethnocultural aspects does reduce the intensity of cleavages. This is reflected in the new convergence to oppose violence and resolve the issue of independence by negotiating with a Spanish government which has already agreed to 'be generous' to the Basques once violence has been abandoned (*The Economist*, 24 October 1998: 52).

Conclusions

When Basque nationalism has been contrasted with Catalan nationalism, it has sometimes been suggested that the latter has been more moderate and less violent because it has had its base in a large Catalan middle class, and has been a predominantly civic nationalism. Basque nationalism, in contrast, is depicted as more exclusivist, radical and violent because of its origin as a nationalism of the 'petty bourgeois radical right' (Hobsbawm 1990: 119), and because of its character as a backward-looking ethnocultural nationalism. But Basque nationalism is not predominantly ethnocultural, and it should be noted that the most radical and violent version of Basque nationalism has been that espoused by its most civic proponent, ETA, which depicted the Basques as 'all workers who live in our soil, without distinction of origin'.

The exclusivist and radical aspects of Basque nationalism have therefore been explained here as deriving, not from its ethnocultural nationalist aspects, but rather from its reactive character as an ideological predisposition, which can be traced back to the construction during the latter half of the last century, of a clear ideological dichotomy between the Basque 'us' and the Spanish 'them'. This offered a simple diagnosis of a complex pattern of interactions which was changing the social structure in frightening and disorientating ways, and led a significant proportion of Basques to define their identity in exclusivist terms (both civic and ethnocultural), and their political goal in self-determination terms. Initial tension between Basques seeking cultural renewal and Basques seeking political autonomy, was ameliorated by the combined ethnocultural and civic symbolism of the Basque language. The political disunity of the 1970s and 1980s occurred when the nationalist ideology failed to offer one simple diagnosis of the 'transition' situation, and instead offered competing civic and ethnocultural diagnoses. A new nationalist convergence began to re-emerge when the experience of the Basque Autonomous Community began to provide a constructed 'institutional definition of nationhood' which could recombine visions of cultural revival and political autonomy; so that the reactive basis for Basque nationalism is now finally beginning to be modified by an internally generated self-confidence focused on a new optimism for a negotiated, rather than a unilateral, route to self-determination.

The persistence of Basque separatism invites suggestions of the fixed character of instinctual loyalties, while the variations in its political manifestations invite a focus on the fluidity of rational interests. But the politics which connects the continuity of Basque nationalism with its diversity is perhaps illuminated by the constructivist view which depicts it as an ideological myth filtering the changing complexities which arose from encapsulation by the Spanish state.

5 Globalisation and nationalism

The case of Singapore

Globalisation seems to pose two kinds of threat to nation-states. First, if it is the case that they developed as political units which were functional for early industrialisation, then they are likely to be weakened or severely disrupted as the new economic globalisation increasingly requires new, larger or reconstituted political units. Second, if they developed as institutions whose coercive and normative powers enabled them to achieve the 'cultural branding of their flocks', then their capacities for such social control might similarly be weakened or severely disrupted by the new cultural globalisation.[1] But globalisation is not just an external force impacting upon nation-states, it is also a process which the policies of nation-states can promote and guide. The relationship between nation-state and globalisation thus depends to a significant degree upon the effectiveness and appropriateness of the economic and ideological management strategies which state élites employ.

Moreover, if, as has been suggested previously, the strength of the nation-state really does depend on the extent to which its citizens subscribe to the vision of a converging civic and ethnocultural national community, then the fate of nation-states in the context of globalisation, might depend crucially upon the ways in which state élites employ the challenges and resources offered by globalisation, in constructing their ideas of civic nationalism and ethnocultural nationalism.

The Singaporean state is exceptional in that its progress towards being one of the most globalised economies in the world has been accompanied by its transition from a weak nation-state to a strong nation-state. It is examined here in order to show the connections between the state's management of globalisation, and its management of the potential tensions between civic and ethnocultural nationalisms. The examination of this case does not imply any replacement of one set of generalisations concerning the tendency of globalisation to weaken nation-states with another set arguing any general strengthening: rather, the intention is to suggest that the impact of globalisation is variable, and does not depend directly or solely on the economic management capacities of the state élites, but also on their strategies for the management of nationalist ideologies.

Globalisation and the nation-state

The suggestion that globalisation weakens the nation-state, derives from an understanding of the state as a unit of economic management. But the variable impact of globalisation, and the fact that it might in some cases and some respects strengthen the nation-state, are more accessible once the nation-state is understood as a unit of ideological management.

Both modernisation theorists and some neo-Marxists have located the origin and nature of the modern nation-state primarily in terms of its functionality for the development of commerce and industry. There are many variations of the argument, but the core theme is that, beginning in the seventeenth century, the industrialisation process involved the investment of rural surpluses in new urban centres. This transfer could only be achieved by the development of cultural homogeneity between urban cores and their rural hinterlands to facilitate the necessary social mobility; and by the emergence of centralised state control, first to ensure the necessary labour discipline, and then to manage the processes of economic change. The sovereign state thus governed the mobilised cultural nation, and functioned as the autonomous manager of the integrated national economy. The emergence of the nation-state was both a precondition and an outgrowth of the first phase of capitalist development.

The term 'globalisation' is also variously conceptualised, but refers in general to the latest phase of capitalist expansion (most usually periodised from the early 1970s), involving the shift from *inter*national to *trans*national networks of trade, investment and finance, so that the movement of economic resources is increasingly outside the control of any one state. It seems to follow, as a matter of definition, that the nation-state which was functional for the first phase of capitalist development, is no longer so functional for the current phase. The encapsulation of national economies within larger regional and global networks, seems to imply the erosion of the nation-state. This is both because the idea of a distinctive national economy ceases to make sense; and also because the ability of the state to function as an autonomous economic manager is undermined by the economic muscle and mobility of international capital, and by the related entanglement of the state in international trade agreements (Cerny 1994, Ohmae 1995, Schmidt 1995, Ross 1995). The outcome is that:

> the nation-state's economic sovereignty is thinned, followed closely by its capacity for independent policy-making. The nation-state no longer presides over anything approximating the concept of 'national economy'. Assets of many a supranational corporation exceed today the GNP of an average nation-state; and with capital moving freely through boundaries that look tight only in world atlases, multinationals find it easy to blackmail nation-states into submission to whatever they define as the interests of the economy.

> (Bauman 1995: 152)

But this conclusion that all nation-states are necessarily weakened by the globalisation process, albeit in varying degrees, is open to doubt on both factual and theoretical grounds. National economic boundaries remain significant (Wade 1996). Nation-states can and frequently do act in ways detrimental to the interests of global capital; imposing restrictive controls, promoting protectionism or implementing anti-pollution legislation. Moreover, in those cases where the interests of international capital and state élites do coincide, this can in various ways empower the latter. One needs, then, to be careful to distinguish factors which impinge on a nation-state's international sovereignty or autonomy from those which influence the state's internal sovereignty and its degree of autonomy from domestic societal pressures. Thus 'it can be argued almost in the same breath both that the state is being or has been weakened by the changes related to globalisation, and that it has been strengthened by precisely these changes' (Smith 1992: 256). Several observers have noted that the increased permeability of national economies and societies may vary in its impact on nation-states in different regions. It poses new challenges which generate the restructuring of nation-states, and sometimes and in some respects their strengthening, rather than their irrevocable weakening (Weiss 1997, Drucker 1997, Pooley 1991, Llambi and Gouveia 1994, Hirst and Thompson 1995, Cable 1996, Shaw 1997, Mann 1997).

The fact that capital has outgrown the nation-state shell within which it reached maturity, does not of itself signify that the nation-state can no longer be functional for capital. Thus, proponents of the 'economic functionality' view of the nation-state stress that it may indeed still perform a crucial role in the global economy by pursuing 'positive nationalist' strategies so as to determine and control the specialised role of domestic labour and capital in the international division of labour (Rodan 1989, Potter 1992, Cable 1996). As Hirst and Thompson have argued, 'Nation states are now simply one class of powers and political agencies in a complex system of power from world to local levels, but they have a centrality because of their relationship to territory and population' (1995: 430). This centrality rests on the nation-state as the sole source of political legitimacy, able to control and mobilise its own populations, and to grant legitimacy to other agencies.

To say this is to recognise that the power of the nation-state influences the global economy, rather than simply the reverse. The 'location of the state in the global economy' is not simply given by the structure of the global economy, but is also something which is decisively influenced by independent variations in the character and strategy of different states. If some nation-states are able to influence, attract, co-opt, ally with, or threaten, international capital, and if, in addition, some of them have significant autonomy from domestic capital, then it might be useful to employ a conceptualisation of the nation-state which does not define it in terms of economic functionality.

The understanding of nationalism as a legitimatory ideology employed by aspiring élites seeking governmental power, and of its potential resonance with societies undergoing disruptive change, was outlined in Chapters 1 and 2, but may be briefly summarised here. Aspiring élites may employ various legitimatory ideologies, but in the absence of the possibility of appeals to traditional divine right or colonial mandate, élites have frequently portrayed the disaggregated society as a mythical kinship community, so as to portray themselves as its mouthpiece. The strength of the nation-state then depends on the extent to which the invented civic and ethnocultural myths of common kinship succeed in mobilising societal support. This in turn depends not only on the cultural resonance of the myths, but also on the extent to which state élites are seen as fulfilling their promises as guardian of the invented nation. The first promise was that of maintaining territorial order, so that commerce and industry could flourish in civil society, but increasingly, state élites began to legitimate their authority by portraying themselves as economic managers able to deliver development towards the attainment of social justice. The nation was increasingly redefined as the social justice community, in which all individuals would have equal status and opportunities because of their position as equal citizens, and their access to its ethnocultural values. Henceforward, both the authority of the state and the strength of national cohesion would depend primarily on the judgement of civil society as to the developmental nationalist legitimacy of the state élites.

The ability of state élites to mobilise society around development promises does depend in part on their ability to deliver real economic benefits. But it depends more fundamentally upon the state élites' ability to persuade their citizens that development involves current investment for future benefit, so that contemporary socio-economic inadequacies and inequalities will be accepted as necessary sacrifices conducive to the goal of the social justice nation. This means that the state's authority over society depends crucially on the strategy which state élites employ in seeking developmental legitimacy. The more they rest their authority on the delivery of immediate social justice, the more the limitations on their autonomy as managers of the domestic economy can undermine their legitimacy, and the more easily can contemporary inequities in welfare erode national cohesion. On the other hand, where state élites employ a 'mobilisation' strategy which promises development and social justice for the imminent but unspecified future, and depicts current economic benefits as proof that faith in the state is warranted and further progress assured, contemporary economic problems need not of themselves erode the cohesion of the nation-state and the nationalist legitimacy of the state élites.[2]

Once such a constructivist view of the nation-state is adopted, the variable impact of globalisation on the nation-state becomes more understandable. It is not globalisation *per se* which might weaken the nation-state, so much as the way in which state élites respond to globalisation in the articulation of their development promises and their portrayal of the social justice nation. And since social justice involves the equitable treatment of minorities alongside the pursuit of economic growth, the relationships between ethnic assertions and national identity will also depend primarily upon how the state élites manage their developmental legitimacy.

The fact that states which seek foreign capital will do so more effectively if they offer tax incentives, cheap efficient labour and political stability which make them more competitive, and that the adoption of such a strategy serves in some respects to inhibit the subsequent policy options of such states as regards both economic and social management, is not contested here. But the impact of this upon differe. states, and the responses of different states, might sometimes serve to enhance state legitimacy and national identity so as to strengthen the nation-state. In the Singapore case, it is suggested that globalisation has promoted the development of both its economy and its national cohesion, primarily because the state élites' economic strategies of globalisation have been legitimated and facilitated by their ideological strategies of collectivist nationalism.

Singapore: globalisation and civic nationalism

The economic globalisation of Singapore was initially facilitated and legitimated by the People's Action Party (PAP) regime's promotion of a collectivist and developmentalist civic nationalism. This provided a justification for authoritarian rule, and was based both on a civic institutionalist framework, and on the inculcation of patriotic pride.

At the time of Singapore's independence in 1965 it was a weak nation-state. First, the break with Malaysia removed the Singaporean urban core from its rural hinterland, so that there was no such thing as an integrated and bounded Singaporean economy and the state's economic management strategy was in collapse (Rodan 1989: 88). Singapore was thus not a nation-state in the sense that the state did not constitute the autonomous and effective manager of a distinct national economy.

Second, Singapore was not a nation-state in the ethnocultural sense. Rather, it was a 'plural society' comprising several distinct racial, religious and linguistic communities, and lacking any overarching cultural values.[3] As such, and as the ethnic disturbances of 1964 and 1969 made clear, it had no natural cohesion, but instead had to be held together by state force, in the form of coercive and authoritarian rule by the PAP regime.

Third, Singapore was not a nation-state in the constructivist sense, in that the PAP did not, at that time, even attempt to articulate myths of national identity as a means of legitimating their governmental power. Instead, they used an ideology of 'survivalism' which specifically stressed the lack of national identity, the absence of a viable national economy, and the vulnerability of the society to international and internal threats. They sought legitimacy by inculcating a siege mentality, in which it was precisely the lack of state power and of national cohesion which made political acquiescence by civil society so imperative.

To say that Singapore was not a nation-state at the time of decolonisation, is to indicate that the PAP government, which led it, lacked nationalist legitimacy. They could claim some democratic legitimacy as a constitutionally elected government, but such legitimacy was limited by repressive policies towards political opponents, the press, students and labour. They could also claim some 'performance legitimacy' as regards their achievement of self-government, but this was called into question by the 1965 expulsion from the Malaysian Federation. Any long-term hope of achieving stronger performance legitimacy based on economic development, merely highlighted the need for a strategy which could contain public discontent during the necessary period of investment and sacrifice required in the early stages of development. The promotion of the 'siege mentality' played a stopgap role, but the inculcation of a sense of crisis against a series of threatening 'others', served in the longer term merely to highlight the need for a stronger sense of 'us'. The PAP government was thus faced with two major tasks: to develop a strategy for state-led economic development and to develop an effective legitimation strategy to generate the necessary political authority for such development.

The selected strategy for economic development focused upon globalisation. From the late 1960s onwards, the PAP regime took the initiative in attracting international capital to invest in Singapore and sought to convince Singaporeans, both labour and local capital, that this was a credible route towards social justice. The consequent globalisation of Singapore's economy has been rapid and extensive. As a result of the state's strategy of alliance with international capital, foreign equity investment in Singapore and Singapore's equity investment abroad both increased rapidly (Bellows 1995: 53, 60), while imports and exports have risen to constitute 155 per cent and 134 per cent respectively of GDP (Ramesh 1995a: 244). The outcome of the state-directed globalisation process has been sustained economic growth of over 8 per cent per year (up to 1997), and the emergence of Singapore as 'the world's most globalised economy' (Ramesh 1995a: 242). The basis for the productive alliance with international capital has been the provision by the Singapore state of tax incentives, infrastructural facilities and relatively low-cost and disciplined labour.

But has the alliance strengthened or weakened the Singaporean nation-state? In an important study showing how the Singapore government has enforced the social control necessary to attract capital, Christopher Tremewan notes 'the PAP-state's weakness in the partnership with foreign capital' (1994: 234). This refers to the impact of the alliance in reducing the state's autonomy as economic manager, illustrated most clearly by the weakening of its initiatives in the direction of a high-wage policy in the early 1980s (Tremewan 1994: 35–8). Second, however, the state has been strengthened in the sense that, in its concern to control labour, it developed institutions which have significantly expanded its social-control capabilities. Third, Tremewan suggests that the state is now being weakened in terms of its internal legitimacy in that 'the increasing levels of exploitation required by capital continue to demand greater and different regulatory efforts', which can only be implemented through 'high levels of state violence' which are responses to, but in turn stimulate, new forms of resistance (1994: 233–4). The implication is that the elaborate structures of social control are fragile, in that 'each new crisis threatens to unravel the entire system of regulation' (Tremewan 1994: 233).[4]

Tremewan's uncertainty as to the strength of the Singapore state, and particularly his suggestion that the 'high levels of state violence' indicate some weakness in the legitimacy of its rule, can perhaps be pinpointed more precisely by examining the relationship between globalisation and nationalism.

The Singapore government's choice of globalisation as a strategy for economic development had as its corollary the choice of collectivist civic nationalism as the dominant strategy for regime legitimation. It has been noted that civic nationalism refers to the inculcation of a sense of pride in the public institutions of a state and civil society, and to the idea of a community of citizens of equal status irrespective of differences in their ethnic attributes or origins. But it has also been noted that civic nationalism may emerge either in a liberal form advocating the equal rights of each individual citizen, or in a collectivist form asserting the distinctiveness and priority of the whole community of citizens. In this latter form, as the assertion of 'the theoretical sovereignty of the people' with a collective will, civic nationalism offers a legitimation for authoritarian rule since it justifies the notion that the state élites must be the interpreters of that collective will, so that 'the select few dictate to the masses who must obey' (Greenfeld 1992: 11). Civic nationalism is also an attractive ideology for legitimating state-led development since its vision of community is a forward-looking one, so that the equality of all citizens, which is its hallmark, is portrayed as being in the process of formation; as being imminent. This means that public disquiet at any present inequalities of status or rights, can be contained by the promise that they are the necessary contemporary sacrifices for the attainment of the nationalist vision.

The development of Singaporean civic nationalism and the development of the globalised Singaporean economy, have interconnected in three key respects. First, the inculcation of civic nationalism has legitimated the authoritarian suppression of individual liberties and welfare, which were deemed necessary for attracting foreign capital and for accumulating investment resources. Second, the proliferation of public institutions, designed by the state to promote the social control necessary for globalised development, has provided the institutional focus for the emergence of a sense of civic national identity. Third, civic nationalism has also been promoted by the state's investment of development resources in technologically glossy public amenities, designed specifically to instil patriotic pride in the populace. Each of these three aspects of the links between nationalism and globalisation can be briefly examined.

Civic nationalism and authoritarian rule

Once civic nationalism was articulated by the state élites as signifying that contemporary restrictions on individual liberty and welfare could be justified as necessary for the future collective good, it provided the core justification for the authoritarian government practised by the PAP regime. Demands for developmental sacrifices from the populace, and particularly from the working classes, which could otherwise have precipitated continued political unrest, were significantly contained once such sacrifice had been defined by the nationalist ideology as a civic virtue. This civic nationalism was forward-looking; in Hill and Lian's words, 'Nation building began in earnest – it involved historical amnesia, looked towards the future and was integrated in institution building' (1995: 3).[5]

The regime's globalisation strategy engendered rapid and unstinted economic development, which has resulted in rising living standards. Nevertheless, the state's concern that Singapore remain globally competitive has led it to ensure that workers' real wage increases remain well below productivity increases, and that state expenditure on welfare assistance remains low (Ramesh 1995b, Asher 1993). Significant economic disparities have persisted therefore, and might even have increased during some phases of growth. The extent of discontent arising from this has, however, been limited by the state's provisions in areas such as housing, education and health care,[6] and probably by the persistence of an immigrant mentality which measures social justice in terms of comparison with the past rather than just by comparison across social groups. But the state's ideological justifications of the need for sacrifice from workers have also played a crucial role.

State policies relating to a wide range of social and political, as well as economic matters, have been repeatedly depicted by the government as imperatives required for Singapore's successful negotiation of the global economy. The portrayal of Singapore in terms of its weakness in the face of international capital is in this way employed as a legitimatory ideology to restrict the scope of political thinking and political debate. As John Gray has noted, 'the rhetoric of globalisation serves to restrict public perception of policy options' (1994a: 18). Singaporeans are repeatedly reminded that their economic security is fragile; they must either work harder to get ahead of the pack, or be left behind; they must keep on climbing the slope, or slide down. The imagery varies but the consistent message is that the economic security of each individual is fragile, and depends upon improving productivity, 'focus[ing] our energies on increasing the size of the economic pie, instead of dissipating them on fruitless disputes' (Government of Singapore 1991: 61), and accepting the need for meritocratic hierarchy.

The impact of economic inequalities on state legitimacy has thus been minimised, and the PAP regime is widely perceived as having progressed towards its development and social justice promises. The ability of the PAP regime to mobilise strong electoral support (nearly 65 per cent in 1997) is clearly only a very inaccurate measure of this.[7] It overstates the extent of support for the regime to the extent that voters have responded to official intimidation and incentives (Chin 1997); but it also might understate the legitimacy of the state in the sense that votes against the PAP may arise not only from perceptions of state illegitimacy, but also from concerns to strengthen democratic debate and articulate competing interests. Nevertheless, there is widespread agreement among observers that Singaporean voters have repeatedly endorsed the PAP regime primarily because of their 'fundamental aspiration for economic security and material improvement which the PAP had a record of providing' (Rodan 1989: 128).[8]

This promise of continued material progress is communicated and dramatised by the state in the vision of Singapore as a moral community in which images of affluence are repeatedly associated with images of social cohesion and national virtue.[9] The regime repeatedly justifies its calls for sacrifice by linking them with the vision of the mature, gentle nation, united by sophisticated technology and communitarian harmony. The regime repeatedly works to convince Singaporeans that this vision of the social justice nation is already beginning to appear, and is within their grasp, so long as they do not lose faith and lessen their discipline. Thus, rapid improvements in private and public affluence become the visible evidence of progress towards mature nationhood. Globalisation promotes state legitimacy and national cohesion, therefore, in the sense that it can be cited to explain both the facts of collective development and the need for collective sacrifice, and also to restrict political debate which might question state policies and nationalist ideologies.

Social control and national identity

Political élites influence the construction of civic nationalism, not just through their ability to promote the language of community and sacrifice, but also through their provision of public institutions which provide the frameworks within which the populace interact, perceive their interests and develop their sense of identity. The PAP regime in Singapore has developed a set of institutions to ensure the social control necessary for globalised economic development. In the process, Singaporeans have been tied into a state-focused network of economic, social and political interactions which provides an 'institutional definition of nationhood' and a 'fundamental form of political identity' (Brubaker 1996: 24)

In order to attract international capital, the state has imposed labour discipline, has restricted direct welfare provisions, controlled labour costs so that economic inequalities have been maintained, and been unresponsive in various ways to the claims of local capital. But the adoption of these policies has implied an expansion of the corresponding role of the state in ensuring that they did not lead to social unrest and political instability. The erosion of the state's autonomy as economic manager has thereby been counterbalanced by the increase in its social management role. The state has built an extensive network of linkages with civil society involving the National Trade Union Congress (NTUC) and its affiliated trade unions; the PAP and the parliamentary institutions, including the Nominated Member of Parliament scheme; and the local community institutions including Community Centres, Citizens' Consultative Committees, Management Committees, Residents' Committees and Town Councils. These various bodies enable the PAP regime to identify and co-opt grassroots leaders (Hill and Lian 1995). The state has also created a 'social control economy' which centres on the state administration of state-subsidised education, housing and health care, and employer-subsidised superannuation (the CPF – Central Provident Fund – scheme). The building of these 'intermediations' strengthens the state by reducing the 'isolation of power' which is the major source of fragility for authoritarian regimes,[10] and ensures that globalisation does not generate social unrest. This response of the state to globalisation means that from the perspective of Singaporean citizens, there does indeed exist a distinct 'Singaporean national economy', managed by the state. All Singaporeans are active participants in this network of economic interactions relating to CPF, housing loans, education, health, public transport and taxation; and their involvement in this state-focused 'national economy' provides a basis for national identity. It does this by creating a community of individuals who directly benefit from the subsidies provided and administered by the state, and who thus come to share common life experiences, a sense of common identity and a culture of political acquiescence and materialism. Involvement in these public institutions thus both ensures social control, and also ensures the development of a community united by a belief that their self-interests coincide. The fact that 87 per cent of the population live in government housing estates gives the government numerous opportunities to enhance the legitimacy of the state and also to 'incorporat[e] the population, ideologically and materially, into a commitment to a society transformed by rapid industrialisation' (Chua 1995: 136).

While the nation originates as an ideological myth invented by state élites, rather than as a distinctive economic community, its subsequent strengthening involves the mobilisation of society around that myth and the institutionalisation of national identity. This process is facilitated by globalisation, since, although this reduces the Singapore state's capacity for controlling the forces influencing its macro-economy, at the same time, it impels the state to increase its capacities for the control over its own populace, and thereby to create the institutional framework around which civic nationalism can develop.

Patriotic pride

The state élites have specifically sought to reinforce the development of a civic nationalist sense of identity based on the collectivist ideology and the institutional framework noted above, by fostering a sense of patriotic pride in Singapore's modern image and international reputation. The Singaporean state invests heavily in promoting this image through ideological indoctrination in the media, the schools and public ceremonies; and promotes a series of technological achievements (such as the port, the airport, military hardware, the MRT – mass rapid transit – train) as symbols of national identity. These evoke pride in the country's economic achievements, the glossiness of its public amenities, the regional and global status of its political leaders and the modernity of its defence forces. While it is difficult to gauge the success of such indoctrination, its effectiveness might be extrapolated from the regime's ideological effectiveness in other areas, such as the 'speak Mandarin' campaign, and from the likelihood that assertions of pride in the 'national home' are particularly likely to resonate with individuals who have experienced the kind of improvements in the family home which the HDB (Housing and Development Board) upgrading schemes have achieved. But the propaganda goes further. Even those Singaporeans who privately feel that they are working harder than ever without significant improvements in their standard of living, are, nevertheless, likely, because of the hegemony of communitarian language in Singapore, to identify with images of national development and progress, and to take pride in them. The identification of self-interest with state-interests, is translated into the subordination of self-interests to national community interests.

It is sometimes suggested that the authority of government in Singapore, and more generally in the Asian NICs (newly industrialised countries), has derived primarily from a performance legitimacy derived from the facts of economic growth. It should be noted, however, that economic growth does not of itself necessarily promote either national unity or state legitimacy. Indeed, it is frequently argued that economic development undermines authoritarian regimes because it inevitably generates the growth of middle-class pressures for liberalisation, as well as working-class unrest with inequalities, so as to constitute a politically destabilising force (Alagappa 1995). The suggestion here is that economic growth has enhanced the legitimacy of the PAP regime, not because individuals evaluate the PAP on a factual-performance basis, but rather because the regime has successfully inculcated a collectivist civic nationalism which subordinates class and individual interests to visions of the common good.

Ethnocultural nationalism and corporatist rule

From the early 1980s, civic nationalism was supplemented by the regime's promotion of ethnocultural nationalism, which sought to co-opt the diverse ethnic identities into a Singaporean ethnocultural identity based on Asian values.

Civic nationalism can accommodate economic inequalities so long as these are seen as not detracting from the equality of status of all citizens, and so long as they are understood as contributing towards the attainment of the social justice nation. But civic nationalism becomes vulnerable when it is suggested that such economic disparities coincide with ethnic differences, so that the economically deprived ethnic minorities begin to announce their suspicion that the claim to civic nationalism might be shallow and might camouflage an underlying ethnocultural nationalism which favours the ethnic majority and discriminates against themselves. This situation faced the Singapore government by the late 1970s, when average Malay incomes began to decline significantly in relation to average Chinese incomes, so that Malays, who had been promised a 'special position' in the Constitution, and who saw their co-ethnics across the causeway receiving economic benefits from positive discrimination, began to believe 'that their problems and disadvantages ha[d] been imposed on them on a racial basis by the Chinese majority' (Li 1988: 179). There was thus the danger that the Malay community might begin to make use of the ideas of 'minority rights' which had gained inter-national currency. This coincided with other signs that globalisation might be introducing various ideas to Singaporean society (including Islamic, Buddhist and Christian revivalism, a hedonistic youth culture, as well as liberal individualism) which could, if unchecked, undermine the social and political control upon which the regime relied. The response of the Singapore government was to launch a campaign to reinforce the collectivist and deferential political culture, in order to create a stronger cultural bulwark against these disruptive implications of globalised development. The government had already begun inculcating Singaporeans during the 1970s, into state-approved versions of Indian, Malay and Chinese traditional cultures, so as to depoliticise these ethnic attachments and provide a cultural ballast which would prevent the spread of 'rootless individualism'. But this had the unintended effect of increasing the sense of distance between each of the different ethnic segments, and also the distance between the ethnic cultures of the majority of Singaporeans and the Anglophone culture of the political élites. The combination of the strategies of depoliticised meritocracy and depoliticised ethnicity, thereby threatened to weaken the sense of civic community upon which élite legitimacy relied. The government responded, from the early 1980s onwards, by progressively developing a new Singaporean ethnocultural nationalism, which could supplement the existing civic nationalism, and provide an overarching cultural identity, which would be strong enough both to tie the various ethnic cultures together and also to demarcate a unique Singapore identity against the encroachments of globalisation.

This development of a Singaporean ethnocultural nationalism may be understood as a facet of globalisation, rather than merely as a reaction against it. Globalisation is sometimes characterised as a process of cultural homogenisation which erodes national identities, but it has been powerfully argued by Roland Robertson and others that homogenisation and heterogenisation are interwoven. Contemporary assertions of nationhood occur because of, not despite, globalisation tendencies, since 'there is indeed currently something like an "ideology of home" which has in fact come into being partly in response to the constant repetition and global diffusion of the claim that we now live in a condition of homelessness or rootlessness' (Robertson 1995: 35). Rapid modernisation and globalisation may generate feelings of insecurity, rather than a new cosmopolitanism, so that individuals become increasingly susceptible to images of the kinship community. Moreover, the nation-state is 'a major agency for the production of diversity and hybridisation, constructing "hybridised national cultures" and establishing their own unique difference' (Robertson 1995: 41). In practice, this assertion of difference may manifest itself either in ethnic claims, or in those of the nation-state; and the relationship between the two does not then depend upon the cultural globalisation processes themselves, so much as on the way in which ethnicity is portrayed in the discourses on the nation-state culture.

Singaporean society and culture have been dramatically influenced by globalisation through the opening up of the society to 'Western' media, commodities and lifestyles, interactions with a large expatriate population, and, for some, the availability of overseas travel and education. The Singaporean state élites have reacted, as have state élites elsewhere, by depicting these aspects of globalisation as a threat to indigenous identity and culture. A state-initiated nationalist ideology has been articulated which invents and propagates myths and symbols of a virtuous Singaporean identity in contrast to a demonised 'Western' other. Myths of cultural and political harmony have been counterposed to depictions of 'Western' society as being culturally and politically decayed. Instead of the earlier siege strategy, which stressed the weakness of Singapore in the face of external powers, the new nationalist imagery depicts Singapore as the increasingly strong nation-state with the resources, both cultural and material, to withstand the threats. In such ways, even the threatening aspects of globalisation can provide ideological ammunition for the construction of nationalism.

From the late 1970s onwards, the PAP government has been concerned with the inculcation of moral values. The reasons for this were cogently stated in Goh Keng Swee's Report on the Ministry of Education, 1979:

> A society unguided by moral values can hardly be expected to remain cohesive under stress. It is a commitment to a common set of values that will determine the degree to which the people of recent migrant origin will be willing and able to defend their collective interest.
>
> (quoted in Hill and Lian 1995: 196)

The government began by linking the teaching of the 'mother tongue' language in the schools (additional to English), with the teaching of 'Moral Education' incorporating Asian and Western ethics. This then developed into the teaching of religion, with particular attention being paid in the early 1980s to Confucian ethics. But when this was perceived as having the unintended consequence of promoting ethnic disunity, the government sought to shift the focus from religious values to the inculcation of more secular communitarian ethics, which focused upon the theme of a distinctive Asian ethnocultural nationalism.

This campaign has been intensively promoted through the education system and the mass media from the late 1980s to the present day. It seeks to erode an ethos of individualism and to promote the idea that deference to community authority, at the level of both the family and the nation, constitutes the Asian virtue which unites Singapore. The 'Asian values' were specified most clearly in the 1991 White Paper on Shared Values. During 1990, while its Maintenance of Religious Harmony Bill was being processed, the government began identifying the 'core values' which were deemed to be common to members of each ethnic community. These were listed and defined by the state in the form of ethical values for the individual, but they were intended as a national ideology which 'through deliberate effort, [will] retain and strengthen our identity, one which is distinct from other societies' (Lee H.L., 1989, quoted in Hill and Lian 1995: 214). Five 'Shared Values' were specified:

1   nation before community and society above self;
2   family as the basis unit of society;
3   regard and community support for the individual;
4   consensus instead of contention;
5   racial and religious harmony.

While this list was never explicitly adopted as a national ideology, the government has continued its campaign to promote the idea that the distinctive ethnic and racial composition of Singapore provides the basis for an equally distinctive cultural identity. The promotion of this 'Asian values' identity is presently focused upon the idea of distinctive 'core family values' (love, care and concern, mutual respect, commitment, filial responsibility and communication) as focal points for a sense of national identity (Hill and Lian 1995: 155). The state promotes the idea that all the ethnic cultures are inherently compatible in their stress on the cohesion and authority of the Asian family, by making this theme of family central to the idea of a Singaporean nation, depicted in ethnocultural terms as the family writ-large.

While none of the specific formulations of core, shared, family, Asian values, have become central nationalist symbols, the cumulative impact of these campaigns has been significant in instilling belief in a distinctive national culture which prioritises community over self, and which is seen as common to the Islamic Malay, the mainly Confucianist Chinese and the Hindu and Sikh Indian segments. The institutional basis for this ethnocultural nationalism is the set of state-sponsored Chinese, Indian, Malay and Eurasian ethnic associations,[11] which channel state resources to the economically deprived members of each racial community, who might otherwise be most likely to articulate their ethnic affiliations in opposition to the PAP regime. These institutions also ensure the inculcation of the state-sanitised version of ethnicity which underpins Singaporean ethnocultural nationalism. The state has thereby sought to shift public perceptions away from the view that ethnicity was divisive, so that to be more Singaporean was to be less Indian, Malay or Chinese. Instead, it fosters the recognition that ethnic identities are the anchor on which national identity can be built, since family, ethnic community and Asian nation are depicted as forming a compatible hierarchy of ethnocultural identity (Brown 1994).

This 'ethnic engineering' can be seen as part of the wider social-control strategy, and also as a strategy for managing globalisation in the context of enhancing economic linkages in China and in the South-East Asian region. The concern to foster economic links with China has been a significant factor in the Singapore state's active promotion of Chinese culture and language, from the early 1980s onwards. Hitherto, it had been taken for granted that Singapore's location in a Malay-dominated region would inhibit the state from any such pro-Chinese stance. However, the potentially destabilising impact of such a shift has been avoided by the state's strategy of portraying it as merely balancing the state's earlier initiatives aimed at the Malay minority. Thus the promotion of Mandarin and Confucianism and 'East Asian virtues' are portrayed as part of a wider strategy of promoting the 'Asian values' of all the constituent Singaporean ethnic communities.

Ethnic diversity, which had earlier been perceived and portrayed by the state as weakening the country's national identity, has been ideologically managed so that it contributes both to the state's control over society and also to the growth of a national ethnocultural identity in which images of multiculturalism (multi-ethnicity) and mono-culturalism (Asian culture) can be combined. Threats of ethnic diversity can still be usefully deployed by the state, when required, to justify limitations on democracy; but not now to justify a weakness of national identity.

By the 1990s, the depiction of Singaporean identity in civic nationalist terms, as a meritocratic society of equal citizens united by a common pride in its modern public institutions, had been supplemented by the depiction of Singaporean identity in ethnocultural nationalist terms, as a society united by its distinctive Asian virtues. Moreover, the PAP regime seems to have avoided the possibility of the tensions between the two forms of national identity becoming politically salient. The promotion of ethnocultural nationalism did indeed marginalise those Singaporeans who had not been educated in their approved 'mother tongue' (monolingual English speakers, Chinese-dialect speakers, or those from families which do not fit into the official categories). But the state has acted to contain or ameliorate such problems by appropriate policy initiatives, including giving new recognition and resources to Chinese clan associations, and to a Eurasian Association. More generally, whereas the earlier civic nationalism had, in effect, favoured English speakers, the rise of ethnocultural nationalism has favoured Mandarin speakers; but the lack of any polarisation between civic and ethnocultural nationalism is indicated by the widespread ambiguity as to whether the state's promotion of Mandarin (and to a lesser extent of Confucianism) has constituted an ethnocultural bias in favour of the Chinese majority, or a fair rebalancing of earlier policies which had promoted the teaching of the Malay language. Civic and ethnocultural nationalisms have largely been interwoven rather than counterposed.

It might therefore seem tempting to conclude that, by the end of the 1990s, the state élites had succeeded in legitimating their economic globalisation policies by inculcating the populace with a strong sense of national identity. The civic nationalist idea of a sovereign community of equal citizens has apparently been interwoven with the ethnocultural nationalist idea of a unique community united by a belief in its common Asian ancestry and heritage, so as to provide a strong basis both for legitimating the PAP regime, and for promoting national unity. But such a depiction of Singapore would be misleading. Nationalism succeeds when it resolves the uncertainties engendered by rapid and disruptive socio-economic change, and generates a sense of security within the community of common kinship. How then are we to explain the anxiety, fear and insecurity which permeate modern Singapore society? If the PAP regime has been promoting a sense of security through its effective nationalist policies, then some other countervailing factor must be at work undermining that sense of security, and thereby weakening both the sense of national cohesion, and the nationalist legitimacy of the regime.

Nationalist legitimation versus state intimidation

The PAP has in some degree undermined its nationalist legitimation strategy by seeking to supplement it with a strategy of state intimidation. The result is that the sense of security provided by nationalism is partially undermined by the sense of insecurity instilled by state intimidation.

The shift from the overt depoliticisation of authoritarian rule in the 1970s to the politics of managed participation in the 1980s and 1990s, might have been expected to engender a reduction in the PAP government's use of coercion against its critics. But this has not been the case. The government has continued to control elections by threatening potential opposition voters with loss of developmental amenities (Chin 1997), and by launching attacks against even moderate critics so as to try to ensure their departure from the political arena; as most notably with Tan Wah Piow, Vincent Cheng, Tang Fong Har, Teo Soh Lung, J.B. Jeyaretnam, Francis Seow, Tang Liang Hong and Chee Soon Juan (Chee 1998: 241–86).[12] Those who stand as opposition candidates at elections are particularly vulnerable. Tang Liang Hong was accused of making 'Chinese chauvinist' remarks and the eventual outcome was that he fled the country and was sued by the PAP leaders for S$8.075 million. Chee Soon Juan was dismissed from his university position and found it difficult to find alternative work in Singapore. J.B Jeyaretnam has been fined and sued numerous times. Francis Seow was interned, investigated for tax evasion and fled to the USA. The dominant explanation for such intimidation refers to the argument that the globalised development of the Asian NICs has engendered a rising tide of liberalism and democracy with which the growing middle classes in particular are imbued. Rising expectations and demands for political participation and liberty put pressures on incumbent authoritarian regimes, which cannot be fully accommodated by strategies of shallow democratisation, so that incidents of state coercion increase, at least until more fundamental democratic reforms are achieved.

This analysis might make sense for South Korea and Taiwan, but in the case of Singapore there is little evidence of any increasing political pressures on the governing regime, which might explain the need for state coercion (Jones and Brown 1994). Indeed, there is a remarkable consistency to the PAP's use of such policies throughout its forty-year period of government. This raises the possibility that the PAP's employment of coercion against political critics is not so much a response to incidents of opposition which threaten its legitimacy, as an attempt to enhance and supplement such legitimacy by instilling the community with a sense of awe at the invincibility and absolutism of the ruler's power (Jones, in Bell *et al.* 1995). The use of coercion against critics might not be designed primarily to defeat those critics, but rather to intimidate the populace so as to maximise their compliance. The regime's legitimacy on democratic, nationalist or performance grounds, could thus be supplemented by the authority arising from the display of power. The suggestion, then, is that the PAP regime has sought to supplement its strategy of legitimating its rule through the inculcation of a collectivist and developmental national identity, by periodic 'crusades' against selected critics, whose public humiliation and political destruction are designed to evoke awe and respect.

If this analysis is accurate, however, it might not be the liberalising pressures of globalisation which explain the limited impact of the regime's nationalist ideologies in legitimating its rule; but rather the (unintended) incompatibility between the two strategies which the regime has employed to sustain its power. While state intimidation may evoke respect for the firm ruler in some, it evokes fear and insecurity in others. The sense of security engendered by the inculcation of a sense of Singaporean national identity, is thus partially weakened and undermined by the sense of insecurity engendered by the strategy of state intimidation. The result is a society imbued with a permanent sense of anxiety, such that many Singaporeans retreat from public political life into the private apolitical sphere, seeking security either in personal relationships or in such 'escapisms' as religion, consumerism, *kiasu*ism[13] or gambling.

Conclusions

Globalisation clearly implies new problems and opportunities for nation-states, and the way in which they confront these depends partly on their variable relationships with international and local capital. But it would be 'more than absurd', as John Dunn has noted, to suggest that 'the practical capabilities of states today in any general fashion fall short of those of their predecessors' (1995: 4). The global economy may indeed need management at the global level, but, if so, the only available instrument of cooperation is the nation-state, and problems of effective cooperation between nation-states should not be confused with the weakening of the nation-state itself (Dunn 1995).

In the Hobbesian model, the strong sovereign state is that in which a centralised government exerts effective control over civil society so as to ensure order within its territory, such that international and local capitalists can go about their business, and the society can enjoy 'peaceful and commodious living'. This authoritarian state, able to exercise coercive power, attains legitimacy in so far as civil society retains its fear of insecurity and recognises the effectiveness of the state in preventing disorder. Thus the strength of the Hobbesian state does not depend either on the autarky of its economy or the autonomy of its economic management (or on any conventionally understood democracy), but rather on the strong legitimacy of the state as the guarantor of order.

The present discussion of the nation-state modifies the Hobbesian model in two respects. First, it is recognised that the state which seeks to facilitate capitalist development must provide not only order, but also the kind of infrastructure, labour discipline and tax regime which international capital requires. The strong state is thus the state which can impose the required labour discipline without thereby undermining its legitimacy and its ability to maintain order. Second, it is argued that the strong state is one which reinforces its legitimacy by articulating an ideology of collectivist and developmental nationalism in such a way as to mobilise effectively the society around myths of national identity and destiny, so that the consent of the populace is obtained not only because of belief in the need for order, but also because of belief in progress towards the social justice nation. The strong state thereby becomes the strong nation-state. There is thus a tension between the classic Hobbesian authoritarian state which relies on sustaining the fear of insecurity to maintain order and unity; and the nation-state which relies on evoking and guaranteeing a sense of security in affiliation to the national community. The sense of security which ties the nation-state together, is potentially undermined by the sense of insecurity which ties the authoritarian state together.

So long as the nation-state is defined as the autonomous economic community, then it becomes difficult to avoid the conclusion that all nation-states are necessarily weakened by globalisation. But once the nation-state is understood as an ideological construct, the contingent impact of globalisation is clarified. Globalisation might indeed weaken the nation-state either by restricting the policy options of state élites, eroding the cultural distinctiveness of the national community or strengthening the liberal and democratic voices which undermine authoritarian regimes. But none of these are universal or necessary implications. In the Singapore case, it is suggested that the state élites have chosen policy options which enhance both the process of globalisation and their own capacities for control and legitimacy; and that globalisation has stimulated the development of a sense of Singaporean civic and ethnocultural distinctiveness. The countervailing forces have not arisen from the liberalising impact of globalised development, but rather from the regime's own lack of faith in their nationalist ideologies and their consequent employment of strategies of state intimidation. Whether globalisation undermines the strength of the nation-state, depends primarily on the state's capacities for ideological management, rather than simply on its strategies of economic management.

6 Reactive nationalism and the politics of development

The case of Ghana[1]

It has previously been suggested (in Chapter 3), that the political character of nationalism might depend primarily upon whether it is constructed by political élites on a reactive basis, or is internally generated on the basis of civic pride or ethnocultural affinity. It was also suggested that the former reactive type of nationalism is most likely when it is articulated by marginalised classes, and resonates with societies which are undergoing some 'crisis of self-confidence'. Such reactive nationalism was depicted as illiberal both in its demonising of specified threats or enemies, and also in the likelihood that it would take a collectivist form, rather than an individualist one, so as to facilitate an authoritarian mobilisation against such threats.

It was also suggested (in Chapter 2), that state élites have frequently sought legitimacy by depicting the state as the engine of development; detracting attention from present inequities and deprivations by depicting the nation as the imminent social justice community. The Singapore case was clearly unusual, however, in that the success of state élites in mobilising support for its intertwined visions of civic and ethnocultural nationalism had been greatly facilitated by the economic growth arising from globalisation. But could a state élite maintain such a vision of civic and ethnocultural nationalist development, and thereby sustain their own political legitimacy, in the face of economic collapse?

The purpose here is discuss the relationship between nationalism and economic collapse, in the context of one case, that of Ghana. The aim is to examine some of the linkages between reactive nationalism and its collectivist and developmental politics, in order to show how reactive, collectivist and developmentalist nationalism varies in its utility for political legitimacy, depending upon whether the threats against which it is ideologically constructed promote the entwining, or the disentwining, of the civic and ethnocultural nationalist visions.

Since nationalism is approached here from the perspective of political legitimacy, we need to begin by pointing out that the legitimacy of authoritarian regimes in developing countries is often seen as relying primarily upon their 'performance'. This indicates that the authority of governments, and thence of the state, depends upon their record of being able to deliver desired private and collective goods to the populace. A failure in this regard will therefore be reflected in an immediate loss of support and legitimacy (Alagappa 1995: 41). Such an understanding of legitimacy would seem to explain why economic collapse precipitated a corresponding collapse of the state in such recent cases as those of Rwanda, Liberia, Sierra Leone and Somalia. But it is important to note that economic collapse does not always lead to political conflict. The case of Ghana is instructive in that it has experienced a regressive cycle where economic collapse was indeed accompanied by a significant erosion of state authority, and by some civil disorder. But it has also experienced a subsequent period of political consolidation, in which both regime and state legitimacy have been rebuilt, despite continued erosion in the living standards of many Ghanaians. In order to examine and explain this, we need to look more closely at the nature of Ghanaian nationalism.

Political legitimacy and nationalism in Ghana

The shift from Ghana's political instability prior to 1982, and its stability since that date, cannot fully be explained in terms of a change in the 'performance legitimacy' of the successive regimes. Regime legitimacy has also been derived from the reactive basis for Ghanaian nationalism, as each regime has sought to mobilise support for itself by a garrison strategy, proclaiming a crisis in which national unity is threatened by specified enemies.

The legitimacy of governments arises out of interactions between rulers and those ruled, and governments seek to influence this relationship through a mix of appeals to shared values, procedural rules, consent and performance criteria, in order to convince the ruled of their right to govern. Success depends partly on their choice of legitimation strategy and on their manipulative skills, but it also depends partly on the nature of the challenges and demands they face. Legitimacy is therefore always contingent, so that rulers must repeatedly seek to cultivate it. Moreover, while it is possible to distinguish, for purposes of analysis, the legitimacy of the state, regime and government, the distinction between them is particularly fragile in the case of developing countries like Ghana, in part, because of the relative newness of this demarcation, but more crucially because of the extent to which political power is, in practice, concentrated. In the discussion which follows, therefore, it is suggested that the relationship between regime and state legitimacy is a permeable one, in that the strengthening or erosion of the legitimacy of successive regimes tends to breed a corresponding identification with, or alienation from, the state (Chazan 1983). The focus here is on isolating and examining two aspects of legitimacy, relating to economic performance and to national identity, in order to try to explain the shift from political regression to political consolidation in Ghana. As a preliminary, however, the reactive basis of Ghanaian nationalism needs to be outlined.

The reactive character of Ghanaian nationalism derives from the fact that it was articulated by a series of marginalised groups, and then resonated with a post-World War II society experiencing a collapse of its traditional authority structure, and an erosion of its social cohesion. Ghanaian nationalism was initially articulated by the

Western-educated élites who formed the Aborigines Rights Protection Society, and later the National Congress of British West Africa.[2] These men found their aspirations for upward mobility in the colonial Gold Coast hierarchy restricted, and therefore sought status as spokespersons for an 'African nationalism' which was at first primarily cultural in focus. However, the fight for decolonisation brought with it a more civic basis for Ghanaian nationalism, which was increasingly evident in the calls for the independence of the Gold Coast in the rhetoric of the overseas-based West African Students' Union, and then in that of the more moderate United Gold Coast Convention. It was, however, the nationalist language of Kwame Nkrumah and his fellow Convention People's Party (CPP) activists, which resonated most effectively with the wider Gold Coast population, offering a vision both of ethno-cultural regeneration and of civic pride.

It seems likely that Nkrumah's radical nationalism grew out of his experience of failure in higher education in the USA and the UK, and his feelings of inferiority in relation to the more moderate West African nationalists with whom he interacted, most of whom, unlike Nkrumah, did achieve their various medical, legal and other qualification goals (Sherwood, 1996). The activists of his CPP, who comprised the bulk of the locality-level mobilisers of Ghanaian nationalism, were similarly marginalised men, the new generation of elementary school-leavers. They were the 'primary-school teachers, clerks . . . petty traders [and] storekeepers . . . And their immediate following was even more humble . . . [T]hose who lacked the all-important Standard VII certificate were hardly employable. Some remained in the villages . . . many more travelled to the "capital town" . . . where they struggled through adolescence in a series of unskilled jobs' (Austin 1970: 16–17).

These educated and semi-educated commoners became politically active through agitation against the traditional authority structure, the locality-level chiefs whose positions had been weakened by their involvement in the native authorities created by the colonial administration. This meant that most villages and towns became disrupted and divided, in the 1930s and 1940s, by chieftaincy disputes. But these disputes were symptomatic of a 'social revolution' arising from the combined impact of urbanisation, the spread of commerce, colonial administration and education. The sudden emergence of the post-World War II problems of unemployment, inflation and the 'swollen-shoot' threat to cocoa farming, then acted as catalysts, ensuring that 'those who had hitherto been marginal men, were now tantamount to public opinion' (Apter 1963: 166). Educated commoners who had been agitating against their local chieftaincies became the local activists of the CPP, and transmitted the argument that the fundamental cause of the various grievances was British colonial rule, and that the solution was 'self-government now'. 'They were organised, and they were many. They had a goal – self-government. They had a devil – British imperialism. They found a God – Kwame Nkrumah' (Apter 1963: 166).

The collectivist and illiberal political implications of this reactive and *ressentiment*-generated nationalism became apparent when Nkrumah's CPP government began employing appeals to the imperative of national unity as the justification for restrictions on political opposition and civil liberties. Visions of nationalism were deployed to promote the idea that these restrictions were the necessary present sacrifices for the attainment of a future social justice community, once neo-colonialism was defeated. Nevertheless, Nkrumah did not seek legitimacy solely by making future-oriented promises of the milk and honey which would flow, first from self-government, and then from the attainment of autonomous development. He also got significant support on the basis of his 'performance' achievements. The 1950s was a decade of improving living standards (Rimmer 1992: 66–8), and virtually every village and town in the Gold Coast received some amenities from state funds, in the form of Tarmac roads, water-pipes, drainage ditches, medical clinics or schools. These private and collective goods proved the ability of the CPP government to deliver. When Nkrumah's regime began to lose support during the 1960s, it was thus feasible that this might be explained simply as the erosion of performance legitimacy, since this was when the flow of amenities dried up and living standards began to erode. However, Nhrumah's loss of support might also be explainable as an erosion of his legitimacy arising from new tensions between the civic and ethnocultural visions of Ghana. His mobilisation of national unity through the demonising of colonialism and neo-colonialism, was increasingly supplemented by the identification of new internal enemies and threats, which, as will be seen, threatened to undermine the claims that ethnocultural community and civic community could be reconciled in Ghanaian nationalism.

A similar question arises in relation to the fluctuations in popular support for Ghana's present political leader, Jerry Rawlings. Can these fluctuations be explained in terms of performance legitimacy, or in terms of changes in the type of threats and enemies against which Ghanaian nationalism has been constructed? The 'performance legitimacy' argument needs examining more carefully in terms of its applicability to the Ghanaian situation, before the alternative argument, relating to the construction of nationalist ideology, can be developed.

Prior to 1982, Ghanaian politics was characterised by chronic governmental instability and a progressive erosion of the power, legitimacy, authority and autonomy of the state (Chazan 1983: 331–60). When Jerry Rawlings took power in his *coup* of December 1981, it seemed inevitable that he too would soon fall victim to 'a state apparatus that had virtually ceased to function', most obviously because he was inheriting an economy which had 'an unerring capacity for dissipating public support for rulers' (Chazan 1983: 321–2). But Rawlings has now retained power for nineteen years, longer than any other ruler of Ghana, including Kwame Nkrumah. Moreover, he has retained power through democratic elections for the last eight of those years, being returned as President in two fair elections, with majorities of 58.6 per cent and 57.4 per cent, on the basis of extremely high turnout of voters (77.9 per cent in 1996).[3] Even Nkrumah's CPP in its heyday only got 57 per cent on a 50 per cent turnout.

At first sight, it might be thought that the most appropriate explanation for this sea-change in Ghanaian politics would be to see political legitimacy as deriving from economic performance. When economic growth gave way to economic decline, from about 1960 onwards, the economy began to slide into bankruptcy (Rimmer 1992). Each successive regime gained initial support by its promises to halt the slide, only to lose that support and be removed by *coup* when it failed. Jerry Rawlings inherited the same mantle, and when the massive inflation and food shortages continued after this accession to power, he was faced, in the early 1980s, with a series of counter-*coup* attempts, and retained power only by employing authoritarian means and imposing a 'culture of silence' (Agyeman-Duah 1987).

The sea-change occurs, according to this 'performance legitimacy' approach, because of the success of the World Bank's structural adjustment reforms, which the Rawlings government began to implement from 1983 onwards. The result was a reversal of the economic decline, and the achievement of real GDP increases of 3 per cent per annum from 1984 to 1990, and 4.3 per cent from 1990 to 1994. The rebuilding of state legitimacy might seem to follow from the delivery of economic performance.

But there are difficulties with such an argument. By the end of 1996, when the large majority of voters expressed their support for Rawlings, and an unprecedentedly high proportion of Ghanaians registered their trust in the state by turning out to vote in the elections, economic growth was falling, inflation was shooting back up to 70 per cent, partly because of a series of devaluations, and unemployment was continuing to increase.[4] Thus the growth of GDP has not, in the judgement of several observers, implied any corresponding growth in living standards. Kwame Frimpong concludes that 'The lot of Ghanaians has . . . been worse than before the implementation of structural adjustment' (1997: 103). Richard Jeffries agrees that 'the real living standards of many Ghanaians, especially in the urban areas, had . . . deteriorated', and while he considers that rural living standards did not continue to fall as much as in the 1970s, 'it would be wrong to suggest that structural adjustment policies as such have produced any very marked improvement in the real incomes of most rural dwellers' (1998: 194, 205).

Even supportive observers of the structural adjustment programmes recognise that 'the effects . . . on workers in formalised employment were evidently mixed. A number of those workers lost their jobs, and for a time at least suffered further deprivations . . . Those who remained in employment became better off . . . up to 1986, but it is likely that they lost much of their gains in the later 1980s (Rimmer 1992: 195). Critics of structural adjustment agreed; 'Reforms in Ghana have been pushed through without any social safety net. Structural adjustment has put people out of work and abolished free education . . . Opening up Ghana to imports has destroyed some local industries' (Christian Aid, in Adams 1995: 35). The change achieved by the Rawlings regime is not that it has improved living standards, but that 'with the notable exception of a small minority in the business community and in private professional practice, people basically have had to learn to live on less' (Shillington 1992: 125).

Proponents of the political economy approach to Ghanaian politics, have, in most cases, been fully aware that the reforms imposed by the Rawlings regime, while halting the economic decline, have failed to raise the living standards of most Ghanaians. Given the general assumption that political legitimacy rests primarily on economic performance, and the particular assumption that Rawlings's shift to structural adjustment in 1983 meant that he had staked his legitimacy on his skills as economic manager (Jeffries 1991), they have sometimes been forced to conclude that the legitimacy of the Rawlings' regime remains weak and fragile, and have thus found it difficult to explain the increasingly impressive evidence to the contrary. Thus Kwame Ninsin, assuming that 'Ghanaian politics is governed by instrumental considerations', and finding that 'the economy remains as fragile as it was in the 1950s', concluded that 'by 1987 the PNDC had not been able to resolve satisfactorily the problem of legitimacy that confronted it on the assumption of power' (1991: 63, 57). Jeffrey Herbst, writing just prior to Rawlings's 1992 electoral victory, which showed solid support from rural areas, argued that the economic recovery programmes had not generated significant income gains for the rural populace, and that they had been both politically and economically marginalised. He concluded, therefore, that 'the PNDC cannot look to the rural areas for strong political support' (Herbst 1993: 93). Donald Rothchild, writing soon after the 1992 election, recognised the economic growth achievements of the 1980s, but also the severe hardships of the less advantaged, and concluded that Rawlings's electoral victory derived from 'public acquiescence and even . . . some acceptance, but this approval was half-hearted and largely contingent on further achievements in securing and distributing resources' (Rothchild 1994: 60). For Richard Jeffries, writing in 1997, the widespread support for the government, displayed in two 'free and fair' elections, is not disputed; but it is not easy for him to reconcile this with the regime's 'weak economic performance' (1998: 190). On the one hand it appeared that 'the main factor in explaining the NDC's victory would . . . seem to be that it had delivered the goods to much of the rural population' (1998: 205); on the other hand, however, it seemed that rural electors, as well as other groups, 'did not, obviously, all vote simply in response to economic benefits' (1998: 206). The Ashanti Region had arguably received more projects than most other regions, and its cocoa farmers had prospered more than most farmers; yet Ashanti rural dwellers voted predominantly for the opposition NPP (1998: 206). Moreover, 'The urban middle and upper strata have . . . tended to prosper under the NDC [Rawlings's party], yet voted predominantly for the NPP [opposition party]' (1998: 206). Something else other than economic performance legitimacy, was clearly at work, and it related to 'the issue of trust' (1998: 195).

Mahamadu Bawumia's study of the 1992 elections sought to show that the reason why rural voters had supported Rawlings more than had urban voters, was because the government's Structural Adjustment Programme had favoured rural households over urban households. But when he compared election results from the Ashanti and Volta regions, he was forced to the conclusion that the argument did not quite work, since 'ethnic perceptions sometimes affect considerations of economic improvement . . . thus it may be more a question of *perceived* fair treatment, rather than economic improvement as such' (Bawumia 1998: 68, emphasis added).[5]

It is indeed the case that Rawlings has built popular support for his regime because he is widely *perceived*, by Ghanaians, as having delivered on his promises of improving Ghanaian living standards. This perception comes in part from the regime's provision, as in the 1950s, of public amenity and infrastructure projects in each region and many localities, which are seen as evidence that the regime does care. But, whereas in the 1950s such provision of amenities coexisted with real improvements in personal incomes, this has not occurred in the 1980s and 1990s, other than for the upper- and middle-income groups in the mining and cocoa sectors. It appears, therefore, that to a significant extent, Ghanaians are measuring their welfare in terms of the community rather than the individual, and in terms of the future rather than the present. There is indeed more 'trust' than 'instrumentalism' in this politics.

Ghanaian perceptions of Rawlings, and of the state, are indicated by the 1991 survey conducted by Richard Jeffries among urban lower-income groups who were not from the home region (Volta) or ethnic group (Ewe) of Rawlings. He found, first, that 'nearly all respondents employed in the formal sector felt that they were economically worse off than they had been five years previously' (Jeffries 1992: 210) Second, however, the large majority of respondents were in favour of the ERP (economic recovery programme) in that it 'had been good for the country' (Jeffries 1992: 214). He also found that 'most respondents did not primarily evaluate the performance of the PNDC government by the criterion of whether it had improved their individual economic situation', but rather referred to 'collective goods and government probity' (Jeffries 1992: 216), and evinced a 'high level of patriotism' on the basis that 'we are getting back our national pride' (Jeffries 1992: 217). The large majority perceived the performance of the government in terms of the leadership qualities of Rawlings (Jeffries 1992: 217).

This personal appeal of Rawlings has sometimes been described simply as charisma, but it is apparent from these findings that his appeal resides in his claim to symbolise the collective national will of 'the people'. The strong implication is that the ability of the Rawlings regime to build up its own support and the legitimacy of the state, might be due as much to the success of its nationalist ideology strategy, as to that of its economic strategy. It will be argued here that both the Rawlings regime, and its predecessors, have sought to compensate for limitations in their economic performance legitimacy by identifying and exaggerating a series of threats, which are portrayed as undermining the society, so that national unity can be generated reactively against those threats. This deliberate construction of reactive nationalism, for purposes of political legitimation, will be referred to here as a garrison nationalist strategy. The success of the Rawlings regimes, and the failure of their predecessors, can then be traced to their differing formulations of that reactive garrison nationalism.[6]

Each government of Ghana has begun its rule by proclaiming the severity of the crisis facing the nation, and by identifying the enemies and threats against which the nation was called to rally under its new leaders. Each regime probably hoped that such appeals to garrison legitimacy were only temporary and would soon be replaced or at least supplemented by more long-term legitimacy deriving in part from performance criteria. But their subsequent failures to deliver material benefits meant, in each case, that appeals to garrison legitimacy were repeatedly revived. If the regime could convince the populace that the failures to revive the economy derived not from their own inadequacies of policy or implementation, but rather from some other culprit, then economic collapse could be turned from a problem into a resource; it could, potentially, become the imperative for the mobilisation of the nation against the national enemy, under the incumbent regime as the 'commander of the garrison'.

The garrison nationalist strategy involved, then, the assertion by a government of a real or incipient crisis such that, for the time being at least, internal disagreements must be put to one side if the society is to survive intact. Hardship and discipline, which might otherwise be regarded as grievances, are now proclaimed as the virtues necessary for defence of the garrison. Support for the regime is identified with commitment to the nation and its survival. The imperative of the need for unity against the common enemy is thus used as a lever for containing internal divisions and quelling opposition to the regime.

Thus, in order to generate its legitimacy, and that of the nation-state, the regime must exaggerate and dramatise the spectres which threaten society, and must identify credible enemies. The obvious starting point for most poor countries, including Ghana, is to explain internal economic problems by blaming them upon global capitalism or Western governments, demonised in such terms as colonialism, neocolonialism or imperialism. But if such threats are to be credible, they need to be made concrete by the identification of those features internal to the society which facilitate the threat and undermine the nation's unity. These internal enemies may be class groups portrayed as compradors, ethnic minorities identified as subversive threats, political opponents depicted as unwitting instruments of foreign interests, or undesirable cultural traits which are characterised as weakening the nation's resilience.

But each regime must choose its enemies with care, and it is unlikely to be able to get away with inventing them, if only because the populace is 'not nearly as naive as many politicians and scholars believe' (Hayward and Dumbuya 1984: 667). The success of the garrison strategy will therefore depend primarily on whether the internal enemies specified by the regime are ones which resonate in the ideological vocabulary and the everyday experiences of the people.

The success of the Rawlings regime in Ghana, and the failures of its predecessors, may thus be examined from an angle other than that of economic performance legitimacy. It may be examined by focusing upon differences in their nationalist ideologies, and in particular upon differences in their choice of enemies.

Garrison nationalism and ethnic scapegoating: Ghana prior to 1982

In the face of economic decline, Ghana's leaders, between 1960 and 1982, sought to revive their support and legitimacy by employing a garrison nationalism which portrayed tribalism as a major threat to national unity. But this choice of 'enemy' had the unintended effect of further eroding regime legitimacy, by disentwining the civic and ethnocultural visions of the nation.

There was a widespread impression, at the time of Ghanaian independence in 1957, that decolonisation and nationalism were synonymous. It was suggested that the emergent Ghanaian national identity could be characterised in ethnocultural terms, as the clustering of related chieftaincy and linguistic systems around an Akan core; and also in civic terms, as the sense of ownership of the administrative and socio-economic structures inherited from the colonial regime. The problematical aspects of both sources of national identity would be resolved by the nation-building functions of the state, and in particular, by the symbolic role of Kwame Nkrumah as the father of the nation, and as the saviour (*Osagyefoh*) of all sections of society against the enemy of colonialism.

As has been well documented, this effort to mobilise Ghanaian nationalism by means of the symbolism of charismatic leadership, had some limited initial success in the 1950s (Apter 1963), but the charisma was undermined by the failure of Nkrumah to deliver on his promises that decolonisation would bring unity, social justice and prosperity. The reserves which had fuelled the distribution of amenity resources in the mid-1950s, had largely disappeared by the end of that decade. Nkrumah responded by constructing a new external enemy against which national cohesion could be restored, in the form of 'neocolonialism', but this was initially too amorphous an enemy to convince ordinary Ghanaians. Nkrumah tried to make the spectre of neocolonialism more convincing by linking it with 'the enemy within', portraying his political rivals as neocolonial agents whose activities were therefore subversive of national unity (Finlay 1967). But this further undermined his credibility, since these rivals were in many cases the ethno-regional patrons on whose access to state resources the hopes of most Ghanaians were focused. The failure of this strategy was perhaps reflected in the various demonstrations of support for Nkrumah's removal from power in the 1966 *coup*.

The potential fragility of Ghana's national cohesion does not stem directly from linguistic and ethnic disunity, but more from the continuing salience of regionalist rivalries for the power and resources of central government, and from the ways in which these rivalries are sometimes articulated in ethnic terms by competing élites (Berman 1998).[7] As noted in Chapter 1, the fact that government resources have been allocated on a regional basis, when combined with a patron–client political culture, has generated a 'home boy' view of politics, whereby each local or regional community comes to believe that their only hope of resources is through someone from their locality or region gaining access to state power and patronage. Thus, while Ghana's unity has never been severely threatened by ethno-regional separatism, or by intense ethnic animosities, its national cohesion has indeed been weakened by the widespread perception that élite rivalries have had 'home boy' loyalty implications, and by the ammunition which those élite rivalries have provided for ethnic stereotyping. Such ethnic stereotyping had been fostered in some respects by the colonial regime, but it only became a major aspect of regime legitimation during Nkrumah's rule.

Kwame Nkrumah's government employed a garrison strategy to try to mobilise society for a socialist (statist) transformation of the economy. This implied the need to justify the imposition of authoritarian one-party rule by undermining the credibility of political opponents. Economic problems were blamed in part on neocolonialism and on the self-seeking of state and party élites, but it was the lack of commitment to Nkrumahism which was stressed as the main factor inhibiting the nation's defence against these threats. From the outset, Nkrumah had depicted his political party, the CPP, as a nationalist movement, and had proclaimed himself as a nationalist committed to combating 'all provincial and tribal differences' (Nkrumah 1962: xv, Austin 1970: 43). Political opposition was thus labelled as anti-nationalist and therefore seditious, and, from the late 1950s onwards, the Northern Peoples' Party, the Ewe-based Togoland Congress and the Ashanti-based National Liberation Movement had each been labelled by the regime as ethno-regional, and thence 'tribalist' in nature. During the 1960s, accusations of tribalism focused increasingly on the Ewe community of the Volta region, who were portrayed as a source both of subversive oppositionist plots and of secessionism.

This depiction of tribalism, and in particular of Ewe tribalism, as the 'enemy within' which threatened to undermine the nation's defence against its neocolonial enemies, served several purposes both for the later Nkrumah regime, and for those which succeeded it – the National Liberation Council, the Busia government, General Acheampong's National Redemption Council, Akuffo's Supreme Military Council and Dr Limann's government. Indeed, it appeared as a particularly useful legitimatory ideology.

First, the portrayal of tribalism as subversive of national unity had high resonance in a society where everyone could be characterised as belonging to some ethnic group, and as either conniving at or participating in ethnic favouritism in at least some area of their social life. The resultant ambiguities and anxieties about the legitimacy of ethnicity, were thus never far below the surface. Governments had merely to tap these anxieties and guilt feelings by loudly condemning the illegitimacy of tribalism for it to provoke a cathartic search for scapegoats on the one hand, and a reaction of moralistic nationalism on the other.

Second, tribalism offered an apparently convincing explanation for a wide range of conflicts and disagreements in society, since there was almost always an ethnic correlation to political alignments. The differential access of the various linguistic groups to educational, economic and political resources meant that it was almost inevitable for tensions between different occupational, rank and status groups, or regions, to involve, *pari passu*, the alignment of members of different ethnic groups against each other. It would, in other words, have been rather surprising if most political cleavages did not involve an inter-ethnic dimension, as well as involving class, occupational, generational or other dimensions. The power of the tribalist ideology derived, then, from the ease with which governments were able to depict politics in this way. They did not always have to make direct accusations of tribalism in order to mobilise the unity of society against ethnic divisions; they could sometimes appear merely to point to the fact of multi-ethnicity and its correlations with political alignments, and 'let the facts speak for themselves'; as if the mere existence of linguistic divisions implied, of itself, the dominant role in politics of ethnic antagonisms.

Third, if accusations of tribalism were to be effective in mobilising national unity and regime support, then they had to be directed against élites who could be perceived as influential enough to constitute real threats to the society, rather than just against a marginal ethnic minority which might be seen to lack sufficient political influence to constitute a viable threat. The Ewes were indeed portrayed frequently as a peripheral and low-status minority community, but garrison ideologies, never-theless, pointed the finger not so much at the ethnic community as a whole, but rather at the 'few Ghanaians who for their own selfish or other ends . . . have been distorting government policies to confuse the masses' (Acheampong 1973: 148). Ewe tribalism appeared to be particularly attractive as a scapegoat enemy, since Ewes had been sufficiently mobile for them to be well represented among the military, administrative and commercial élites, while the involvement of some Ewes in movements opposed to the retention of the present Ghana–Togo boundary, facilitated the depiction of the wider Ewe community as sympathetic to secessionist plots, so that they could be depicted as a threat to the unity of the nation.

For these reasons, Ghanaian governments, in search of instant legitimacy, found the attractions of tribal scapegoating too much to resist:

> it has the virtue of performing multiple functions at apparently low political cost. It promotes national unity (and thence regime support) against both a minority group and an alleged threat (secessionism) to the nation's territorial boundaries. It serves to apparently explain, and thus to either defuse or promote, elite rivalries; depending on how it is employed. Finally, it has moral force because of the pejorative connotations of 'tribalism' which all may safely condemn. The political cost appear[ed] to be low in that the use of the 'Ewe threat' has not provoked a united hostile response from the target group; partly because of an Ewe sense of weakness which has engendered disappointment and apathy rather than hostility, and partly because of the very extent of Ewe integration into Ghana's social and political life, which has both muted the communal hostilities, and inhibited the alienation which might otherwise have developed.
> (Brown 1982: 67–8)

Garrison nationalism was not based solely on the spectre of tribalism during the 1970s, but this, nevertheless, emerged as one of the most consistent themes. Each new regime accused its predecessors of being ethnically biased and of sowing 'the seed of tribal conflict' (Acheampong, quoted in Smock and Smock 1975: 249); and increasingly, the spectre of Ewe tribalism was employed to explain political opposition. Similarly, Ghana's economic decline was blamed on an alleged link between smuggling, Ewe secessionism and Togo's 'financial activities to wreck Ghana's economy' (Brown 1982: 63). After the elected government of Dr Limann came to power in 1979, it tried to mobilise support against its major critic, Jerry Rawlings, by portraying him as an Ewe tribalist *coup* plotter (Baynham 1985: 640). Limann was trying to maintain support for his regime and promote a sense of national unity, by employing the 'Ewe threat' as 'Ghana's version of the permanent plot' (Bentsi-Enchill 1980).

It is quite evident, given the regime instability of the 1966 to 1982 period, that these attempts by the various regimes to generate effective legitimacy, did not succeed. Unable to sustain legitimacy by appealing to the success of their economic performance, or evidence of popular support or the acceptability of their constitutional procedures, they attempted to generate legitimacy quickly by putting the blame on tribalism, seeking to generate regime support and national unity by depicting the country as under threat from ethnic rivalries, and especially Ewe tribalism. But the outcome was to promote rather than to inhibit the country's disunity, and to precipitate rather than prevent the regimes' demise.

The reasons are clear. However attractive the spectre of Ewe tribalism was to the successive regimes as an instant recipe for generating garrison nationalism, its employment as ideology served to increase rather than decrease the political salience of ethnicity, and to further alienate political opponents of Ewe origin. Moreover, the more Ewe élites were marginalised by predominantly Akan governments, the less convincing it became to depict Ewe tribalism as a significant cause of Ghana's economic and political problems. Ghanaians increasingly perceived that problems of élite corruption and incompetence arose from the behaviour of the state élites themselves, who were predominantly (and increasingly) non-Ewe. Moreover, the depiction of Ewes as the enemy was probably not validated by the everyday experiences of most Ghanaians, given the high degree of trans-ethnic social interactions, and the low levels of ethnic antagonism. Even the attempt to portray Ewes as secessionist threats to national unity probably backfired, given the minute and ineffective character of secessionist activity in the 1970s, and the low level of interest in it among Ewes (Brown 1980a).

The vision of Ghana as an ethnocultural community had gained its credibility from the claim that all the country's ethnic segments shared a common West African culture, and could potentially unite around a common Akan core. The demonising of tribalism weakened this ethnocultural nationalist vision both in that it focused attention on the marginalisation of the non-Akan northern and Ewe communities, and also in that, by counterposing 'tribe' and 'nation', it undermined the process whereby the former might provide a building-block for the construction of the latter. The intertwining of Ghanaian civic and ethnocultural nationalism was thus weakened by the shift in the ideologies of state élites, which instead of engendering hope in a vision of political and ethnocultural unity, rather engendered fears of disunity.

By 1982, therefore, the rapid decline of Ghana's economy had been accompanied, in a 'regressive cycle' (Pellow and Chazan 1986), by the repeated failure of state élites to establish their legitimacy and authority. Instead of the appeals to garrison nationalism mobilising the society to unite under the regime to defeat the threats of tribalism, these appeals had the unintended effect of pointing attention to the regimes' own role in weakening the national garrison. Perhaps the tribalists were not the opponents of the regime who were pointed to, but rather the regime itself; and perhaps it was not just the smugglers or compradors, or even the neo-colonialists, who undermined the economy, but rather the institutions, strategies and personnel of the state.

Ghana in the post-1982 period

Rawlings has succeeded in restoring both regime and state legitimacy, by employing a garrison nationalist strategy directed against enemies identified as élite corruption and the remoteness of the state. The society's disillusionment with the failure of previous élites to deliver their developmental promises, has been channelled by Rawlings into a Rousseauean nationalism. This new nationalist strategy means that, while the politics of regionalist rivalry continues and is perceived in ethnic terms, it does not undermine the nationalist legitimacy of the regime.

The Rawlings regime legitimated itself on a reactive garrison nationalism basis from the outset, as indicated in its use of the term 'National Defence Council'. The country's economic and political collapse were blamed on the domination of previous regimes by 'a pack of criminals' (Ray 1986: 19) who had been corrupt and self-seeking, on the fact that the state was widely perceived as being a 'remote, alien institution' (Ray 1986: 24), and on imperialism. These problems could only be tackled, according to the new government, if the society could be mobilised to root out corruption, to effect a political revolution which would incorporate the masses into decision making, and to reconstruct the economy on a socialist basis. Later on, when the regime arrived at the judgement that it had no option but to implement the economic recovery programmes of the IMF and the World Bank, the language of socialism and anti-imperialism was dropped, and attention was therefore focused more specifically upon the two other threats, élite corruption and the alienating distance between state institutions and the lives of ordinary people.

In this initial period, the regime had no need to manufacture or exaggerate a sense of crisis, given that economic collapse was evident in the massive inflation and food shortages.[8] The sense of crisis was further evidenced by the series of nine counter-*coup* attempts against the regime between 1982 and 1986 (Ray 1986). Given the repeated warnings by earlier regimes of Ewe tribalist plots against incumbent governments, it could have been expected that Rawlings's accession to power, and the fact that his key advisers and senior colleagues were also members of the Ewe minority, would be met by some political or civil instability. There was indeed an ethno-regional dimension to each of these plots against the new regime, but instead of blaming them on anti-Ewe tribalism, the regime portrayed them as instigated by disgruntled self-seeking individuals. The fact that Rawlings did not accuse his political opponents of being tribalists probably served to strengthen the perception that he himself was not a tribalist. This portrayal of the plots appeared to corroborate the regime's claims that the main threat to the nation was indeed the self-interested behaviour of individuals, and that the state of crisis still persisted, so that discipline and obedience remained imperative. Moreover, as Richard Jeffries notes, there has been 'no discernible ethnic or regional favouritism in the PNDC's distribution of development projects' (Jeffries and Thomas 1993: 360). There soon developed a widespread perception, that 'All our previous governments have been tribalists, but Rawlings is a non-tribalist' (quoted in Jeffries 1992: 222).

The identification of élite corruption as the primary enemy against which the nation had to mobilise if it were to survive, was one which Rawlings had already signalled strongly in his 1979 intervention which was proclaimed as a 'housecleaning exercise'. Moreover, this was a perception of politics which had by this time become conventional wisdom among ordinary Ghanaians. All Ghanaian governments had in fact sought to legitimate themselves by highlighting the corruption of their predecessors, but this had not hitherto proven to be an effective strategy. Corruption had initially been widely condoned, since it had been the ostentatious wealth of Ghanaian élites which had made them attractive as home-boy patrons, in that their wealth both proved their power to attract resources, and also provided a role model towards which aspirations could be aimed. However, the increasingly overt corruption of the Acheampong regime had led many Ghanaians to the conclusion, by the late 1970s, that the only possible explanation for development failures must lie with the patrons themselves – the 'old guard' who had diverted resources from their client communities and into their own pockets. It was the spread of this diagnosis of Ghana's problems which explains why the progressive immiseration of the 1970s did not lead to any real radicalisation on the part of the rural and urban poor, but instead generated a 'defensive communalism' characterised by disillusionment and the rejection of 'old corrupt politicians' (Brown 1980b). Since the state itself was understood as no more than the sum of its patronage activities, the loss of faith in 'old corrupt politicians' soon manifested itself in disillusionment with the state. As Chazan has noted:

> some kind of disengagement from the state was taking place. This withdrawal was only minimally directed at physical removal from the Ghanaian context. Much more rampant was an emotional economic, social, and political detachment from the state element.
>
> (1983: 334–5)

But this disillusionment was accompanied by nostalgia; the corruption and decline of contemporary politics being visualised in terms of the idealisation of a previous era of amenity development and economic growth. For most Ghanaians, this meant a growing nostalgia for the immediate post-independence period, and a new mythologisation of Nkrumah – portrayed not as dictator but as populist hero (Brown 1980b).

Rawlings tapped into the alienation from the state, and this longing for a new populist hero, by portraying himself as the spokesman for the masses, mobilising the anger of the nation against the state. As Nugent has noted, 'The Rawlings regime made a bold departure by diagnosing the state as an integral component of the crisis rather than a self-evident solution to it' (1995: 51). Rawlings claimed that 'Ghana is in crisis . . . [because] all our previous governments worked in the interests of a local elite, and foreign masters . . . Therefore the solution to our problem of hunger in the midst of plenty is to regain our sovereignty, and for the masses of our people to exercise this power, ourselves, on our own behalf' (Rawlings, quoted in Hansen 1991: 29–30). This identification with the nation against the state was formulated in various ways. Initially, in 1979, Rawlings depicted his *coup* as an action to prevent the anger of the people leading to widespread civil conflict, by taking limited action to punish those individuals, including officers of the Acheampong and Akuffo governments, who had misappropriated state resources. As Folson has noted, this did not imply either a political or an economic revolution, but it did imply a 'moral purge' whereby house-cleaning would lead to a moral cleansing, and a reassertion of the vision of the nation as a social justice community (1993: 78).[9]

The 1981 *coup*, however, was justified in rather different language, as a political revolution based on popular sovereignty – a move towards peoples' democracy in which government would be based on 'the consent and authority of the people . . . the farmers, the police, the soldiers, the workers – you, the guardians, rich or poor' (Rawlings, quoted in Shillington 1992: 80). It was directed against not just individuals who had acted illegally, but against those who 'live in idle comfort and welcome any oppression that will sustain them' (Rawlings, quoted in Folson 1993: 79). On some occasions this formulation of the revolution appeared, at least to those on the left, to involve a mobilisation of workers against the bourgeoisie and petty bourgeoisie, but Rawlings sought to contain the resultant violent incidents perpetrated by defence committees, by stressing, increasingly, the need for all Ghanaians to cooperate as one community (Hansen 1991: 79–83). Rawlings's solution was, finally, to legitimate the revolution as being a rejection and reversal of the management policies of all previous Ghanaian regimes which, he now argued, had been the fundamental cause of corruption. Instead of aberrant immoral individuals being the enemy, the enemy was being depicted, by 1983, as the policy failures of the state. It was the faulty policies of all previous regimes which had led to the type of controls which culminated in the *kalebule* chits, and which had made corruption endemic throughout society.[10] The revolution was depicted, therefore, not as a class revolution, but rather as a revolution to cultivate a spirit of loyalty to Ghana, and support for the necessary financial discipline and moral rectitude which were implied by 'responsible financial management' (Folson 1993: 87). The particular virtue of this formulation of the revolution was that it could portray the erosion of standards of living which was implied by the adoption of the World Bank's structural adjustment programme, as a national regeneration.

Rawlings thus legitimated himself on what Folson has termed a 'Rousseauist' nationalist basis, expressing the disillusionment of the ordinary Ghanaians with both the old-guard patrons and the institutions of the state (1993: 94). He set about building new political institutions of popular democracy at local and district levels, and announced his rejection of old-style élitist politics. This strategy meant that the widespread distrust of the state, which had weakened the previous regimes, could potentially be translated into a legitimatory strength for his regime.

Rawlings had, from an early stage, voiced his concern to develop a 'Ghanaian form of democracy' which would reinforce this sense of national unity, rather than democratising on the basis of the kind of competitive party elections which had fostered the élitist and corrupt patronage politics in the past. To this end, the 1982

People's Defence Committees and Workers' Defence Committees gave way to the 1984 Committees for the Defence of the Revolution, and then the 1988 partly elected District Assemblies, each of these being on a non-party basis. Rawlings initially envisaged similarly non-party regional and national assemblies, on the lines of Museveni's Uganda. However, in the face of domestic pressures, and probably pressures from the international agencies (Jeffries 1992: 225), Rawlings gave in and agreed to multiparty elections. He did have the advantages of incumbency in these elections, including the ability to distribute public amenity development projects to key constituencies on the eve of the elections (Nugent 1995: 246–7). Moreover, the elections comprised only the type of 'shallow democracy' sufficient to legitimate support for the desired neoliberal policies (Bienefeld 1995). But Rawlings managed the elections skilfully, so as to retain and promote his 'Rousseauist' legitimacy. He used the campaigns as a platform for reinforcing his image as a 'common man' and a 'non-tribalist' who could articulate the will of 'we Ghanaians', especially in contrast to his main opponents who could be depicted in 'old guard' terms, as 'intellectuals' out to 'mislead ordinary Ghanaians' or as untrustworthy self-interested élites (Jeffries and Thomas 1993: 340). The main opponents in 1992 were Hilla Limann, the discredited ex-President, and professor Adu Boahen, whose image was that of a member of the intellectual élite. In 1996, Rawlings's main opponent was J.A. Kuffour, a lawyer and businessman who had held office in the previous government of Dr Busia. While the elections campaigns were, as always, dominated by local issues, this theme of 'us' versus 'the big men' was central in most constituencies. Even when the local party activists of Rawlings's party were themselves 'big men', they depicted themselves as 'the candidate[s] of the virtuous poor', unlike 'the lawyers and those big men [who] didn't mind the ordinary people', from whom 'J.J. [Rawlings] came to deliver us' (Nugent 1995: 258–9).[11]

Rawlings's success in mobilising a sense of national unity, in rebuilding state legitimacy and in generating widespread popular support for his regime, can be inferred from the results of these two elections. In particular, the efficient and transparent organisation of registration and voting for the 1996 elections was undoubtedly important in promoting the legitimacy of the state in the eyes both of the voters and of international observers. The fact that voter turnout was over 70 per cent in all regions of the country, was also significant, since it indicates that a vote against Rawlings did not signify any alienation from the state. Particularly significant in this regard is the fact that the only region which did not return a majority vote for Rawlings, the Ashanti Region, nevertheless had a voter turnout of 79.8 per cent, somewhat above the national average.

But it is the Ashanti vote which deserves particular examination, since it raises the question as to how the national identity strategy of the Rawlings regime has affected the relationship between ethnic rivalries and national identity (and thence the relationship between ethnocultural and civic nationalisms). It has already been noted that the Ashanti vote against Rawlings cannot readily be explained in terms of rational economic self-interests, since the region has done particularly well in terms of public amenity resource allocation from the Rawlings regime, and also in terms of the incomes of the Ashanti cocoa farmers. The easiest explanation of the vote would be to postulate the existence of a deep-rooted primordial antagonism between Asantes and Ewes. But this seems to be misleading. It is certainly true that there is a tendency to mutual ethnic stereotyping in relationships between Ewes and Asantes, which employs myths of pre-colonial conflict to construct images of contemporary untrustworthiness. These stereotypes were stimulated by the earlier anti-Ewe scapegoating ideologies which had been employed by the previous Akan-dominated regimes, but their impact has been to foster a sense of social distance rather than a strong social antagonism, and Asantes clearly do not regard Ewe tribalism as a viable cause of Ghana's economic woes.

The results of the 1992 and 1996 elections do illustrate the existence of a political rivalry between the Ashanti and Volta regions, but this is probably not primarily ethnic in origin or in structure, and is both generated and contained by the structure of the elections. Both in 1992 and 1996, voters were faced with a choice of leading presidential candidates between an Ewe and an Asante; Rawlings versus Adu Boahen in 1992 and Rawlings versus J.A. Kuffour in 1996. In both cases, Rawlings got over 90 per cent of the (predominantly Ewe) Volta region vote, while his Asante opponents got over 60 per cent of the Ashanti regional vote. But the 94 per cent vote for Rawlings in the Volta region indicates that it is not ethnic loyalties which are determining voting behaviour. Since only 73 per cent of Volta region voters are Ewes, the 94 per cent regional vote for Rawlings indicates that the non-Ewes who occupy the north of the region, and who in 1969 had voted for the Asante candidate, are in the 1990s also voting solidly for Rawlings, presumably on a regionalist home-boy basis, rather than on ethnic lines.[12]

Ghanaian elections have traditionally been viewed as competitions between local, district and regional communities for state patronage, with election candidates being perceived as potential patrons (Nugent 1995).[13] Thus the distinctive voting patterns in the Volta and Ashanti regions do not signify that the Ewes and the Asantes are any more tribalistic or regionalistic in their political orientations than other Ghanaians; merely that, more clearly than for other Ghanaians, the elections gave them a choice of regional patrons. Moreover, while it seems likely that many Ashanti voters continue to distrust Rawlings as an 'Ewe tribalist', this does not now translate into a rejection of his nationalist vision identifying élite corruption as the threat against which Ghanaian nationalism must be constructed. Political rivalries between Ewes and Asantes persist, but now that they are not ideologically manipulated, they need no longer undermine national unity, or threaten the legitimacy of the state. The fact that nationalism and ethnicity are no longer counterposed, means that the state élites can begin to reconstruct an ethnocultural vision of unity. This is reflected in Rawlings following the lead of Nkrumah by wearing traditional Akan costume, thus promoting Akan culture as the core ingredient for a Ghanaian ethnoculture. 'The kente cloth, the state sword and the state chair, all of which dated from the [Nkrumah] First Republic, were symbols of the supposed linkage between modern democracy and indigenous political culture. According to this conscious symbolism, the President was to be regarded as the chief writ large' (Nugent 1995: 261).

There is no doubt that Jerry Rawlings has received widespread popular support, and the legitimacy of the state has been rebuilt, because he is believed by Ghanaians to have begun the process of national economic recovery, and this belief is indeed fuelled by physical evidence of economic performance – most obviously in the provision of public amenities such as roads and electricity supplies to many localities. But the purpose has been to suggest that such amenities are significant not because they constitute the economic resources upon which regime legitimacy depends, but rather that they are perceived as symbols of an impending national development. This is not the instrumental politics of economic self-interest, but rather the ideological politics of communitarian mobilisation. Moreover, the collectivist nationalism of the Rawlings regime ensures that it remains relatively illiberal and intolerant of dissent,[14] but its stability, legitimacy and support, do not seem to depend upon the delivery of economic growth or of civil liberties, so much as on the rebuilding of a sense of national identity.

Conclusions

In the case of Ghana, successive regimes have relied primarily on garrison nationalism, rather than solely on performance legitimacy. They have repeatedly sought to mobilise national identity by directing attention to 'sometimes imagined threats to [their] rule'. But whether or not this is a 'tragedy', as Jeff Haynes has suggested with respect to Rawlings (1991: 425), depends upon their choice of threats. So long as the strategy of garrison nationalism involved the scapegoating of one ethnic minority segment, the Ewes, this both weakened state legitimacy (by eroding the unifying vision of ethnocultural nationalism) and also promoted political instability (by generating perceptions of ethnic plots).

The shift to a garrison nationalism directed against 'corrupt élites' has served to reverse the erosion of state authority, and has promoted an ethnically neutral civic nationalism which inhibits the divisive impact of ethnic rivalries. Rawlings has managed to channel mass disillusionment with the state so that it provides the basis for a Rousseauean nationalism, subsequently institutionalised through competitive elections. These have enabled Rawlings to mobilise the support of a large majority by identifying himself as the spokesman of 'us Ghanaians', and portraying his opponents, not in ethnic terms, but as 'élites'. To this end, he has supplemented civic nationalism with the symbolism of ethnocultural nationalism, by sometimes clothing himself in Akan regalia.[15]

In Ghana, therefore, it has not been primarily the objective economic performance of the regime which has provided the basis for its success, but more the fact that the regime has articulated a communitarian vision of national development which has resonated with mass perceptions, and has facilitated some reintwining of the civic and ethnocultural visions of the nation. It is frequently suggested both that economic globalisation has in varying degrees eroded the strength of nation-states, and further that the World Bank's structural adjustment policies have undermined the sovereignty of the debtor nation-states of Africa. If this is interpreted to mean that state élites have felt constrained in their choice of economic policies, then Ghana is clearly a case in point. But policies of economic deprivation do not necessarily erode the legitimacy of the state or the cohesion of the nation. This depends upon the type of ideological strategies employed by political leaders, and upon whether their ideological formulations resonate with the cultural perceptions of the populace. As Hayward and Dumbuya have noted, 'What is remarkable, is the degree of popular support achieved by national élites in the face of devastating economic and political crises . . . [M]uch of this is due to the successful manipulation of myths and symbols in ways which have enhanced the legitimacy of élites, their parties and their regimes' (1984: 671).

This should not be interpreted to imply that economics and politics are completely disconnected, since economic hardship clearly constitutes a major stress factor which makes all forms of politics, including state legitimation, more difficult. Nevertheless, it is clear that economic hardship might have the effect of either alienating popular support for a regime and undermining the strength of the state, or of providing a resource which a regime might be able to employ to its own advantage. The ability of a regime to generate political support from economic hardship depends in large part upon the credibility of its ideological formulation of the nation, its enemies and its goals.

7   Contentious visions

Civic, ethnocultural and multicultural nationalism

> Civic nationalism offers a vision of a community of equal citizens; ethno-
> cultural nationalism offers a vision of a community united by a belief in
> common ancestry and ethnocultural sameness; and multicultural nationalism
> offers a vision of a community which respects and promotes the cultural
> autonomy and status equality of its component ethnic groups.

It has previously been argued that the strength of modern nation-states depended
upon the belief that the state was the engine of development towards the vision of
the social justice nation, in which the civic nation and the ethnocultural nation
would converge. Contemporary disparities between the civic community and the
ethnocultural community were thus defused by the extent of the belief that civic
integration was intertwined with ethnocultural assimilation. The recent problems
of the nation-state have thus been conceived as arising from disillusionment with
the capacity of state élites to deliver this developmental promise. As belief in a future
convergence of the civic and ethnocultural communities eroded, the contemporary
tensions between them became more visible and politically salient.

As unassimilated ethnic minorities began to reject offers of assimilation, several
states have sought to prevent conflict by accepting new ideas of minority rights.
In many countries, therefore, the state now has to deal with contentions between
three distinct visions of community – civic, ethnocultural, and multicultural.[1] The
resultant politics vary markedly between different countries because of differences
in their ethnic composition, and in the character and responses of their governments.
In all cases, however, the emergence of multiculturalism raises major issues for the
sense of national community, in that it challenges both the civic idea that the nation
is a community of equal individual citizens whose distinct ethnic attributes ought
to be politically irrelevant, and the ethocultural idea that the nation is a community
whose members ought to be culturally assimilating. In some cases, multiculturalism
has become sufficiently well articulated to offer a new vision of a social justice
community – a society united by its commitment to the equal rights of each component ethnic minority. The tension between civic nationalism and ethnocultural
nationalism, is thus seen as being joined by a new tension with multicultural

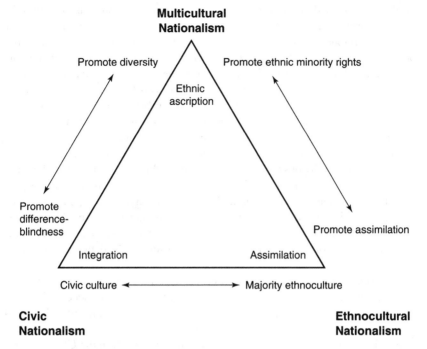

Figure 2 The competing nationalist visions

nationalism. The purpose here is to summarise briefly the three nationalist visions, which are indicated in Figure 2. Chapter 8 will then examine the types of nationalist politics to which they give rise.

Nations are frequently depicted as if they were the arenas or the frameworks within which politics occur. This is misleading, not only because it confuses the distinction between state and nation and attributes to nations an essentialist character which they do not possess, but, more pertinently, because it distracts attention from the extent to which politics is *about* nations, rather than simply *within* them. It is suggested here that the three distinct understandings of the nation are presently confronting each other head on. The next chapter then examines how the weakened state is caught in the cross-fire, having grave difficulty in discovering either the authority or the strategy, which might ameliorate the tension and facilitate an accommodation.

The visions of civic and ethnocultural nationalism have been examined previously (in Chapters 2 and 3), but are briefly summarised here, in order to elucidate the potential tensions between them, and also those with the multicultural nationalist vision.

Civic nationalism offers a vision of a kinship community of equal citizens which is formed on the basis of contract, commitment, loyalty and love. Individuals of various ethnocultural backgrounds may enter this community at adulthood, or through migration, by committing themselves to loyalty to the public institutions and way of life of their residential homeland. Civic nationalism can thus accommodate ethnocultural diversity within the nation, so long as the state remains ethnically blind in its public institutions and policies, and so long as individuals direct their political loyalty to the state, rather than to their ethnocultural groups. The potential problem of ethnic diversity is thus resolved by the process of civic integration.

Ethnocultural nationalism: while civic nationalism can accommodate the diversity of ethnic values, attributes and origins of its members who have all committed themselves to the homeland, ethnocultural nationalism cannot. Ethnocultural nationalism is based on the myth of common ancestry, and of inherited ownership of an ancestral homeland. It focuses on the belief that the community shares some distinctive racial, religious or linguistic attributes, which are then seen as the 'proof' of common ancestry. Individuals who have not inherited such attributes, may nevertheless be able to acquire them (through intermarriage, religious conversion, language acquisition, etc.) and this process of assimilation implies the corresponding acquisition of belief in the common history and ancestry of the adoptive community. The potential problem of ethnic diversity is thus resolved by the promise of assimilation.

Multicultural nationalism: whereas there is widespread awareness of the ideas of civic and ethnocultural nationalism, it is not so generally accepted that the term 'multiculturalism' might also refer to a form of nationalism. Indeed, the term is sometimes used to refer to the rejection of ideas of identification with a nation-state. Christopher Lasch, bemoaning the loss of community in the USA, identified two such features of multiculturalism. First, it offered an apparently cosmopolitan denial of patriotism, 'conjuring up the agreeable image of a global bazaar in which exotic cuisines, exotic styles of dress, exotic music, exotic tribal customs can be savored indiscriminately, with no questions asked and no commitments required' (Lasch 1995: 6). Second, it split the nation up and eroded the discursive lifeblood of community:

> rival minorities take shelter behind a set of beliefs impervious to rational discussion. The physical segregation of the population in self-enclosed, racially homogeneous enclaves has its counterpart in the balkanization of opinion. Each group tries to barricade itself behind its own dogmas. We have become a nation of minorities . . . This parody of 'community' – a term much in favor but not very clearly understood – carries with it the insidious assumption that all members of a given group can be expected to think alike. Opinion thus becomes a function of racial or ethnic identity.
>
> (Lasch 1995: 17–18)

But this is a critic's view. Proponents of multiculturalism do not see themselves as closet ethnocultural nationalists, simply seeking political barricades behind which to defend the integrity of their ethnic minority. They seek, rather, to establish an encapsulating social justice community which is bound together by common values relating to the celebration of ethnic diversity, and the commitment to inter-ethnic equity. They seek a national community within which the diverse ethnic communities can flourish, and within which disadvantaged ethnic minorities can be guaranteed the rights and resources necessary for the attainment of their full development. Such a community has been depicted by Iris Marion Young as 'the social and political ideal of togetherness in difference':

> A society and polity where there is social equality among explicitly differentiated groups who conceive of themselves as dwelling together without exclusions . . . The polity should foster institutions and procedures for discussing and deciding policies that all can accept as legitimately binding, thereby creating a public in which the groups communicate. But . . . this public is heterogeneous, which means that the social groups of the society have a differentiated place in that public, with mutual recognition of the specificity of the groups in the public. . . . The primary moral ground for this heterogeneous public is to promote social justice in its policies.
>
> (1995: 161, 165)

This vision of the multicultural nation as a social justice community is manifested most clearly in the call for existing states to recognise and promote the collective rights of each ethnic minority group within the society to variously specified forms of autonomy, resource allocations, or political representation (Kymlicka 1995a: 6–7).

The initial summary of the multicultural nationalist vision needs some elaboration. All ideologies function in politics as recipes for certainty, but their tenets are, nevertheless, always in flux as they are subjected to examination and debate. Four aspects of ongoing debates about multicultural nationalism deserve to be briefly noted. The purpose is not to express doubts as to the coherence or persuasiveness of the multicultural nationalist vision, but rather to pave the way for expressing doubts as to the amenability of multicultural nationalisms to corporatist management by the state.

Identity

The individuals' sense of identity, and their capacity for moral development, are seen, in some versions of the multicultural vision, as being intrinsically derived from their immersion in the ethnic community of their parents. Other versions of multiculturalism are more cautious, and claim only that the ethnic community is the primary source of identity. This is so even if, as in Kymlicka's liberal version, the end goal of the individual's moral development might be that of arriving at an ability to evaluate critically the ethnoculture which shaped that development (1989). The multiculturalist argument, that the state ought to protect and enhance ethnic minority communities, rests primarily on this claim that these are the essential or primary communities of identity. Multiculturalist visions thus echo the earlier primordialist view of ethnicity as offering an intrinsically powerful emotional bond, except that multiculturalism suggests a positive evaluation of this, whereas earlier primordialism regarded the ethnic bond as primitive, instinctual and irrational, to hopefully be replaced as modernisation progressed, by the more rational attachment to the civic nation (Geertz 1963). It is widely accepted, even by critics of multi-culturalism, that individuals do need a sense of attachment to some cultural communities, and that they ought not to be forcibly assimilated into them. But it is debatable whether it might be face-to-face communities such as those of kinship and locality which are crucial to a sense of individual identity rather than the imagined communities of ethnicity. It is also debatable as to whether individual identity depends on access to the ethnic culture of their parents, or could be served by assimilation into another ethnoculture (Patten 1999). Some critics of multi-culturalism query whether an individual's need for cultural meaning implies their location solely or primarily within a single 'homogeneous cultural framework', or whether they need access to a plurality of cultural communities so as to provide the 'openness and diversity . . . indispensable to a healthy personality' (Waldron 1995: 108, 112). One ambiguity of multiculturalism is, therefore, that it seems to promise a community which benefits from and celebrates diversity, while also promising to embed the individual members of that community within one ethnic segment.

Group rights

Multiculturalism calls for the state to recognise that ethnic minority communities have legal and moral rights as collectivities. In some cases, all that is being claimed here is that individual rights can sometimes effectively be made only on a collective basis, as with the right to resource allocations or political representation. But the more contentious multiculturalist argument is that 'minority rights' are often group rights which are independent of and have priority over individual rights, and the claim which has attracted most critical discussion is that the state should give ethnic minority communities the right to define and restrict the liberties of their individual members (by, for example, punishing cultural transgressions or restricting out-marriage). Communitarian defenders of multiculturalism make this case most strongly, on the basis of their view that the community precedes and has priority over the individual. The liberal case for multiculturalism is more problematical. On the face of it, it would seem that the liberal state should be seeking to under-mine those cultures which do not value individual autonomy (Patten 1999: 8). Alternatively, it is sometimes suggested that a liberal can support multicultural nationalism so long as the possibility of exit from illiberal ethnic communities exists (Kukathas 1995: 238), or so long as the state retains the right to protect individuals of the ethnic minority whose cultural autonomy the state protects, from any illiberal practices emanating from that culture (Kymlicka 1989, Ch. 9). But these arguments raise, rather than resolve, doubts as to how multicultural nationalism can reconcile its support for the right of each ethnic community to promote its own group cohesion; with its concern also to ensure the right of each individual to grow up in a national community free from ethnic barriers.[2]

The just distribution of power and resources

The multicultural vision of a social justice nation is one in which each distinct ethnic minority community has a fair share of power and resources. It is this vision which ties the different ethnic communities to each other, and thus ties them to the encapsulating nation. In David Miller's words, 'Trust requires solidarity not just within groups but across them, and this in turn depends upon a common identification of the kind that nationality alone can provide' (1995: 140). This sense of nationality would seem to depend upon a 'trust' that the state institutions fairly allocate positions of power to representatives of each ethnic community. Various mechanisms are available to promote this, including federalism, communal electoral rolls, affirmative action and quotas, but the most directly relevant institution would seem to be that of consociational government, where government is by a coalition of ethnic representatives (Lijphart 1977).[3] This has not, however, been directly advocated by all proponents of multiculturalism, and one reason for this has probably been the corporatist and undemocratic requirement that the state, rather than the ethnic minorities themselves, predetermine which communities be represented in the governing coalition, and which criterion of allocation be applied. Arendt Lijphart has recently suggested, however, that 'self-determination' can be applied to consociationalism if proportional representation voting is allowed to determine the identity of the ethnic communities sharing power, and the distribution of power between them (1995).

This does not however solve the fundamental problem that societies comprising indigenous and migrant communities of differing sizes, with differing cultural values, are unlikely to concur in one understanding of a just 'balance' of power. It has frequently been suggested that minority communities, which, in the past, formed ethnocultural nations, but which have subsequently been forcibly incorporated within a modern state (e.g. Maoris in New Zealand, Quebecois in Canada) should be regarded as having more substantial rights to political autonomy or resource reallocations than those accruing to communities formed from individual or voluntary migration, not just because of their differing contemporary circumstances, but also because of rights to compensatory justice, or 'reparations' for previous wrongs by the presently dominant ethnocultural majority. This conception of compensatory justice might not be accepted by present generations who were not the authors of the earlier injustice. It also differs from the understanding of justice which is likely to be used by immigrant minorities seeking to rectify contemporary economic, political or cultural disadvantages. It is therefore indeed unlikely that the different minority communities within a state will agree with each other as to what constitutes a just distribution of power and resources between them. Moreover, the multicultural promise of equality of status for each ethnic minority is not fully realised in the political principle of proportionality, which perpetuates the marginal-isation of the ethnic minorities, each of which, and in some cases all of which, might well be outvoted by the ethnocultural majority. Smaller groups are indeed likely to appeal on key issues to the principle of parity,[4] and consociationalism potentially goes further since it offers government by consensus, which means that any one ethnic representative should have the (disproportionate) power of absolute veto.

The fact that the vision of social justice as 'balance', embodied in multiculturalism, cannot easily be translated into practical 'ethnic arithmetic' formulas of political representation and power allocation, does not of course detract from the emotional power of that vision; however, it does help to explain some of the problems of multicultural politics.

Minorities and majority

Finally, multiculturalism raises a debate as to the status of the ethnic majority. In most states, there are claims that members of ethnic minority communities have hitherto been politically, economically and culturally marginalised because assimilationist ethnocultural nationalism has facilitated the domination of power within modern states by members of the ethnic majority. The consequent prescription suggests that the reassertion of the cultural rights of ethnic minorities, must necessarily involve some reallocation of power and resources, so that by rectifying the economic and status disadvantage of members of ethnocultural minority groups, the cohesion and vibrancy of these communities can be preserved or restored. This designation of members of ethnic minorities as the disadvantaged sometimes leads proponents of multiculturalism to minimise or ignore the existence of disadvantage within the ethnocultural majority. Majority communities are sometimes marginalised by being depicted as having no strong ethnic attachment, or are portrayed as the ethnic community whose previous dominance must now be compensated for by their new subordination. The question arises, then, as to how multiculturalism deals with the fact that recent widespread increases in economic (class) disparities in many countries, frequently cross rather than coincide with ethnocultural lines, so that there are significant numbers of disadvantaged individuals within ethnic majority communities, who might see themselves as excluded from the social justice vision offered by multiculturalism, and who might therefore understandably react against it. It is worth noting, again, that the multiculturalist suspicion of ethnic majority communities, and thence of the state, rests in part on the claim that civic nationalism is merely a cover for ethnocultural nationalism.[5] This is indicated in Kymlicka's response to Michael Walzer's claim that the USA offered an example of a state which sought to be neutral so as to attain a 'divorce between state and ethnicity':

> What Walzer calls the 'neutral' state can be seen, in effect, as a system of 'group rights' that supports the majority's language, history, culture, and calendar. Government policy systematically encourages everyone to learn English, and to view their life-choices as tied to participation in English-language institutions. This is . . . not 'neutral' in its relationship to cultural identities.
>
> (1995b: 10)

It is, in part, the perception of a pre-existing alignment of the state with the ethnic majority, which justifies the multiculturalist concern for the counterbalancing creation of new state institutions and procedures protecting and promoting ethnic minority interests. Nevertheless, in Australia, for example, proponents of multiculturalism have recently sought to correct 'the misconception that [multiculturalism] is concerned mainly with immigration and minority ethnic communities', by claiming that it is 'inclusive', reassuring the ethnic majority that 'Australians whose origin is wholly or partly from Great Britain and Ireland can take special pride in their heritage' (NMAC 1999: 2.6). But such aspirational statements have not usually been institutionalised so as to provide parallel ethnically based supports to the disadvantaged of both majorities and minorities. The implication seems to be that proponents of multiculturalism face the prospect of backlash from the ethnic majority, unless they can either explicitly recognise the need to protect ethnic majority rights,[6] or can manage to intertwine their vision of multicultural nationalism with the civic nationalist vision.

The brief outline of civic nationalism and ethnocultural nationalism, and the summary of the main ambiguities relating to multicultural nationalism, indicate that the three visions of the nation are in key respects incompatible. The multicultural nationalist vision of a democratic nation of equal ethnic minorities, the ethnocultural nationalist vision of an ethnically homogeneous society, and the civic nationalist vision of a community of equal individual citizens differ markedly from each other in their diagnoses of contemporary problems and in their ethical prescriptions for solutions. This means that they also differ as to who they consider as members of the nation. Multicultural nationalism, other than in its Singapore manifestation, grants members of ethnic minorities higher status than members of ethnic majorities in the vision of the nation, in the sense that it only explicitly advocates the group rights of the former. For ethnocultural nationalism, it is clear that those who have assimilated or inherited the dominant ethnically based culture deserve higher status than those who have not. For civic nationalism, individual members of both ethnic majorities and ethnic minorities deserve equal status as citizens, on the condition that they give their primary loyalty to the state and civil society, rather than to their majority or minority ethnic attachments. In a situation where each of these three ideologies is asserted strongly by different individuals within the same country, the prospects for their peaceful resolution, or their violent confrontation, would seem to depend to a significant extent on how the state responds.

But the response of the state to the contention between the three visions of nationalism is conditioned by the fact that this contention has arisen precisely because of an erosion in the authority of the state. Belief in its promises of political integration and ethnocultural assimilation was weakened by its various failures regarding the delivery of equitable development. Moreover, we are repeatedly told that the authority of state élites is being undermined in numerous ways by the various processes of globalisation.

Such apparent weakening of the state does not make inevitable a collapse into tragedy such as that of Yugoslavia, Lebanon, Northern Ireland or the Sudan. It does, however, help to explain some of the problems evident in the nationalist politics even of established democracies. It is no coincidence that the spread of multiculturalist ideas of minority rights has gone hand in hand with the emergence of 'majority rights' movements, such as those of Le Pen's National Front in France, Pauline Hanson's One Nation in Australia or the Hindu BJP in India. Such parties 'fight multiculturalism for moral, social and economic reasons, rather than out of any overt, biological based racism' (Immerfall 1998). They are populist reassertions of ethnocultural nationalism through which marginalised classes within the ethnic majorities are reactively expressing resentment at their exclusion both from the social justice vision offered by multiculturalism, and from the 'superior, elite' status of equal citizenship which they were promised by civic nationalism (Greenfeld 1992: 7). Nevertheless, it is clear that there are countervailing forces at work. In some countries the tension between contending nationalisms is a moderate one simply because of the moderate claims being made by the various communities. But the moderation or assertiveness of the claims might be partly related to the strategies adopted by the state, which, therefore, need examination.

8 How can the state respond to nationalist contention?

Corporatist and pluralist approaches

The purpose here is to examine the ways in which states are responding to the tensions between the three nationalist visions outlined in Chapter 7. State élites are of course never simply the neutral managers or arbiters of these nationalist visions, and several have been willing to employ authoritarian means to impose their own view of nationalist virtue upon aberrant sections of society. The authoritarian imposition of one nationalist vision is not examined here, though its impact was discussed in the context of the Basque case (Chapter 4). But some states which wish to promote one vision of nationalist virtue, nevertheless, seek to avoid political contention by taking measures to accommodate, persuade, coopt or divert proponents of competing nationalist visions.

This gives rise to two strategies, the first derives from the assertion by the state that it is the authoritative manager who can reconcile or contain the nationalist tensions; the second derives from attempts by the state to retreat from such overt management, and to facilitate the dispersal of the nationalist tensions into various state and civil society sites, and thence hopefully their defusion. The managerialist element in states' responses is examined first, by employing the concept of corporatism. The alternative element in states' responses, which seeks to appease and disperse the tensions, is then more briefly examined in the language of pluralism. The dominant argument which arises from these discussions is that the corporatist strategy is likely to overstretch the authority and capacity of the state, and thus might in some ways exacerbate the tensions which it seeks to contain. The pluralist strategy, while never resolving the tensions, might be within the capacity of more states, and might also be useful in beginning the process whereby the contending nationalist visions begin to overlap, or even partially to reintwine. The discussion will be illustrated by references to the Australian case, but these references do not constitute a 'case study' of the kind attempted in some of the previous chapters. This lack of detail concerning the Australian situation is partially compensated for by the brief essay on the Aboriginal issue in Australian politics provided in the Appendix.[1] The intention here, however, is to outline, in rather general terms, the structure of politics which derives from the uneasy coexistence, within most contemporary societies, of the three visions of the nation.

The corporatist strategy

Faced with political tensions between proponents of the three nationalisms, the state might seek some degree of accommodation between them. It can employ two strategies for this. The first of these is the corporatist strategy, where the state proclaims itself as the definitive manager of nationalist politics. This involves the construction of hierarchical intermediary institutions, and also the new deployment of ideological myths which can accommodate these ethnic hierarchies within a reconstituted national community.

In response to the upsurge in ethnic minority rights claims, some states responded by announcing their conversion to multiculturalism, and establishing ethnically specific institutions to facilitate the provision of special resources and rights to the minority communities. But the concept of corporatism suggests that such state responses might have another function, that of containing the ethnic minority claims, so that they do not clash overtly with the civic and ethnocultural visions of the nation.

It is not suggested here that corporatism constitutes the sole response to minority rights claims in any country. The present government of Australia frequently responds in pluralist ways to such claims, and its governments have also in the past employed more authoritarian responses. Nevertheless, key institutional reforms have been undertaken which have corporatist implications, and governments are thereby carried in corporatist directions even when their preferences lie elsewhere.

In Australia, as in many other countries, political discontent articulated in ethnic terms increased from the late 1960s onwards. It involved both the assertion of Aboriginal rights and also the claims of non-English-speaking migrants. Even where discontent was not strongly articulated, political party concerns to woo migrant and minority votes acted as a pressure towards state responsiveness to ethnic minority claims. But the state did not just move towards responsiveness explainable in pluralist terms. In various respects it moved further towards interventionist management, on the assumption that 'political organisations or institutions are needed to maintain harmony among different ethnic communities' (Kukathas 1991: 605).

The concept of corporatism

Corporatism refers to the construction by the state of institutional and ideological frameworks within which potentially disruptive societal groups can be managed, so as to ensure national cohesion. While it has usually been used to refer to a state strategy of economic management, it is here used to refer to a state strategy of ethnic management.

The term corporatism has usually been employed to refer to a state strategy of economic management, and this restricted use of the term arose partly from the belief that the study of efforts to manage *gesellschaft* contractual associations, such as employers' groups, trade unions or workplace organisations, needed a different conceptual approach from that used to study the management of such *gemeinschaft* moral communities as family, ethnic group, church and nation.

But the distinction between *gesellschaft* and *gemeinschaft* had previously been blurred in the corporatist literature which appealed to myths of pre-industrial organic unity. Corporatist depictions of Greek, Roman and medieval society, searching for the 'natural social and civic associations' (Wiarda 1981: 119), did indeed begin with references to family, clan, tribe and church. But the guild, the workplace, and the 'social bonds between landlord and peasant' (Williamson 1985: 19) were also depicted as being moral communities, though ones which functioned as production units, so that ties of traditional obligation coincided with ties of economic interest.

Corporatist thought developed during the second half of the nineteenth century as an attempt to rebuild the moral order which industrialisation and liberalism were destroying, and it looked for ideas of moral consensus both in Catholic visions of God, and in more secular visions of the nation (Williamson 1989: 26). In the twentieth century, this corporatist search for moral communities on which to build societal cohesion reached its apotheosis in European Fascist nationalism; and this bred a reactive retreat from assertions of the moral power of the nation. Thereafter, corporatist writers looked increasingly for moral cohesion in state management of industrial relationships relating to class, trade unions and capitalist–worker relationships.[2] Maniolesco had looked to state-licensed economic corporations which would 'create a new moral environment' among all those engaged in a particular area of production, so as to generate industrial harmony (Williamson 1989: 31). This was echoed by La Tour du Pin's suggestion that the economic and contractual associations relating to production were the primary moral communities which potentially provided 'the fulcrum of individual fulfillment and collective association' but which if not properly managed, also constituted the major site of class conflict (Newman 1981: 9). With this latter formulation of the problem of order, the earlier focus on family, *ethnie*, church and nation could finally be discarded, and replaced with the new concern, by Durkheim among others, to seek order in the state organisation of functional, production-based corporate associations (Newman 1981: 6–8). The culmination of this trend came in the 1970s with Schmitter's seminal formulation of corporatism, in which the concern with moral cohesion disappears completely, and is replaced by the search for harmony in the state's hierarchical ordering of its relationships with functional, production-orientated economic interests (1979).

The identification of the production unit as the basis for the state's intermediations with society had derived primarily from the assumption that economic conflict comprised the central threat to social harmony. If indeed it is now the contending nationalist visions within society which comprise the main threat, then it might make sense to look to the moral community of ethnicity as the basis for the state's management of that threat, as had been indicated by the earlier formulations of corporatism.[3]

If the state is unable any longer to marginalise or demonise ethnic minority claims, then it might well see itself as having no option but to try to assert itself as their authoritative manager. Such management becomes feasible if the state can employ institutional and ideological means to reconstruct the national community in ways which link family, *ethnie* and nation together. The corporatist role of the state then becomes that of managing social cohesion by creating institutions which provide a hierarchical structuring of these moral communities within society, and by creating nationalist ideologies which depict the *gesellschaft* society as if it were an organic moral community.[4] Corporatist theory does not, however, depict the state just as the neutral guardian of the common good. It sees it, rather, in Weberian terms, as a bureaucratic structure with the capacity 'to act independently as a status group', with its own entrenched interests and values (Cawson 1986: 65). The requisite autonomy of the state derives, in corporatist theory, from its ability to deflect adverse reactions against its managerial interventions onto the élites of the corporatist interest associations which it creates or licenses. Thus, corporatism involves the state claiming legitimacy on the grounds that it is the authoritative manager of social cohesion, and this claim is protected by its strategy of routinising the politics of such management in specialised institutions manned by co-opted élites, so as to quarantine effectively the state from the consequences of any resultant contentions.

Writers on economic-focused corporatism repeatedly warned that the term should be used to refer to a particular sector of policy formulation and implementation, rather than to a total system. The present usage of the term is also sector-specific in that the state's corporatist management of nationalist contention does not imply the need to adopt a similar strategy in other policy areas. But such corporatism can never be a peripheral sector of politics, since the way in which the myths of ethnicity and nationhood are engineered is always central for the authority of the state. When the state defines the ethnic minorities whose claims are to be managed, and creates the institutional structures needed for such management, it must also intervene to promote new myths of national identity which can accommodate the multicultural vision, and which can thereby legitimate its interventions.

The state as the definer of inter-ethnic 'fairness'

The state's definition of the social structure in terms of ethnic categories serves to prioritise and cement one particular version of identity. The employment of one state-defined criterion for allocating rights and resources to the licensed ethnic communities then raises the problem that the selected criterion is always subject to challenge by those ethnic segments which would benefit more from another criterion, or from another definition of ethnic categories. Thus, the attempt to engineer corporatist unity is problematic in the sense that the state becomes the target of dissensus concerning the criterion of ethnic 'fairness'.

Instead of responding to ethnic minority claims by demanding that politics be constituted on an ethnically colour-blind civic basis, while reasserting the imperative goal of one assimilated ethnocultural nation, state élites, in Australia, as elsewhere, have moved, albeit in an *ad hoc* way, towards the political recognition of ethnic minority communities. The strategy of managing ethnicity begins by constructing a map of the social structure which legitimates ethnic segmentation, and then claims that this ethnic map of society should be employed as one of the bases for political allocations.

This corporatist response seeks to promote multiculturalism by maintaining and defending the ethnic compartments of the society so that those communities which the state élites define as being under threat, can strengthen and maintain their ethnocultural distinctiveness. But corporatism seeks also to contain the claims of such communities so as to ensure that they do not threaten political stability or societal unity.

In Australia, the definition of Aboriginal was initially left to the various states and territories, so as to distinguish between 'full blood' and 'half caste', and to identify the tribal groups within each region. The contemporary governmental definition, however, is based on self-classification, and on the concept of an overarching Aboriginal and Torres Strait Islander category. This change of definition has promoted the change of state strategy from one of 'divide and rule' control, to one of corporatist management, which is facilitated by the assumption of one common Aboriginal community. Meanwhile, the term 'multicultural' has been employed to refer also to the provision of state services to migrants, and first-generation off-spring, of non-English-speaking backgrounds (NESB). Recently, such state services have increasingly involved measures to educate the English-speaking majority into the virtues and advantages of ethnic pluralism. In both ways, the state directs its resources to managing the cultures of ethnic minorities.

These state definitions of ethnic identity, and their employment as a basis for resource allocations, have the effect of prioritising one identity, and one version of that identity. Instead of celebrating the multiple and fluid identities available to each individual in the society, the state 'aims to preserve a heritage of cultural differences that have been given by a certain kind of history' (Hindess 1992: 23). This cementing of static ethnic categories might well be intended to 'maintain [state] hegemony and class domination' (Jacubowicz 1984: 18), but instead of achieving its aim of depoliticisation, it serves, potentially, to institutionalise the new political contention of ethnic claims.

The dominant justification for the political licensing of ethnic communities, in the case of Australia, has been that the earlier politics of ethnic depoliticisation and assimilation had had the effect of promoting and camouflaging discrimination against Aboriginal, Asian and southern or central European minority ethnic communities, and that this imbalance must be rectified in order to rebuild national unity. This change of stance on the part of the state began with the 1965 ending of the 'white Australia' immigration policy and the 1975 Racial Discrimination Act. Since the avowed aim of corporatism was to rectify an imbalance in favour of the ethnic majority, it followed that this majority, variously depicted as 'white', 'British',

'English' or 'Anglo-Celtic', has been treated as a residual category, whose numerical, cultural, socio-economic and political dominance disqualifies them from any explicit corporatist protection by the state.

It is interesting to compare this with Singapore's implementation of the corporatist strategy. In the Singapore case, the shift in state policy from meritocratic western-isation to the politics of 'ethnic arithmetic' began in 1981 with the formation of the Council for Malay Education (Mendaki), but this was accompanied by new state policies to promote Confucianism and Mandarin, and then in 1991 by the formation of the Chinese Development Assistance Council (Brown 1994). The shift to corporatism thus involved measures to recognise explicitly the majority Chinese community as an ethnic category deserving of state-protection as regards the allocation of rights and resources.[5]

This difference, between the corporatist exclusion of the ethnic majority and their corporatist inclusion, is significant since it directly influences the politics of ethnic allocations. The corporatist strategy involves the assertion, by the state, of an authoritative moral criterion for the allocation of differential rights and resources to specified ethnic communities. In Australia, the employment of the language of compensatory positive discrimination in response to Aboriginal claims has fostered disparate perceptions of the state's role, since there is no agreed formula for balancing past wrongs with present compensations. While some Aboriginal groups have regarded the state's preferential allocations as mere tokenism, some elements of the majority culture have seen them as open-ended subsidies accompanied by the unwarranted surrendering of sovereignty. Similarly, while multicultural policies towards NESB minorities are condemned on the one side for perpetuating 'outmoded egalitarian myths that are inimical to national revival' (Bullivant 1989: 127), they are condemned on the other for failing to build the differential group citizenship and welfare rights required to overcome social exclusion (Jayasuriya 1993).

Such differences in the conception of just relationships between ethnic commu-nities are not easily resolvable through negotiation. In its early stages, Australian multiculturalism emerged as 'identity politics' which stressed 'the private domain of . . . cultural needs and interests'. But this phase soon 'ran into troubled waters', and moved in the direction of social justice rights claims (Jayasuriya 1990: 616). The use of the language of rights serves to translate negotiable interest claims into absolutist non-negotiable assertions. The state seeks to prevent the clash of competing absolutist rights claims by asserting that its own formula of national identity ('official Multiculturalism') is itself an absolutist moral imperative, but in doing so the state comes to be seen by all ethnic communities as partial. Elements in either the ethnic majority or in one or other of the ethnic minorities are likely to claim that they are disadvantaged by the formula. This problem is common to both the majority–exclusion form and the majority–inclusion form of corporatism, but it is potentially less politically dangerous in the latter case since, as in Singapore, the state is able to defend itself against the charges of bias by using the language of equality and universalism (in Prime Minister Goh Chok Tong's words, 'whichever group you belong to, we give you equal treatment'). Moreover, the 'majority–

inclusion' state is less likely to face the more electorally destabilising wrath of the ethnic majority.

The political contentiousness of the state's search for an authoritative criterion of ethnic fairness, is illustrated, as regards Australia, by the failure of the 1998 Native Title Amendment Act to resolve the ambiguities of the High Court's 1992 *Mabo* decision and its 1996 *Wik* decision, so as to reconcile the competing land claims of pastoralist farmers and Aboriginal activists. Land litigation continues, and each side pursues their claims in absolutist language, and portrays the 1998 'compromise' as a sell-out to the other side. Similarly, the state's policy of official multiculturalism becomes a focal point for 'the great divide' (Betts 1999), being portrayed by one side as amounting only to a cosmetic celebration of 'souvlaki' and 'dragon dances' (Davidson 1997), and by the other as promoting 'overemphasis on the rights of particular groups without stressing their corresponding obligations', and as meaning that 'certain people are able to escape criticism about their views or behaviour because of their ethnicity or background' (NMAC 1999: 2.2). The danger, then, is that ethnic corporatism does not have the intended effect of insulating the state from contentious ethnic claims, but does precisely the opposite. The state potentially finds itself at the centre of an 'illiberal' discord.[6] As Martin Spencer has warned, in the context of American multiculturalism, there is also the danger of:

> the loss of the liberal rhetoric of civility and tolerance that has softened the sharp edges of intergroup conflict . . . [and] the failure of leaders from *all groups* to speak out publicly and forcefully against outrages and incivilities practiced against members of *groups other than their own*. The danger here is that the spirit of political correctness may persuade the leaders of the peoples of colour that such an obligation falls only upon the leadership of the culpable White males, and that the chronicle of their own suffering exempts them from moral responsibility in this regard.
>
> (1994: 566)

The state thus puts itself into the untenable position of being the target of ethnic discontent, the negotiator of the non-negotiable, and the 'umpire' who is seen by each team as playing for the other side. Far from depoliticising ethnic issues as intended, the dynamics of corporatism tend to heighten the politicisation of ethnic contention. The state seeks, therefore, to avoid explosion by routinising ethnic politics in corporatist institutions.

The corporatist politics of ethnic institutions

The state's response to this politicisation of ethnic contention is to create corporatist institutions on to which the contention can be deflected. These institutions function as monopolistic intermediation channels which define the

continued . . .

ideological and structural parameters for ethnic interest articulation, and thereby facilitate the state's control of these interests. But the limitation of this strategy is that the deflection of contention onto the élites who hold office in the corporatist ethnic institutions weakens their capacity to control their ethnic constituents.

As the state becomes the target of societal dissensus concerning ethnic justice, it seeks to insulate itself by developing agencies and procedures which will institutionalise and routinise this contentious politics, or at least deflect it from the state élites and onto the officials and the co-opted ethnic élites in the peak agencies. But corporatist ethnic institutions are not mere 'lightning rods for the inevitable outrage and complaints' (O'Donoghue 1996). They also give 'the multicultural ideological apparatus . . . financial and organizational muscle to propagandise the ideology' (Bullivant 1989: 123); they facilitate the state's responsiveness to the more moderate ethnic claims; and they provide arenas within which the more radical ethnic élites can be house-trained. The functions of political control and of interest articulation are thus combined.

In Australia, state funding for the Aboriginal community is channelled from the Department of Aboriginal Affairs, through the Aboriginal and Torres Strait Islander Commission (ATSIC), whose avowed aim is to promote Aboriginal empowerment and self-determination. Its board presently comprises twenty Aboriginal commissioners, seventeen of whom are elected, and it channels resources through thirty-six regional councils comprising elected Aboriginal members. The state has developed institutions which appear to accede to claims for Aboriginal self-determination, but which function according to norms of bureaucratic and financial accountability, so as to contain and constrain such claims (Young 1995).

Funding for non-English-speaking migrant communities was channelled, from 1975, through the Office of Multicultural Affairs,[7] while at the state level, funding is through the Offices of Multicultural Interests, liaising with the Ethnic Communities Councils. These peak multicultural organisations channel funds to over 2,600 ethnic organisations. In 1998–9 the Immigration and Multicultural Affairs Portfolio had a budget of $546m., of which $159m. was allocated to settlement, citizenship and multicultural programmes (NMAC 1999: 127), though the funding is much more modest at state level. These hierarchies have been responsive to ethnic concerns and claims, but they have also functioned in the classic corporatist manner 'to coopt some ethnic leaders' (Vasta 1993: 220).

There is evidence that the creation of corporatist institutions to deal with the contentious issue of ethnic justice does usually serve to deflect some of the societal discontent on to the ethnic élites who are co-opted. This was illustrated recently in Australia when Lowitja O'Donoghue, then the Chair of ATSIC, complained that:

> All too often the national debate . . . look[s] for someone to blame. More often than not the blame falls on the main Commonwealth agency, the Aboriginal

and Tores Strait Islander Commission . . . since it is naively assumed and portrayed that we have sole responsibility in this area of government . . . Always in the background during these recurrent exercises is a considerable body of opinion that resents any form of government assistance to indigenous people, that talks about our being overcompensated, that is always on the lookout for evidence of misspending within the indigenous affairs budget, and is gleeful when it thinks it finds it.

(1996)

But this perception that the co-opted ethnic élites have responsibility for government policies concerning their ethnic constituency is not confined to those from the other segments of society who have alternative criteria of ethnic fairness; it is a perception which necessarily also arises within the relevant ethnic constituency itself, and which undermines the effectiveness of the corporatist strategy.

Corporatism functions effectively only when the state controls the leadership and structure of the associations so that 'interest associations do not represent their members' interests' (Panitch 1980: 172). In other words, corporatism needs co-opted leaders who can control their ethnic constituents, but who are not, in practice, responsive to the variations in the interests, situations and needs of those whom they claim to represent. There is a tension between the fluid debates and factions within each community, and the need for the state to construct and institutionalise a static image of each community in which its values, attributes, goals and leaders are stable and predefined. The co-opted ethnic élites become the target for diverse and competing claims from within the ethnic community, and when the level of state support falls short of their raised expectations, it is the ethnic élites who are held responsible, and thence characterised as either corrupt, incompetent or renegade. Thus in the Australian case, Aboriginal leaders have been subject to accusations from their ethnic constituents that they were putting accommodation with the state above defence of community rights (Kukathas 1991: 608), and this is recognised by the ATSIC leadership:

> If we decide to fund one community for major infrastructure, for example, then another can easily be found which will say its need is at least as great. This means that, almost inevitably, some of the most damaging criticism of ATSIC will come from our own community.
>
> (O'Donoghue 1996)

The societal dissensus as to how to balance competing ethnic claims, is politicised by the corporatist strategy; but the state seeks to protect itself from the resultant contention by deflecting discontent on to the corporatist institutions. To the extent that it succeeds in this, however, it weakens the corporatist institutions on which it relies. The resultant tensions can, in most cases, be partly contained by further managerial responses – the reform or invention of institutions, the holding of official enquiries, the co-optation of new élites, or the reallocation of funds. But corporatism's best hope is to contain the contention within a new myth of organic unity;

to inculcate into all ethnic segments the belief that they share one common national identity which can accommodate their cultural diversity.

The corporatist politics of national identity

The state seeks to locate myths and symbols of either civic or ethnocultural nationalism, with which to build a new ideology of the multicultural nation. However, such myths and symbols are in short supply, and the more the state is seen to engineer actively the national identity, the less traditionally authentic it appears and therefore the less its unifying and legitimating power.

Attempts to reconstruct national identity are located in diverse civil society sites; but the stance taken by the state is always crucial, and is never reflective of societal consensus. The official ending of the 'white Australia' policy in 1966, and the Australian High Court *Mabo* decision of 1992 for example, were contentious landmark initiatives which had direct implications for the depiction of national identity. They propelled attempts to reconstruct national identity so as to accommodate multiculturalism and portray the nation as an overarching identity which could contain and thereby control the claims of ethnic segments.

Such reconstruction of national identity may in theory employ either ethno-cultural nationalism or civic nationalism. Again, the comparison with the Singapore case is useful. In that case the state has had some success in reconstructing the nation as an umbrella ethnocultural community defined in terms of 'Asian values'. The values of each component ethnic community were then defined by the state as compatible with those of the others, and with those of the overarching ethnocultural nation.

In Australia, however, there appear to be no obvious resources with which to construct a vision of an overarching ethnoculture which could unite Indigenous Australians, English-speaking settlers, and non-English migrants (Castles *et al.* 1990: 141–8). The myths and symbols of nationhood cannot be sought in Anglo-Celtic history, since that history is frequently portrayed by the state in terms of shame, as divisive and ethnically discriminatory. In the absence of the feasibility of appeals to common racial origin, there is a restricted repertoire of available cultural traditions which have not been depicted as ethnically based. The hitherto dominant national identity myths such as Gallipoli and Kokoda Trail, and the symbolism of 'Waltzing Matilda', have lost their unifying power as they have come to be portrayed as signifying 'white' and Anglo-Celtic domination. There are some attempts to replace them with appeals to a common culture of 'mateship', a common sense of humour, or an 'Aussie' version of English, which can unite settlers, migrants and indigenese; but charges persist that these also derive from 'white' values, rather than offering a basis for a cultural umbrella which can accommodate multiculturalism, in order to build a consensual national identity.

If it is difficult for Australia to construct a sense of ethnocultural nationhood, which can accommodate multiculturalism, then it might seem more promising to try reconstructing civic nationalism. This attempt begins with the claim that all sections of the society subscribe to some notion of the tolerant democratic society. National unity must be sought, then, in the idea of an overarching civic community, comprising not just equal individual citizens as in the ethnically colour-blind liberal or republican formulation, but comprising also the equal authentic ethnic segments, united by their commitment to the legal and constitutional framework of the nation-state. But even this is problematical since the constitution is itself a contentious issue because of its impact on ethnic relations. In Australia, constitutional debate has recently focused on the contentious issues of a Constitutional Preamble, 'Aboriginal Reconciliation', a bill of rights, and republicanism, each of which provided forums for contention on whether the constitution should be 'colour-blind', or should recognise differential ethnic claims. The partial solution, as Hutchinson (1994: Ch. 6) has noted, has been to invest significant efforts in 'ambitious and self-conscious experiments in nation-building' (1994: 165) which focus mainly on the states' sponsorship and licensing of commemorative festivals, such as the 1988 Australian Bicentennial celebrations, offering unifying symbols and foundation myths to portray the authenticity of the civic nation.[8] Donald Horne has recently commented, however, that such appeals to 'constitution' and 'federation' might seem 'a bit too dry' to act as powerful unifying symbols (1996: 6). Moreover, Hutchinson has noted that such efforts to engineer feelings of civic identity have been only partially successful. In the absence of any unifying war of liberation, the celebration of the multi-ethnic origins of the nation and its development as a political community, serves to unleash 'a storm of ethnic grievances' (1994: 170). The Anglophone majorities and the non-English speakers accuse the state and each other of seeking to engineer ethnically biased historical myths so as to legitimate contentious contemporary status claims.

The Australian state has, since the mid-1970s, espoused a formula for national identity which is designated by the term 'official Multiculturalism'. This policy is used to promote ethnic diversity, but is, nevertheless, phrased in language which is primarily that of civic nationalism, asserting the rights of all individuals to equal treatment and equal liberties free from barriers of ethnicity.[9] This packaging of multicultural values in the language of civic nationalism is an attempt by the state to intertwine the civic and multiculturalist visions. These are depicted as the 'natural' virtues of Australian society, while the previously dominant ethnocultural nationalism has been consistently depicted as an immoral and aberrant (though endemic) racism, with ethnocultural assimilation being equated with ethnic genocide. At the level of social relationships between ethnic communities, Australia remains a remarkably tolerant and harmonious society, but the state's attempt to entwine, managerially, civic nationalism and multicultural nationalism, and to promote the demonisation of ethnocultural nationalism, might well have had a detrimental impact on political debate and political legitimacy. Public debate in Australia on issues of ethnicity, race and nation, is now frequently characterised by mutual abuse (most obviously, but not solely, in the context of the 'Hansonite backlash'), and feedback on the official multiculturalism policy has been 'quite polarised' (NMAC 1999: 41). Such polarisation might correlate, it has been suggested, with the divide between the educated professional middle class and the 'parochial' subordinate classes (Betts 1999). There are also some indications that only a minority might have been convinced by twenty-five years of official multiculturalism, that the civic and multiculturalist visions are in fact intertwined virtues; and that a majority might still see the three nationalist visions as being disentwined and mutually incompatible.[10]

The attempts to interweave civic nationalism and ethnocultural nationalism in Australia, prior to the 1970s, had developed primarily within civil society, where even those indigenous and migrant minorities who were excluded or marginalised, seem to have envisioned a future of integration and assimilation for Australia rather than one of ethnic 'self-determination'. The new attempt at interweaving has been pursued much more as a top-down managerialist formula which seeks to hide the real tensions between civic and multiculturalist tenets behind slogans promoted by a state which is already viewed with scepticism. The result is to highlight, rather than to obscure, the differences between the two visions.

These problems arise partly because nationalist myths can only be persuasive to the extent that the constructed can be disguised as the natural. But the more that attention is drawn to the active role of the state in constructing the artificial nation through its immigration policies, its ethnic legislation and its normative interventions on ethnic relationships, the less powerful is the myth of organic naturalness, and the less easily is national loyalty mobilised. Instead of retreating from the enterprise, however, the state élites continue trying to construct the organic nation; attracted, like insects around the light, to the source of their problems.[11]

The legitimacy of the corporatist state

> The state seeks renewed legitimacy by depicting itself as the neutral corporatist expert, above societal contentions, and capable of managing ethnic politics and national identity. But the ironic impact of the shift to corporatism is to further add to the legitimacy problems facing the state, since the state lacks the capacity to achieve social justice, manage ethnic politics and forge a new national identity.

The intertwining of ideas of ethnocultural assimilation with those of political integration had previously enabled the state to depict itself as ethnically neutral even when, as in Australia, its immigration and language policies favoured white and English-speaking groups, and its legal system ignored or condoned 'racist' cultures. But this claim to ethnic neutrality was challenged by claims that the promotion of the majority ethnic culture was having the impact of eroding minority cultures without generating their assimilation. In now committing itself to replacing its assimilationist national identity with a new multicultural one, the state seeks to rebuild its reputation for impartiality and fairness and portrays itself as the non-political managerial expert.

It is not, however, perceived as being a neutral expert in this way. This is partly because the construction of ethnic justice is inherently contentious and beyond the capacity of the state; but also because the state's interventions to prioritise the designated corporatist interest groups are sometimes seen as contradicting tenets of universality deemed as central to democratic legitimacy (Parsons 1988: 521). In Australia, the government's initiatives on multiculturalism were perceived by many, according to the Fitzgerald Report, as 'social engineering which served to promote rather than reduce injustice, inequality and divisiveness' (Kukathas 1990: 162). The danger is, thus, that the state, instead of successfully employing corporatist means to impose organic unity on the societal dissensus, becomes itself splintered by the segmental claims made upon it. This is the spectre which John Gray portrays:

> From being an umpire which enforces the rules of the game of civil association, the state has become the most potent weapon in an incessant political conflict for resources . . . Civil life soon comes to resemble the Hobbesian state of nature from which it was meant to deliver us . . . Distinct communities and ways of life which had once been constrained to . . . mutual accommodation by moderating their claims on each other and on government have an incentive to engage in all-out legal and political conflict.
>
> (1993: 12–15)

Even if this is too pessimistic, the corporatist management of minority rights claims is vulnerable to the suggestion that the negotiation of inter-ethnic relationships within the state 'should always be allowed, but they can't be imposed . . . We have to work slowly and experimentally towards arrangements that satisfy the members (not the militants) of this or that minority. There is no single correct outcome' (Walzer 1992: 168). If it is indeed the case that the management of contending ethnic rights claims is not subject to any definitive resolution of ethnic balance, then, to the extent that the state proclaims itself as the definitive ethnic manager, it has significantly added to the legitimacy problems which gave rise to state interventions in the first place. The problem is that, while talk of the multicultural nation does indeed promote the state's 'external legitimacy' by projecting an image of multi-ethnic harmony, social justice, political fairness and global cosmopolitanism (Moodley 1983: 330), the weakness of the claims to organic multicultural community merely exacerbates the internal legitimacy problems by exposing the state's inability to deliver on these promises.

Multicultural nationalists accuse it of failing in its promise to promote effectively minority rights, civic nationalists accuse it of failing to uphold civic difference-blindness principles, and ethnocultural nationalists accuse the state of 'reverse racism' and resent the state accusing them of being racists. These problems might indeed be merely the corollary of significant successes in promoting equity and preventing ethnic violence, but they are, nevertheless, politically significant problems, and we need to consider whether they might be reduced through the adoption of an alternative state strategy.

The pluralist strategy

> If corporatism overstretches the authority and capacity of the state, the best hope for the state might be to adopt a pluralist approach which seeks to contain the tension by blurring the distinctions between the three nationalist visions, and seeking ambiguous symbols which promote their interweaving.

The pluralist strategy indicates that the state must treat ethnic minority communities as interest groups willing to enter into the politics of bargaining and compromise. This implies, as Michael Walzer has noted, that ethnic groups will function in the political arena so as to defend ethnic minority cultures against cultural assimilation; promote the recovery of their own ethnic culture and the celebration of ethnic diversity in the wider society; and create institutions which will ensure the perpetuation of the ethnic community (1995). Ethnic minorities are indeed likely to be politically assertive in organising themselves so as to put pressure on the state to discard any ethnocultural nationalist bias in favour of the ethnic majority, and to act instead as the guarantor of ethnic minority claims. But this is not so very different from the kind of politics practiced by other types of minority or marginalised groups within complex pluralistic societies, who must organise and exert pressure in order to try to counteract the influence of more dominant, wealthy and powerful interests. It is certainly true that ethnic communities claim that they are more than interest groups – they see themselves as rights groups defending not just the partial interests of their members, but their very sense of identity. But the language of rights is used by various interests groups (for example workers' rights) in the defence of those interests which they see as most fundamental.

   It is sometimes suggested that this politics of ethnic pluralism might function best where the dominant understanding of nationalism influencing the state is that of civic nationalism, as is sometimes claimed in the cases of the USA and Britain. In these countries, the rise of assertions of multicultural nationalism have mostly been limited in their stridency,[12] and have not been accompanied by widespread support on the part of ethnic majorities for reactive assertions of ethnocultural nationalism. Referring to the experience of immigrants into the predominantly civic nationalist USA, Walzer implies that there is indeed some overlap in the ideas of civic nationalism and multiculturalism: 'On the basis of some decades of experience, one can reasonably argue that ethnic pluralism is entirely compatible with the existence of a unified republic' (1995: 147). He suggests that this compatibility arises because:

> A rough fairness in the distribution of funds is probably ensured by the normal workings of democratic politics in a heterogeneous society . . . Democratic politics can be remarkably accommodating to groups, so long as it has to deal only with individuals: voters, candidates, welfare recipients, taxpayers,

criminals, all without official ethnic tags. And the accommodation need not be bitterly divisive, though it is sure to generate conflict. Ethnic citizens can be remarkably loyal to a state that protects and fosters private communal life, if that is seen to be equitably done . . . A state committed to pluralism however, cannot do anything more than to see to it that opportunities are *available*, not that they are used, and it can only do that by ensuring that all citizens, without reference to their groups, share equally, or roughly equally, in the resources of American life.

(Walzer 1995: 153–4)

This depiction of pluralist politics serves, however, to indicate the limitations of the likely accommodations, since the values and institutions of civic nationalism clearly cannot dissolve the differences between itself and those of ethnocultural and multicultural nationalism. Thus, the granting of superior status to the ethnic majority is not compatible either with the granting of equal status to all, or with the giving of special compensatory status to ethnic minorities. The multiculturalist advocacy of differential group citizenship rights is not compatible with civic nationalism's advocacy of equal individual citizenship rights 'without reference to their groups'. The type of governmental institutions which give voice to the values of the ethnic majority are probably not those which can best ensure that the voice of the ethnic minorities is prioritised. So, if the apparent utility of the pluralist response to multiculturalism does not derive from the ability of civic nationalism to dissolve the incompatibilities between the three nationalisms, how are we to explain it?

Proponents of competing ideologies are rarely able to hold coherent conversations with each other, because of their antithetical premises and visions. This is often a source of political tension, but it may also possibly be an ameliorating factor. It means that the pluralist state, which does not proclaim itself as the sole manager of nationalist contentions, is likely to respond by trying to avoid the issue as much as possible. It is worth noting Brian Barry's comment that 'communal cleavages are so potentially explosive that they can probably only be accommodated in the interstices of politics, while politicians ostensibly fight one another over quite different issues' (1975: 398). So, instead of pursuing strategies which put nationalist confrontations in the spotlight, as seems to be the case with corporatism, the pluralist state seeks to defuse them by allowing them to be dispersed within civil society. This was apparently the case in the Australian elections of October 1998. This had been heralded as a 'race-based election', which would inevitably unleash the acrimony surrounding Aboriginal claims for recognition of native title to land owned by their ancestors. It was, however, characterised by almost universal and studious avoidance of the issue.[13] Not only was it to nobody's clear advantage to raise it, but all sides shared the fear of violence on the streets.

This strategy of avoidance is sometimes supplemented by a deliberate blurring of the quite clear distinctions between the three ideological positions, and by the search for new symbols of nationalism which are sufficiently ambiguous for all sides to embrace. In Australia, again, the proposal to replace the (British) monarchy with a Republican presidency not only served to deflect attention from disputes about race and ethnicity, but was also potentially embraced by some civic nationalists as embodying republican virtue, by some multicultural nationalists as a symbol of the dethronement of 'white Australia', and even by some ethnocultural nationalists who saw it as symbolising the maturation of Australia as an ethnocultural community distinct from and now of equal status to Britain.[14] Appeals to the values of tolerance, equality and justice can also be repeatedly employed to bring all sides together, so long as they remain sufficiently soft focused.

The main feature of the pluralist strategy, would appear to be that the state can remain eclectic, accommodating a mix of institutional procedures and values. This might not immediately appear to be a virtue, however, since it ensures that all sides remain dissatisfied. Proponents of multicultural nationalism fail to see their key principle of differential group rights accepted by the state, or any fundamental restructuring of state institutions which they see as designed by and for the dominant cultural community. Civic nationalists see their key principle of equal individual citizenship rights violated by quotas. Ethnocultural nationalists object to the introduction of state institutions which seem to promote the ethnic segmentation of the society.

But the central virtue of the pluralist approach to the politics of multiculturalism is that the state does not get the full force of blame for these various disillusionments, and all sides have some reason for hope that the state is indeed responding, at least partially, to their pressures, and that things are, at least potentially, moving in their direction. In pluralist politics, there are always some politicians and civil society activists, some aspects of government or opposition policy, some agencies of the state and civil society, which are in line with the goals of each of the nationalisms. Multiculturalists gain hope from the introduction and funding of anti-discrimination agencies, multicultural or indigenous affairs offices, multicultural education initiatives, affirmative action programmes and quotas. Ethnocultural nationalists gain hope from the fact that these programmes hardly dent the overrepresentation of members of the majority ethno-culture in élite positions. Civic nationalists gain hope from the vibrancy of key civic legal and representational institutions which keep politics and culture at least partly separate. In this politics, disagreements are not resolved, rather, 'stability in political life is found in motion, if it is found at all' (Gray 1994b: 731)

It is, thus, the eclecticism of the pluralist state, and the inconsistencies or ambiguities of its stance on multiculturalism, which might hold out most hope for the containment of the nationalist tensions. The politics of pluralism is usually discussed in terms of competition over concrete interests. But the pluralist politics of multiculturalism involves competition over competing ideological visions. Whereas interests are always located in the present, ideology always focuses upon the past and the future, so that it is peoples' beliefs about potential futures and mythical pasts which determine their levels of hope or despair, rather than their cost–benefit calculations as to present welfare. The divergent hopes of progress towards each of the nationalist goals are indeed a fragile basis for political stability; much more fragile than the vision of coinciding civic and ethnocultural national communities which held some of the nation-states together in the past. But if politics is perceived as the containment of disagreements, rather than as their definitive resolution, then pluralism might offer the best hope of successful politics, even in this area of ideological contention.

9 Epilogue
Nationalist ideologies in conflict

The purpose of the book has been to unravel nationalism by isolating and examining its ideological components. It has been suggested that it was the intertwining of the civic and ethnocultural visions of nationalism which facilitated the rise of the modern nation-state, and that it is their unravelling which has engendered the emergence of the multicultural nationalist vision, and thence the potential contention between the three strands of nationalist ideology. Some states are indeed managing, with varying degrees of success, to resolve, defuse or diffuse the resultant political tensions. But the widespread incidence of nationalist conflict is evidence of the difficulties of reintwining threads which have unravelled. The politics of nationalist contention is a politics of ideological confrontation which is inherently resistant to management and compromise. The purpose in this concluding chapter is to briefly summarise the argument of the book, and then to illustrate the ideological power of contending nationalisms by offering four brief essays: on nationalist conflicts in Australia, Northern Ireland, Rwanda and Kosovo.

The constructivist perspective views the nationalist formula for individual identity and collective self-determination rights as a psychological and political ideology. Its simplistic diagnosis and prescription enables otherwise confused individuals to deal with complex social problems, and to acquire a sense of emotional security. Thus, when aspiring political élites sought to legitimate the rise of the modern state by employing the nationalist ideology, the disruptive impact of modernisation processes upon face-to-face communities of family and locality, ensured the widespread appeal of the nation as a surrogate – the mythical kinship community.

Not all modern states were equally successful in legitimating themselves as 'nation-states', and most ensured compliance from at least some members of their societies by authoritarian means. Nevertheless, many individuals in most modern states did identify with their nation-states, because they saw the society they inhabited both as an ethnocultural nation united by kinship myths of common ancestry and common ethnically derived attributes; and also as a 'civic nation' whose kinship was formed by commitment to the contemporary homeland and its institutions. Any tensions between the community defined by the common ethnoculture, and the community defined by common territorial citizenship, were ameliorated by the spread of a 'developmental optimism'. This focused on a vision that assimilation into the core ethnoculture, and integration into the core political community, were both progressing, so as to generate the widespread perception that civic and ethnocultural communities would coincide in the imminent social justice nation.

Such developmental optimism relied crucially on the belief that members of minority cultural groups and peripheral regions could benefit economically and socially from access to the 'national economy' around which the state was focused, so that national (ethnocultural) assimilation and national (civic) integration were always weakest in those cases where such incentives were least. But even in those cases where optimism had promoted the nation in this way, disillusionment with the developmental promises of state élites has increased markedly since the late 1960s. It is the consequent weakening of belief in the intertwined visions of civic and ethnocultural nationalism, which explains current contentions. Ethnocultural assimilation comes to be perceived as ethnic domination, and civic integration comes to be perceived as a centralising invasion of political autonomy. The intertwining of civic and ethnocultural visions of nationalism has thus given way to new attempts to reintwine civic and ethnocultural nationalism in the service of minorities seeking varying degrees of autonomy from the state.

Contemporary nationalist politics involves ideological confrontation between competing constructions of the nation. Groups and individuals within the same state differ as to whether they aim at a civic nation of equal individual citizens, an ethnocultural nation of ethnic sameness, or a multicultural nation of equal status ethnic or ethno-regional segments. They also differ, in some cases, as to whether they seek this vision within the existing state, or through formation of a new state. The resultant politics of nationalist contention involves the construction of incompatible nationalist myths, with each side employing the language of civic, ethnocultural or multicultural nationalism to define itself, articulate and legitimate its claims, and demonise its opponents. These differing identities, diagnoses and visions, provide the resilient interpretative frameworks which transform potentially negotiable rivalries of interest and power into ideological confrontations structured on the basis of mutual incomprehension, with the resultant mutual abuse and distrust inhibiting the search for compromise solutions.

This view of nationalist disputes means that the explanation of current confrontations is not to be located primarily in the chronological examination of the causal impact of past events, but rather in the examination of the mythologisations of the past embodied in the competing ideologies of those conducting contemporary disputes. This does not imply that the short interpretative essays which follow are substitutes for accurate knowledge of the specific administrative institutions, socio-economic structures and historical events relating to each nationalist dispute. They are intended, rather, as a reminder that such objective factors do not of themselves cause the disputes, but function as causal factors only in so far as they are portrayed in the justificatory and mobilising ideologies of those involved, embodied in myths of civic, ethnocultural or multicultural nationalism. For illustrative purposes, four contemporary nationalist disputes are briefly discussed so as to show different patterns of the 'disentwining' of state-focused civic and ethnocultural nationalisms into new contending nationalisms. The case of the Australian Aboriginal issue provides some back-up to points alluded to in Chapter 8, and illustrates the clash between multicultural nationalism and ethnocultural nationalism. Northern Ireland and Kosovo are then discussed as examples of confrontations between differing ethnocultural nationalisms, and the case of Rwanda is examined as a clash between civic nationalism and ethnocultural nationalism. In each case, the aim is to show the incompatibility of the ideological visions adhered to by the contending sides. Ideologies are not just the rhetorical icing on the materialist cake, they construct the perceptions which define the cake. Thus nationalist confrontations are not fundamentally clashes of interest, but of ideologies.

Appendix
Case studies

David Brown with Natalia Norris

Australia

In the 1998 Australian federal elections, 10 per cent of Australians voted for Pauline Hanson's One Nation party, which defends assimilation, calls for reduction in Asian immigration, and opposes as 'reverse racism'[1] the present government's affirmative action programmes for Indigenous Australians.[2] In February 1999 some indigenous activists ceremonially burned the Australian flag and denounced the present government as 'racist scum'. In between these two positions, the voice of a civic nationalism, which might reject both ethnocultural assimilation and multiculturalist affirmative action, remains remarkably muted. The result is that 'race' has become the most contentious issue in contemporary politics, with public discussions of Australia's national identity dominated by mutual accusations of racism.

The present crisis of national identity has its roots in the 1960s. Prior to this, Australian nationalism had developed on the basis of the intertwining of an ethnocultural nationalist identity focused on myths of Anglo-Celtic ancestry, with a civic nationalist identity focused on egalitarian myths of mateship and idioms of rural independence. But the resultant Australian nationalism remained underdeveloped primarily because of a colonial mentality in relation to the British 'mother country'. During the 1960s, however, a new civic and cultural self-confidence seemed to be appearing, which expressed itself in the opening up of Australian nationalism to both non-white migrants and the indigenous minorities. In 1962, Aborigines gained the right to vote;[3] from 1965, the official 'white Australia' immigration policy was abandoned; and in 1967 over 90 per cent of Australians voted to end racial discrimination by removing the words 'other than the Aboriginal race' from the constitutional clause enabling the federal government to make special laws for 'people of any race'.[4]

But these policy changes did not herald a new national solidarity, because they came too late. In particular, the offer of political integration to Aborigines was a belated response to pressures from indigenous activists who had experienced the government's ethnocultural assimilation policies, only to face discrimination.[5] The sense of being strangers in their own land was expressed, for example, in the 1972 establishment of the Aboriginal Embassy on the lawns of Parliament House. This disillusionment led many Aborigines to reject the 'offer' of assimilation, and this rejection generated an increasing awareness, during the 1970s, that assimilationist ethnocultural nationalism might be a form of racism. At the same time, Australia's individualistic civic nationalism was being weakened by the increasing recognition that the 'needs based' social welfare provisions of governments were insufficient to help those who felt socio-economically marginalised, so that assertions of group rights by disadvantaged ascriptive groups – women, migrant ethnic minorities and Aborigines – would be necessary if the civic promise of equal citizenship status were to be attained.

Thus, disillusionment with the assimilationist basis of ethnocultural nationalism has combined with disillusionment with the individualistic basis of civic nationalism to generate the calls for a multicultural nationalism. Such multicultural nationalism demands that the state protect and promote the distinctive communities of its migrant minorities, and recognise the rights of the Aboriginal nations to the land, resources and autonomy, which were taken from them by early European settlement and subsequent assimilationist policies.[6] In the face of this, Australian ethnocultural nationalism has been forced onto the defensive by the accusations of racism, and has moved to the reactive, populist right-wing.

Civic nationalism's promise of equal individual status has indeed been retained as an end-goal vision which both ethnocultural nationalists and multicultural nationalists can embrace, but it has lost much of its power as a guiding principle of public policy in the face of accusations that its individualism only serves to sustain existing structures of power and deprivation, and provides a camouflage for ethnic domination. As the voice of civic nationalism increasingly emerges in the form of new-right, neo-liberal calls for individual responsibility, rather than as a welfare liberal pursuit of individual fulfilment, it sounds increasingly like the voice of the privileged élites, and ceases to resonate with those Australians who feel socio-economically insecure. Marginalised indigenous and migrant minorities turn to multicultural nationalism, while marginalised 'white' Australians turn to ethnocultural nationalism. The intertwining of Australian civic and ethnocultural nationalism has thus given way to the ideological confrontation between Australian multicultural and ethnocultural nationalisms.

From the perspective of multicultural nationalism, the state is condemned for its failure to achieve a substantive and symbolic 'reconciliation', which would acknowledge Aborigines as custodians of the land, recognise their right to self-determination and offer a full apology for the past and present racism of white Australia. Aboriginal culture is celebrated for its spiritual beliefs, communal lifestyle, and unique affinity with the land, with these attributes seen as giving it a moral superiority over the secular individualism and materialism of Western culture. The European invasion of Australia is seen to have condemned the Koori, Murri, Noongar and other Indigenous Australians to genocide through disease, various incidents of mass slaughter and the policy of removing Aboriginal children ('the stolen generation') to white missions. Successive governments' modification of such genocidal assimilationist policies since the 1970s (including the 1989 formation of ATSIC – the Aboriginal and Torres Strait Islander Commission),[7] is regarded by many pro-Aboriginal groups as inadequate and ineffective compensation for the discrimination and dispossession of the past, and is also seen by some as a camouflage for the perpetuation of racism. The most potent symbol of this endemic racism is the refusal of the present government to confirm the restorations of Aboriginal native title to their land which were indicated in the *Mabo* and *Wik* High Court decisions.[8] It is widely believed that, beneath the pretence of a compromise between the claims of pastoral leaseholders and the claims of Aboriginal rights, the 1998 Native Title Amendment Act has effectively reduced Aboriginal land rights. This view was vindicated by the March 1999 decision of the United Nations Committee for the Elimination of all forms of Racial Discrimination (CERD) that the Act might constitute racial discrimination.[9]

Such views are contested and resented by the proponents of assimilationist ethno-cultural nationalism. For them, Aboriginal culture is seen as primitive and backward when compared to the Western civilisation of Australia's European heritage. While the levels of poverty, sickness, crime and drunkenness among Aborigines are recognised as socio-economic problems which ought to be tackled in the same way as should deprivation among other Australians, they are, nevertheless, seen also as proof of the inadequacy and inferiority of Aboriginal culture. It is accepted that violence against Aborigines at the time of European settlement was wrong, but it is noted that this was accompanied by Aboriginal violence against European settlers, and should, in any case, be regarded as a past event which is not the responsibility of present generations, and is not the cause of the contemporary plight of Aborigines. This plight is traced, instead, to a dependency mentality, which, it is argued, has been exacerbated by the affirmative-action programmes that have pumped resources to Aborigines thus promoting corruption and subsidising unemployment.[10] This is, moreover, seen as unfair to other Australian 'battlers' who are not eligible for such resources. From this perspective, the 'Aboriginal industry' which campaigns for and administers these resources, and which supports Aboriginal native title claims to large and undefined tracts of Australian land, should thus be seen as 'a carefully coordinated assault on the conscience of other Australians for the express purpose of producing guilt so as to extract monetary compensation'.[11] Moreover, it is argued that Aboriginal calls for reconciliation, apology and the recognition of custodianship, should be rejected, since they herald demands for Aboriginal national sovereignty which threaten to divide, and therefore potentially to destroy, the Australian nation and its way of life.

The ideological languages of multicultural nationalism and of ethnocultural nationalism thus confront each other, with each side perceiving the government as aligned with their opponents. Mutual distrust between the two perspectives on Australian nationalism, and thence on the government, is presently so acute that there seems little hope that a reconciliation ceremony, constitutional preamble or bill of rights, could enable those on each side to find a language in which they might communicate with, comprehend and respect each other's perceptions.

Northern Ireland

The 1998 Belfast Agreement sought to resolve the Northern Ireland conflict by establishing a Catholic–Protestant coalition government for Northern Ireland, and providing new institutional links both with Eire and Britain. The danger to this peace accord, as to previous attempts at resolution, was, primarily, that many on each side had different criteria of 'fairness', different diagnoses as to the causes of the 'troubles', and therefore different visions as to a solution.

The origins of the dispute have frequently been traced to the 'internal colonialist' policies of the English state towards Ireland, which began in the thirteenth century with the Normans, continued with the Elizabethan 'settlements' of the 1640s and culminated with Cromwell's 'transplantation' policies. These policies generated political rivalries both between the new English settler-landlord classes and the old English (and Irish) landlord classes which they displaced; and also between the new landlords and the tenant farmers (Irish and Scottish) whom they exploited. The resultant discontent of these marginalised and exploited classes was articulated from the late eighteenth century, by members of the new Irish middle classes who were excluded from power and influence by English rule. They developed an Irish nationalism directed against English domination, which emerged first as 'Defenderism', then as the Irish Volunteers, and then as Wolfe Tone's 'United Irishmen'. This Irish nationalism interwove civic ideas of equal citizenship of a free Ireland, with ethnocultural ideas of a Gaelic revival, so as to offer a vision of a resurgent Irish nation. Since English 'colonialism' had involved not just economic extraction, but also an attempt to assert the dominance of the established Anglican church, Irish nationalism could provide a home for all who opposed the Anglican religion of the English settler-landlords; it thus united Catholics with Protestant 'dissenters' (Presbyterians, Quakers, Huguenots and others) in order to oppose the Anglican new ascendancy.

After the 1801 Act of Union, which brought Ireland officially under British rule, this Irish nationalism re-emerged in Fenianism and the Land League, before crystallising in the Home Rule movement, whose goal of a united and independent Ireland came so close to achievement between 1885 and 1913. Home Rule nationalism again accommodated both Catholics and non-Catholics, but, increasingly, uneasily.

It was indeed the likelihood of Home Rule which promoted the unravelling of Irish civic and ethnocultural nationalism, and the ideological reconstruction of the dispute as one between two ethnocultural nationalisms defined in religious terms, Catholic nationalism and Protestant nationalism. The salience of the religious symbolism employed by these ethnocultural nationalisms, has its roots in the dominant role of the Catholic and Protestant legitimations for English political factionalism, which persisted until the marginalisation of the Catholic cause in Britain in the early eighteenth century. In late nineteenth-century Ireland, this religious symbolism strengthened because it seemed to promise legitimation to rival and insecure élites in search of authority, as well as images of communitarian security to a society dislocated by uneven industrialisation and agrarian change.

The 'Protestant' vision of the Anglo-Irish nation had been constructed in the late eighteenth century by Anglican settler-landlords who found themselves politically isolated, both against the peasantry and against the threat of attack from Catholic France. The term 'Protestant' (encompassing Presbyterians, Methodists, Anglicans, and others) resolved this isolation by serving as a symbol to unite the various competing class groups (exploited peasants, marginalised middle classes, and landlords) around myths of a potential threat to their culture and way of life by 'Rome Rule'. In reaction to this, the Gaelic ethnocultural basis of Irish nationalism increasingly adopted the symbolism of Catholicism, in order to mobilise the support of an Irish majority against English Anglican rule. These two visions of the nation, Catholic and Protestant, each offered directly opposing accounts of the causes and nature of the Irish 'troubles'.

The Protestant diagnosis is that they are defending the right of the people of Ulster to self-determination, both against the Irish Republic's territorial claim (particularly the claim to the three Northern Ireland Counties with a Catholic majority) and against the post-1969 terrorist insurrection of the Catholic minority.[12] Northern Ireland is seen as a Protestant nation (a Protestant state for a Protestant people), based both on the rationale behind its formation, and on the democratic right of its two-thirds Protestant majority to control their own destiny without fear of being overrun by the Catholics of Eire.

The Protestant province of Ulster was promised autonomy and British protection in the 1920 Better Government of Ireland Act. Hitherto, it has been seen as unable to fulfil its Protestant destiny not only because of the Catholic insurrection, but also because of the vacillations of Britain in its defence of Ulster autonomy. Nevertheless, the best guarantee of Ulster autonomy, from this Protestant perspective, has remained alliance with England. This is symbolised in the self-designation of Ulstermen as Unionists, Loyalists or Orangemen. Unionist myths refer to English planters taming the wilderness of Ireland with the Bible and the sword, the betrayal of the settlers by the treacherous natives, and the threat to 'freedom, religion and laws' caused by the accession of the popish King James II in 1681. Loyalist myths (more suspicious of the British) depict Ulstermen as standing alone in adversity, fighting against the Catholic threat and constantly betrayed by their supposed protectors, the British, who have repeatedly seemed prepared to abandon 'Loyal' Northern Ireland to a Catholic Republic. Loyalist symbolism includes myths of sacrifice, siege and betrayal as typified by the Siege of Derry and the Battles of the Boyne and Aughrim (1689 to 1691). The term Orangeman refers to the Orange Order formed in 1795, but now extends to all Protestants defending their rights, as embodied in the figure of King William of Orange, on a white horse with his sword unsheathed at the Battle of the Boyne. New symbols repeat the messages, in slogans such as 'No surrender', and the powerful image of the red clenched fist.[13] The battles are seen as having to be repeatedly refought, with forces such as the B Specials in the 1960s, the Royal Ulster Constabulary and the British army, against the guerrilla war launched by Catholics in the 1920s, and, again, against the Catholic insurrection and terrorist campaign launched in 1969.

The Protestant view of Catholics as the enemy of the embattled nation of Ulster, is directly reversed in the Catholic view of Protestants as the enemy of the embattled nation of Ireland. Protestants are depicted as a minority of migrant (Scottish or English) descent who have used gerrymandering techniques to become a manufactured majority in one province. Catholics see themselves not only as the democratic majority of the population of Ireland (80 per cent), but more fundamentally as the authentic inheritors of the ancient Irish nation which 'throughout history . . . has been regarded as a single national unit . . . distinct from other nations cultivating their own system of law, culture, language and political and social structures'.[14] Nevertheless, within Northern Ireland, Catholic Civil Rights groups used the language of minority rights to fight against a 'system of apartheid' which excluded Catholics from power and discriminated against them in employment and housing. The enemies of Catholic nationalism have not only been the Ulster Protestants, but also the British state which pursued a policy of inaction during the Irish Famine, and betrayed Ireland by partitioning it and using British troops and its direct rule to sustain Protestant domination. As the British have blocked the democratic and constitutional route to Irish nationalism, the Catholics have been forced to resort to violence, in the nineteenth century, in the uprisings of Fenianism, from which the Irish Republican Brotherhood emerged, and in the twentieth century in the Sinn Fein ('ourselves alone') movement, through its armed wing, the Irish Republican Army, and its splinter groups.

This Catholic mythology draws on the same events as Protestant mythology, but reverses their moral significance, so as to validate a Catholic sense of grievance by depicting a series of nationalist uprisings led by Catholic martyrs, brutally cut down by stronger Protestant forces. The list is long, but includes the Battles of the Boyne and Aughrim, the execution of the leaders of the 1916 Easter Rising, the 1921–3 suppression of the Irish Republican Army by the 'Black and Tans', and the Bloody Sunday shootings of 1982. Such events symbolise the oppression of Catholics by Protestants throughout history. The systemic nature of this oppression has been variously manifested, in the anti-papist Penal Laws of the seventeenth and eighteenth centuries, the 1921 Partition, the 1922 Special Powers Act, the Prevention of Terrorism Act of 1989 and the 1991 Emergency Provisions Act.[15] The tampering of evidence, which led to the false convictions of alleged terrorists such as the Guildford Four and the Birmingham Six, are new symbols of the discrimination and degradation which Britain has imposed on the Catholics of Northern Ireland.

It is perhaps not the various conflicts of interest and power within Northern Irish politics which form the basis for nationalist confrontation, but the mutual incomprehension and distrust which arise from adherence to antithetical ethnocultural nationalist ideologies.

Rwanda

Political instability in central Africa has, at its core, the eruptions of violence in Rwanda and Burundi, involving Hutus and Tutsis. But rather than characterising the conflict in primordialist terms of tribal antipathy between two racial groups, it is understood here as a confrontation between a Hutu ethnocultural nationalism and a Tutsi–Rwandan civic nationalism. Thus the terms Hutu and Tutsi do not indicate the actual alignments of the dispute. They rather indicate the ideological perception concerning those alignments, so that, for example, the slaughter by one Hutu faction of another, could be justified and understood as necessary for the defence of loyal Hutus against Hutu traitors who had sold out to the Tutsi enemy.

The ideologies of Hutu and Tutsi identity had been inculcated by the German and Belgian colonial administrations, and had their roots in their racial and racist preconceptions whereby the Tutsis were regarded as culturally superior 'bronze Caucasians', while Hutus were regarded as inferior Bantu Africans. The form in which the ideologies have developed and the politics for which they have been employed, have their origins in economic tensions which have focused on acute rivalry for scarce resources as the economy has collapsed, and in the political tensions which have been generated by corrupt, faction-ridden and dictatorial governments. By the time of the late 1950s, when these tensions first erupted into violence, an understanding of Rwandan politics in terms of rivalry between a Hutu majority (about 85 per cent) and a Tutsi minority (less than 14 per cent) had achieved hegemony.

The subordination of the Hutu majority under colonial rule, had meant that their identity developed reactively against the state and emerged in an ethnocultural nationalist form. The Hutu perception saw Hutus and Tutsis as two distinct racially based nations, locked in a zero-sum conflict within the same state and territory. Tutsi perceptions of identity, on the other hand, developed when their pre-colonial status as patrons was transformed into a cemented-power monopoly over Hutus by Belgian colonial rule, so that when Tutsi nationalism developed, it was associated with the Rwandan state, and took on a civic nationalist complexion. This means that from the Tutsi perspective, the terms Hutu and Tutsi, were used to refer to distinct class or caste communities within a (potential or emergent) Rwandan nation.

Hutu ethnocultural nationalism distinguishes the Hutu and the Tutsi on a racial basis, with the Hutu depicting themselves as a people of Bantu origin who have farmed in Rwanda since the tenth century, and the Tutsis as a cattle-breeding people of Hamitic origin, who arrived in the fifteenth century. The racial stereotypes depict the Hutu as shorter and more robust, while the Tutsis are depicted as tall, clever and dishonest. The power of such stereotypes was illustrated during the 1994 massacres, with Hutu forces attempting to 'cut the Tutsi down to size' by chopping their legs off at the knees.[16]

In Hutu mythology, the pre-colonial period is depicted as one in which a potentially harmonious relationship between the Hutu, Tutsi and Twa communities was destroyed by Tutsi oppression. This oppression involved nineteenth-century Tutsi attacks on Hutus in North and West Rwanda, which are symbolised in the mythologisation of one particular expedition, the *inkemba*, where the Tutsi are depicted as pillaging and burning Hutu villages. This Tutsi oppression was then institutionalised through the kingship system which involved the Tutsi king, the *mwami*, and his three advisors, the cattle chief, army chief, and land chief. According to Hutu versions of history, the cattle chief and army chief, who were Tutsis, were favoured, while the position of land chief, belonging to a Hutu, was subordinated. This oppression of the Hutus was exacerbated through a system of *ubuhake*, an unequal clientelist relationship, which locked the Hutu into economic dependency on the Tutsi. Hutu propaganda portrays the Tutsis in the colonial period as the cruel auxiliaries of the colonial administration, who relished their work and benefited from exploiting Hutus, particularly through the practices of *batake* which was a corveé or land tax and *ubureetwa* which was a corveé imposed specifically on Hutu. In 1957, the Manifesto Bahutu directly challenged Tutsi overlordship and signalled the Social Revolution of 1959 which saw the realisation of Hutu Power through the electoral victory of *Parmehutu* (the Hutu Emancipation Movement), followed by the independence of Rwanda in 1961. Subsequent politics is understood as involving repeated attempts by Tutsis to reverse the Social Revolution, and to enslave the Hutus again.

The Hutu claim is that they were able to prevent such enslavement until 1973 through the efforts of the first Prime Minister Gregoire Kayibanda (regarded from the Hutu perspective as the father of democracy). He led the 1959 revolution and dedicated himself to defending the interests of the rural masses. In the face of new Tutsi threats, Hutus were defended, from 1973 to 1994, by General Habyarimana and his governing party, the National Revolutionary Movement for Democracy (MRND). Habyarimana's death in 1994 was blamed on Tutsis, and on Hutu traitors, who were specified in the death lists drawn up by the ex-President's wife.

But the claim was that the Tutsi menace could only be defeated by destroying the Rwandan Patriotic Front (RPF), seen by Hutus as a Tutsi dominated army of exiles which has been seeking a Tutsi resurgence since 1990. For extremist Hutu groups in particular, such as the Coalition for the Defence of the Republic (CDR) and the *Inyarahamwe* militia ('those who attack together'), the violence against RPF Tutsis and treacherous Hutus which revived in 1990 and again in 1994, symbolised the defence of the Hutu race against a diabolical Tutsi plot. Their aim was to rectify 'the mistake of 1959', when Tutsis were allowed to escape from Rwanda following the Social Revolution, and then launch attacks on the new democratic regime. This time, the Hutu victims would finally exterminate their Tutsi oppressors.

The Hutu have used the term *inyenzi* (cockroaches) to symbolise the status of the Tutsi as vermin, who 'have infested Rwanda and must be eliminated',[17] so that Hutu children were taught they had the right to oppress the Tutsi – 'What's wrong with killing an enemy? Kill the snake!'.[18] For this reason, Hutu élites called upon the population to perform *umuganda* – voluntary collective work – by killing Tutsis.

The above Hutu view of racial confrontation is not directly reflected in Tutsi propaganda, since, for those who identify themselves as Tutsi, the terms Hutu and Tutsi do not symbolise distinct races, but rather different social castes or classes. According to a local Tutsi proverb, 'a Tutsi is a Hutu with 10 cattle'.[19] The Tutsi talk of the *Banyarwanda* (the people of Rwanda) – 'We speak the same language, have the same culture, live on the same hills, we are the same people'.[20] None the less, the Tutsi define themselves as of higher status; superior, intelligent and brave. The Hutu are correspondingly depicted as impatient, lazy, slow witted, servile and greedy. As a warrior caste, the Tutsi regard themselves as possessing the quality of *itonde*, stoicism and courage. By contrast, the Hutu are regarded as uncouth peasants lacking courage.

The Tutsi perception of the relationship between the people of Rwanda is symbolised in an eighteenth-century myth used to justify the caste system:

> The *mwami* [king] testing his sons gives them milk to guard. Gatutsi [Tutsi] stayed awake all night and returned the full pot of milk to his father the next day. Gahutu [Hutu] who became tired, dozed off and let the pot spill half its contents onto the ground. Gatwa [Twa] became thirsty and drank all his father's milk. As a result the *mwami* chose Gatutsi as his successor, pronouncing that he was 'forever exempt from physical labour'. Gahutu was made his serf and Gatwa was expelled from society, assuming the status of an untouchable.[21]

This myth reflects the Tutsi recognition that the relationship between the *mwami* and their subjects was unequal, but that the *ubuhake* relationship between ordinary Hutus and Tutsis rested on common kinship and a division of labour which was mutually beneficial. According to Tutsi mythology, the balanced nature of political and social relationships was further reflected in the fact that the land chief was a Hutu, the cattle chief a Tutsi and the army chief a Twa. They blame the colonial administration for abolishing the role of the land chief and changing a reciprocal relationship between Hutu and Tutsi into one which produced Hutu subordination and alienation.

Tutsi mythology refers to the 1959 Social Revolution as the Hutu Revolution, the first of the massacres of the Tutsi by Hutus. These massacres continued in 1961 with the *coup* of Gitarama, when Belgians connived with Hutu groups to remove the *mwami* from power, leading to 10,000 Tutsi being killed and another 130,000 fleeing into exile. Rather than being seen as the father of democracy, Kayibanda is regarded by the Tutsi as the person who prevented democracy in Rwanda by implementing single-party rule and corruptly concentrating power and industry in his home region. From this Tutsi persective, both Kayibanda and his successor, Habyarimana, sought to camouflage their favouratism of some Hutu clans and factions over others, by employing anti-Tutsi rhetoric.

Whereas Tutsi nationalism had primarily employed the symbolism of the Tutsi monarchy in the 1950s and 1960s, by the 1990s, the Rwandan Patriotic Front (RPF) was employing the symbolism of democracy, as well as the United Nations validated symbolism of minority rights. The RPF describe themselves as reclaiming the motherland and instituting democracy, repatriating Rwandese refugees and implementing welfare policies to ensure peaceful coexistence. Their commitment to unity is signified in the claim that 50 per cent of RPF leadership was Tutsi and 50 per cent Hutu. They depict their 1990 advance not as an invasion, but as a war of liberation against military dictatorship. The RPF army portrays itself as the defender warriors of Rwanda – an allusion to the *abatabazi* pre-colonial warriors who would sacrifice themselves to defend Rwanda. The term *inyenzi* (cockroaches), is also used by Tutsis to refer to the RPF. In contrast to Hutu pejorative usage of this term, however, it is employed as a positive reference symbolically linking the RPF with the nineteenth-century guerrilla movement created by the *mwami* as a resistance force against colonial invaders. The term genocide was quickly adopted by the RPF to refer to the 1994 killings, despite the fact that it was not just Tutsis who were killed, but any political opponents of the regime. In Tutsi mythology, the term victims refers to both Tutsi and Hutus targeted in the killings. Survivors, however, is a term only applied to Tutsi.

An emergent Rwandan civic nationalism was never able to accommodate an emergent Hutu ethnocultural nationalism. The intensity of economic, status and power disparities, and the physical and emotional insecurities which these disparities engendered, have ensured the susceptibility of Rwandans to the two antithetical nationalist ideologies which insecure élites have propagated. The structural basis for the conflict is thus no longer the rivalries for state power and resources themselves, but the mutual distrust, misunderstanding and fear, which is embedded in the two constructed ideologies. The inability of the decolonising state to intertwine civic and ethnocultural identities so as to generate a sense of security, led those subject to the uncertainties of deprivation, to seek security in simple formulas of countervailing Hutu and Tutsi rights, enemies and destinies.

Kosovo

During the early 1980s, tensions in Kosovo between Albanian ethnocultural nationalism and Serb ethnocultural nationalism, became increasingly violent, and after 1997 this was manifested in armed conflict between the Kosovo Liberation Army and the Yugoslavian (mainly Serbian) troops and police. It was the effort at international mediation of this dispute which led to the NATO bombing of Serbia in March 1999, precipitating the flight and deportation of Albanians from Kosovo.

Conflict between the different nationalities in the Balkans can be traced to the decline of the Ottoman and Austro-Hungarian empires in the latter part of the nineteenth century. In this context, dislocated societies were susceptible to the legitimatory myths of nationalism which rival élites began to employ. The post-1945 reconstitution of Yugoslavia under Tito's leadership was a conscious attempt to build a Yugoslav nationalism which could avoid the clash of ethnocultural nationalisms that had engendered the collapse of the previous Yugoslavia. Tito's initial strategy was to intertwine a civic nationalism based on Yugsolav Communism with an overarching Slavic ethnocultural nationalism, so as to minimise the opportunities for élite manipulations of ethnic and regionalist rivalries. But by the mid-1960s this strategy was clearly running into trouble, in part because it was implemented 'from the top down', with the help of significant centralised state force.

Tito responded by progressively modifying his strategy, moving towards increasing federal decentralisation based on a multicultural Yugoslav nationalism. This sought to build upon (rather than replace) the ethnocultural and regionalist nationalisms, by offering a vision of a state in which each distinct nation and nationality had its own republic or province, and received a fair share of power, autonomy and resources. This shift towards multiculturalism involved, as one aspect, the reduction of Serbian domination over the Albanians in the Province of Kosovo, culminating in the formal recognition of Kosovo as an autonomous province, and implicitly as an Albanian homeland, in 1974.

The core dilemma for Yugoslav multiculturalism was, however, the tension between the civic nationalisms and ethnocultural nationalisms within each of the component republics and provinces. While each republic and province was the 'homeland' for members of a particular ethnic nationality, it did not contain all such members, and it also contained members of other nationalities. Thus, for example, 10 per cent of Serbia's population was non-Serb, while 40 per cent of Serbs lived outside Serbia. A Serbian civic nationalism would thus exclude Serbs outside the Republic's boundaries, but would incorporate non-Serbs within those borders; Serb ethnocultural nationalism, on the other hand, would give Serbs higher status than non-Serbs within Serbian borders, and would potentially incorporate Serbs living in other republics within a 'Greater Serbia'. A parallel situation applied within Kosovo, which contained a majority (about 75 per cent) of Albanians, with Serbs and Montenegrins the largest minority groups; but most Albanians lived outside Kosovo, as citizens of the neighbouring country of Albania. Thus while a Kosovo civic nationalism would include the Serb and Montenegrin minorities, Kosovar ethnocultural nationalism would refer only to the Albanian majority and would potentially refer also to visions of unification with Albania.

The potential tensions between the civic and ethnocultural nationalisms of each component nationality, could be contained so long as Yugoslav multicultural nationalism offered a vision of fair ethnic balance, and this was accomplished most successfully from the mid-1960s until Tito's death in 1980, in part because Tito was able to offer each nationality the hope that existing imbalances might be rectified in their favour. Thus, the fact that Kosovo was granted the status of autonomous province in the 1974 Constitution, but not that of a full republic, was a deliberately ambiguous signal. The fact that Kosovo gained its own representation in the federal Presidency and had similar autonomous powers to the republics, encouraged Kosovars to regard this as granting independence from Serbia, and as a step towards full republic status, which would carry with it the right, if necessary, to secede and join Albania. But the new constitution also reassured Serbs by defining Kosovo as a province of Serbia, rather than a province of Yugoslavia, thereby indicating that Kosovo could never secede and that Serbia would still be able to protect its interests there.

The ambiguities of the 1974 Constitution concerning Kosovo's status were, however, insufficient to prevent the new wave of élite rivalries which were generated by its impact on Serbian influence at the federal centre. The Constitution exacerbated the tension between Serbian civic and ethnocultural nationalisms by reducing Serbia's proportional representation and power in the federal Presidency. This threatened Serbia's ability to act as a protector of the non-Serbian Serbs, and so stimulated an upsurge of ethnocultural nationalism when these Serb minorities were threatened. This appeared to be the case in the late 1970s when the Kosovo economy began to markedly decline, and insecure Serbs began to leave. Serb ethnocultural nationalism began as calls to protect Serb interests in Kosovo (and Vojvodina), and then developed into calls for the 'restoration' of these provinces to Serbia; calls which provided the basis for Slobodan Milosevic's rise to power in 1987.

The Albanian claim to Kosovo rests on the assertion that it is part of the Albanian homeland of their ancestors, that they have always lived there and that throughout modern times they have formed the majority of the inhabitants. They cooperated with Serbs to oppose Ottoman rule in the Battle of Kosovo in 1389, only to be rewarded by Serbian claims that it must protect itself by creating a Greater Serbia from which the Muslim 'Albanians and Turks' must be expelled. Kosovars see this project as having been launched in the middle of the nineteenth century, and pursued consistently thereafter:

> Serbia compiled the project 'Nacertanija' in 1844, which anticipated the occupation of ethnic Albanians territories and emigration by force . . . From that time to the present day Serbia has continued with the expulsion of the Albanians . . . Serbian and Montenegrin monarchies perpetrated their policy of extermination and genocide and even ethnocide on the Albanian people . . . The Yugoslav kingdom continued the colonisation of Kosova and other land of ethnic Albanians by Serbs and Montenegrins . . . The forceful annexation of Kosova to Serbia and Yugoslavia influenced further on the emigration of the Albanians. Repression continued to be exerted in different ways and it was always done on purpose of the emigration and assimilation of the Albanians . . . Every expression of thought, feeling and culture dealing with the Albanian nation, was condemned.[22]

Serbian suppression and colonisation of Kosovo after 1912, the reimposition of Serbian rule after 1945 and the destruction of Kosovar autonomy after 1989, only confirmed and intensified Albanian fears that the Serbian aim was 'an unprecedented genocide in the Europe of twentieth century [sic]'.[23]

But Serbs had been told a different story. They see themselves as the original inhabitants of Kosovo, and the Albanians as later arrivals who were a minority until Serbs were forced to flee the area under Ottoman rule. The Battle of Kosovo has been depicted by nineteenth- and twentieth-century Serbian nationalists as the national foundation myth, establishing the national identity and cultural superiority of the Serb people in the 'Kosovo Covenant' which translated military defeat into spiritual liberation. This portrayal of Kosovo as the sacred Serb homeland was reinforced by its religious status as the home of the Patriachate of the Serbian Orthodox Church, and thus as 'an inalienable national treasury, indispensable for the identity of the Serbian people'.[24] Serbian rule of Kosovo liberated the Albanian population from the yoke of Ottoman rule, and enabled them to access the superior Serb culture. Albanians who did not wish to accept this, were reminded that Albania is their homeland, not Kosovo. The 'Albanian national minority' disregarded the rights of the Serbs in Kosovo by staging a 'separatist's rebellion' in 1981, aimed at achieving a 'Kosovo Republic' with the right of secession,[25] and the unification of all Albanians in a 'Great Albania'.[26]

In the recent crisis, Serbs and Albanians in Kosovo were fully trapped within these two hegemonic ideologies. Serbs saw that their land and security was threatened by Albanians who in turn believed their own land and security to be threatened by Serbs. To each side, the behaviour of the other side was inhuman. The ideological myths of each side seemed to be merely common sense. That is the tragedy of nationalist conflict.

These brief essays have tried to make explicit the ideological myths of each side in the selected nationalist contentions. This is intended to illustrate the general point, that the unravelling of nationalism into its competing civic, ethnocultural and multicultural visions constitutes a powerful causal factor, which transforms some of the diverse interest rivalries and power disputes within nations, into ideological confrontations between nations. The aim of the book has been to explain this nationalist politics by arguing that the strength of nation-states depended upon the psychological and political power of their entwined civic and ethnocultural nationalist visions. The intention has then been to show how the disentwining of these visions promoted nationalist contention; and how this is exacerbated or ameliorated depending upon the ideological strategies employed by the various nationalist élites.

Previously, many nation-states sought to provide a sense of security by intertwining the civic and the ethnocultural visions of community, so as to accommodate the difference between the two memberships. Many of them failed in this endeavour, with the result that today's contentious nationalisms frequently seek security by disentwining the two so as to expose and politicise the gaps between communities of ethnocultural sameness and communities of territorial commitment. In a world of difference, this makes the world of difference.

Notes

Introduction

1 It is noted by Margaret Canovan, for example, that 'the boundaries of Englishness became elastic and the difference between "English" and "British" largely imperceptible'. But 'contemporary developments [relating to Northern Ireland, demands for Scottish independence, and the issue of the European Community], by directing attention to questions of nationhood, (threaten) to tear off the comfortable blanket of silence in which the ambiguities of English/British identity have been cloaked for the past two centuries' (Canovan 1996: 77, 79-80).

1 The conceptual languages of nationalism

1 See also Margaret Canovan's comment that 'nationhood [is] a sticky cobweb of myths and mediations, guaranteed to repel the clear minded' (Canovan 1996: 139). It is important that these comments as to the complexity and ambiguity of the concept are made precisely by those who are *not* repelled, and who *are* clear-minded.

2 The relationship between ethnicity and nationalism is treated differently in each of the three approaches, as indicated in this chapter. For a more detailed discussion of how various writers on nationalism can be located within differing conceptual approaches, see Smith (1998).

3 This leads various writers to conclude that the primordialist approach is dead or irrelevant. See, for example, Rogers Brubaker's comment that it is 'a long-dead horse that writers on ethnicity and nationalism continue to flog' (Brubaker 1996: 15 n.4), or John Armstrong's comment that 'the notion of national identity as a *primordial* phenomenon has been generally discarded by scholars' (Armstrong 1995: 35). It is suggested here, however, that the rarity of explicit avowals of primordialist explanation should not be seen as signifying any weakening of its influence. This is indicated by Armstrong's note to his comment quoted above, which refers to the influential work of Arendt Lijphart, who rarely uses the term 'primordial', but whose work is nonetheless built on primordialist assumptions.

4 In a recent article, Francisco Gil-White used the terms 'primordialist' and 'circumstantialist' to refer to competing depictions of the psychology of ethnic actors, rather than competing explanations. He found, not surprisingly, that ethnic actors were 'heavily primordialist' in that they expressed belief that they and their co-ethnics shared common descent (Gil-White 1999).

5 Smith himself does not regard 'perennialism' as a form of primordialism, but it seems that a clear distinction between the two has to rely on a selective definition of primordialism as referring only to the claim that modern nations and ethnic communities are based on factual 'lines of physical descent' (Smith 1998: 192). But this would

exclude those primordialists such as Clifford Geertz, who Smith classifies as 'cultural primordialists' (1998: 151).

6 Anthony Smith is careful to distinguish his own explanation of nationalism, which he characterises as 'ethno-symbolism', from the primordialist and perennialist approaches. Smith's focus on the role of the intelligentsia in promoting ethnic symbols of nationalist ideologies in the modern era, does indeed seem to locate him in the 'constructivist' camp discussed below (see p. 20). But his other focus on the ethnic origins of nations, in which ethnic communities are depicted as pervasive, ubiquitous and durable cultural collectivities which provide a powerful sense of identity to their populations, has some important similarities with Clifford Geertz's primordialist focus on the 'cultural givens'. At the risk of oversimplifying Smith's nuanced arguments, it seems that he avoids conceptual confusion by viewing ethnic groups in largely cultural primordialist terms, while viewing the nationalisms into which they sometimes transform, largely in ideological constructivist terms.

7 'Ewe' is pronounced 'evy'.

8 The terms 'circumstantialist' and 'instrumentalist' are sometimes also used to denote this approach.

9 This has been argued by Mike Innes, referring to the work of the social psychologist Solomon Asch, that 'As a matter of course we trust the word of others . . . We proceed in this way because any other process is inefficient . . . On such a process is the nature of community built' (Innes 1997: 20).

10 This discussion of the Ghanaian Ewes is pursued in Chapter 6 of this book.

11 The issue of whether the ability of nationalism to perform these functions means that it thereby deserves the designation of an 'ideology', is a contested one, as noted by Freeden (1998). Freeden's own judgement is that nationalism should be regarded only as a 'thin-centred ideology', rather than a 'full' ideology, on the grounds of an alleged 'structural inability to offer complex ranges of argument' (1998: 750).

12 John Davis (1996: 446) notes that, given Gellner's recognition of the 'absurdities' of myths, it is 'hard to explain his antipathy to psychoanalysis, though Hall and Jarvie (1996: 18) indicate that this might have stemmed in part from his scepticism of psychoanalysis as therapy.

13 Brown (1994: Ch. 1) contains a discussion of ethnicity in psychoanalytic terms.

14 The phrase 'seek out a name' is used by Stephen Frosh in the context of a discussion of the work of Cornelius Castoriadis.

2 New nations for old?

1 As noted in Chapter 1 (see p. 25), Marxism treats nationalism partly in situational terms, and partly in constructivist terms.

2 For examinations of how the language of nationalism has come to dominate the language of patriotism, see Viroli (1995), and Dietz (1989).

3 The use of the term 'ethnocultural nationalism' in preference to the term 'ethnic nationalism', is discussed in Chapter 3. The term 'cultural nationalism' is sometimes also used, but is avoided here simply because it might seem to imply that civic nationalism does *not* have a cultural component.

4 The alleged 'weakness' of civic nationalism is discussed more fully in Chapter 3.

5 Brubaker then stresses the political tensions within these new nations, between ethnocultural and territorial allegiances.

6 The debate is not avoided by the depiction of some states as 'democratic', since it re-emerges in the debate between those who define democracy in terms of particular forms of electoral, party, bureaucratic and constitutional institutions; and those who define it in majoritarian, pluralist or consociational terms which refer to the influence upon government of the specified social groups.

7　The state may be seen as the agency of a divided group either in the pluralist sense, or in terms of some notion of factionalism. Where a cohesive social group, which has captured the state, corrodes internally into rival factions (as perhaps happened in the case of the Apartheid regime in South Africa), it is likely that it will use myths of nationalism, *a fortiori*, to camouflage this. In the pluralist state, government is based on the claim that the diverse interests can all be aggregated or negotiated through bargaining, with the state institutions as the arbiter. Thus the state is not itself depicted as fractured, but rather as comprising the 'umpire' institutions whose neutrality is defined in relation to the unified nation.

8　The languages of order, justice, democracy and development, among others, are usually employed in conjunction with ideas of nationalism, in order to convince the populace that the state functions for the common good, rather than for any narrower agency or institutionalist ends.

9　As indicated previously, 'ethnocultural nationalism' and 'ethnicity' are closely related concepts, but are not identical. The term 'ethnicity' refers to a sense of identity to a cultural community, which is perceived as a community of common descent. The term 'ethnocultural nationalism' refers to a claim to political rights for a cultural community, which is legitimated in terms of such claims to common descent. But there is no assumption that the two terms need refer to the same cultural community; in other words, it is quite feasible for an ethnocultural nation to contain several constituent ethnic communities; for example, the Han Chinese ethnocultural nation contains several distinct language groups which function for some purposes as ethnic communities.

10　The relationship between civic and ethnocultural nationalism on the one hand, and liberal and illiberal nationalism on the other, is discussed in Chapter 3.

11　Mann's extensive and influential work on the development of European nationalism is outlined in summary form in Mann (1996), from which these quotations are taken. In common with several other writers, Mann does not use the terms 'cultural' and 'political' nationalism to refer to the distinction between claims made by an ethnic community and claims made by a state–territorial community, but rather to refer to a distinction between assertions of cultural virtue, and claims to independent statehood.

12　The Singapore case is examined in Chapter 5.

13　This formulation of the issue is indicated by Anthony Smith: 'When the civic or the ethnic elements come to predominate, the unity and power of the nation is impaired, and citizenship and ethnicity may be brought into conflict' (Smith 1995: 100).

3　Are there two nationalisms?

1　See for example Alter (1989: 37), 'integral nationalism . . . is encountered under various titles. Radical; extreme; militant; aggressive-expansionist; derivative; right-wing; reactionary; excessive'. Guibernau refers to ethnocultural nationalism as 'Romantic nationalism' (1996: 55–7).

2　The term 'political' is used for example by John Hutchinson (1994), and 'social', by James Kellas (1991). 'State' is the term used by Meinecke (1972).

3　The term 'ethnicity' is used here to refer to a sense of identity based on myths of common ancestry. The term 'ethnocultural nationalism' refers to the claim that a community of common ancestry should have some rights of autonomy.

4　Kymlicka uses the term 'ethnic nationalism' to refer, in effect, to racial nationalism which is exclusive. He then uses the term 'ethnocultural nationalism' to refer to nations seeking to promote cultures based on language and common history, and which are defined as inclusive (Kymlicka 1999: 132–3).

5　The charge that, in the liberal West, the ideology of civic nationalism might sometimes serve to camouflage ethnic domination, is no doubt true. But it is equally true that in other kinds of societies, myths of ethnocultural assimilation are sometimes used to camouflage the (civic) integration of non-ethnics.

6 On Herder (1744–1803), see Meinecke (1972: Ch. 9). On Fichte (1762–1814), see Kedourie (1993) and Greenfeld (1992). On Weber, see Guibernau (1996).
7 Smith first suggested this distinction in 1971: 'All nationalist movements, then, can be placed along a continuum. At one end, we have the *"Ethnic"* movements with a high degree of cultural distinctiveness; at the other, the *"Territorial"* movements bound only by aspirations and a common territorial-cum-political base' (Smith 1971: 218).
8 Though it is in fact this aspect of Kohn's argument which he had criticised (Smith 1991: 81).
9 See the debate on this issue between John Hargreaves and Michael Keating, in the context of Keating's depictions of the Catalan, Quebec and Scottish cases as civic nationalisms in Hargreaves and Keating (1998).
10 This is not to suggest that the theorists previously referred to do not examine these issues, merely that these are not elucidated by this particular aspect of their conceptualisations of nationalism. Thus, Greenfeld (1992), for example, does seek to explain the complexities of French nationalism in terms of the two models of nationalism, but it is indicative that her study actually shows the interweaving of three stages of French nationalism, none of which correspond with the models.
11 This suggested argument is pursued in the discussion of the reactivity argument: see pp. 64–6 and thereafter.
12 It must be said, however, that Fichte's conception of individual freedom involved a Rousseauean vision in which the will of the individual is fused with the will of the nation. Fichte's notions of German superiority ('only the German . . . is capable of real and rational love for his nation') has similarly illiberal connotations (Kedourie 1993: 61 and 77–8).
13 The major issues of this debate are examined in Kymlicka (1995b).
14 Greenfeld relates the character of nationalism to variations in the type of tensions which emerged in hierarchical societies, and the type of 'images of social order' imagined by emergent élites (1992: 490). She thus recognises the element of élite choice, but sees their interpretations of nationalism, whether liberal or collectivist, primarily as the articulations of particular cultural traditions.
15 Including Herder, Fichte, Meinecke, Kohn (German Czech), and Alter.
16 She argues that the architects of the classic case of a liberal civic nationalism, that of England, were the new aristocracy. The growing middle classes played a role subsequently, as its main propagators (Greenfeld 1992: Ch. 1).
17 She uses the term *ressentiment* consistently to refer to reaction to other nationalisms, but locates that reaction primarily in the groups who articulate the national consciousness. She never uses the term to refer to the frustrated status expectations of élite groups in the absence of any externally directed resentments (Greenfeld 1992).

4 Constructing nationalism

1 The main such distinctiveness relates to the disproportionately high percentage of Basques with blood group O and the rhesus-negative gene.
2 The only evidence given by Conversi, however, refers to depictions of such 'proto-nationalism' in the early nineteenth century (1997: 44–5).
3 The percentage of native Basques identifying themselves as 'only Basque' was 50.6 per cent in 1979, 40.5 per cent in 1988 and 43.8 per cent in 1991 (Medrano 1995: 175). Support for Basque nationalist parties has averaged 40 per cent of votes in general elections between 1977 and 1993, and 64 per cent of votes in regional elections between 1980 and 1994. Support for the radical nationalism of *Herri Batasuna* has fluctuated between 15 per cent and 18 per cent of votes (see n. 5 below). It should be noted that about one-third of the electorate are migrants.
4 According to figures used by Clark, 47.5 per cent spoke Euskara in 1934, and 19.1 per cent in 1975. But the del Campo survey, referred to by Clark, further shows that in

1975, Euskara was spoken fluently by 30.4 per cent of the native-born Basques. In 1934, there were 570,000 Euskara speakers, and in the mid-1970s, despite more than a doubling of the regional population, the number of Euskara speakers was 450,000 (Clark 1979: 140–5). During the 1980s, the promotion of Euskara in schools led to an increase in its use. The number of speakers rose to 540,000 in 1991, i.e. about 26 per cent of the population (Montana 1996: 232).

5 In the 1931 municipal elections, Basque nationalist parties got 35.74 per cent of votes, and in the 1936 general elections they got 35.06 per cent. Medrano gives no overall figure for the 1933 general elections, but indicates that it was slightly higher than the 1936 result (Medrano 1995: 85 Table 7). The voting figures from 1970 onwards are given in Medrano as a percentage of the eligible electorate, and in Ross as a percentage of actual votes (Medrano: 172 Table 20, Ross 1996: 505 Table 3). It should be noted that the abstention rate for the 10 elections between 1977 and 1993 averaged 31.3 per cent. In the post-Franco period, the Basque Nationalist Party (PNV) remains the main nationalist party. *Herri Batasuna*, the political arm of ETA (*Euskadi Ta Azkatasuna*), has been the second most popular nationalist party since its formation in 1978. *Euskadiko Ezkara* (EE) was formed in 1977 in a factional split from ETA, but in 1993 it merged with the Spanish Socialist Party (PSOE). *Eusko Alkartasuna* (EA, Basque Solidarity) was formed in 1981 under the leadership of Carlos Garaikoetrexea, the first President of the Autonomous Basque government of 1980.

6 The *Fueros* were the political institutions of the Basque provinces which gave them a degree of self-government. Each Basque province was governed by a 'broadly chosen General Assembly with a smaller permanent Deputation'. The provinces were exempted from Spanish conscription, taxation and customs duties (Carr 1966: 63). The interests of the rural Basque élite were threatened by the abolition of the *Fueros* since this meant the replacement of the *Juntas Generales* 'elected through procedures that privileged the traditional rural areas', with the less autonomous *Diputaciones Provinciales*, which were elected by direct ballot 'and subordinated to the central government' (Medrano 1995: 70).

7 Carlism developed out of court factional rivalries between King Ferdinand VII and his brother Don Carlos. Carlism came to symbolise the conservative Catholic opposition to liberal centralising constitutionalism. This resulted in the Carlist wars of 1822–3, 1833–41 and 1870–5.

8 Shubert indicates that there were 60,000 immigrants into Vizcaya between 1880 and 1900, where 'industrialisation was most rapid, and most wrenching' (1990: 127).

9 The mining and iron industries which developed in the Basque Country from the 1850s onwards, were dominated by a few Basque families, as well as by some foreign-owned companies. The Basque capitalist élite had major financial and industrial interests in Spain which were decisive in the development of the Spanish economy in the early twentieth century. As Carr notes, with a few exceptions, 'the really rich men in Spain after 1900 were Basques' (Carr 1966: 406).

10 Shubert notes that in Vizcaya, native Basques working mainly in small workshops or as artisans or white-collar workers, founded the Basque Workers' Union. Migrant workers clustered in metal working and mining formed the socialist Metal Workers' Union and Miners' Union (1990: 128).

11 In 1967, apart from Madrid, the Spanish provinces with the highest per-capita income were the Basque provinces of Vizcaya (65,000 pasetas), and Guipuzcoa (63,000) (Medhurst 1972: 5). Horowitz notes that 'the percentage of total tax revenues in Spain paid by those in the Basque region is more than three times the percentage of state expenditure there' (1985: 249–54).

12 It has been suggested by Medrano that because of their economic and career links with Spain, 'the participation of the Basque bourgeoisie and intelligentsia in the anti-Francoist movement [was] negligible' (1995: 135). This seems misleading, since, although some capitalists and officials did participate in the Franco regime (Medrano

1995: 127), other members of the 'bourgeoisie and intelligentsia' participated substantially in the active resistance activities of the PNV and ETA. Medrano understates this by depicting the class position of ETA activists, not in terms of their own middle- or lower-middle-class occupations, but those of their more working-class fathers. Medrano elsewhere defines class position in terms of the individuals' occupation, rather than that of their parents (1995: 135–4).

13 In Guipuzcoa, 1977 unemployment was 4.3 per cent, and support for nationalist parties was 28.1 per cent. In 1979, unemployment was 10.5 per cent and nationalist support was 32.7 per cent. In 1982, unemployment was 18.8 per cent and nationalist support was 47.4 per cent. For the Basque Country as a whole, the unemployment rate rose from 4 per cent in 1976 to 23.5 per cent in 1986 (Medrano 1995: 122).

14 It provides the focus of analysis by, for example, Medrano (1995).

15 In 1983, Basque imports from the rest of Spain were 54 per cent of Basque GDP, and exports were 72 per cent of Basque GDP. Imports from Spain were 86 per cent of Basque imports, while exports to Spain were 76 per cent of Basque exports (Medrano 1995: 122). Between 15 per cent and 25 per cent of those in the Basque Country support the goal of full independence (Medrano 1995: 176).

16 In 1980, when the first Basque Government was formed, PNV got 38 per cent of the vote, and HB got 17 per cent. The dominant nationalist party since 1980 has been PNV, which has led the regional government, and also regularly won five to eight seats in the Spanish parliament. Their governmental dominance within the Basque region derives partly from the fact that HB refused to take its seats in parliament.

17 The Spanish government response of repression in the face of ETA violence led, as ETA had intended, to increased support for radical Basque nationalism. But the Spanish government response of political concessions and amnesties also served only to promote further nationalist demands. This cycle of confrontation was at its peak at the time of the February 1981 *coup* attempt (Letamendia 1995: 191–2).

18 The figures given in Medrano are for those identifying themselves as only Basque: 36.8 per cent in 1979, 31 per cent in 1988 and 30.8 per cent in 1991. But the data is also given separately for native Basques and non-natives. This shows that 50.6 per cent of native Basques identify themselves as solely Basque in 1979 and 43.8 per cent in 1991. The equivalent figures for non-native residents of the Basque Country are 12.4 per cent in 1979 and 7.5 per cent in 1991 (Medrano 1995: 175). De Rafael does not give a figure, but refers to studies showing that 47 per cent of Basques 'identified with their region', and a 1990 study showing 20 per cent of Basques had 'pure nationalistic feeling' (De Rafael 1998: 57–8). Keating quotes a figure of 26 per cent identifying themselves as solely Basque in 1988 (Keating 1996: 130).

19 For a discussion of Arana's nationalist 'inventions' and his legacy, see Conversi (1997: 53–73).

20 Santiago Arana, the father of Sabino Arana, was mayor of a town near Bilbao and a deputy of the Junta General of Vizcaya. He owned rural and urban property and ran shipping and (wooden) shipbuilding concerns. He financially supported the Carlists in the Second Carlist War and was in exile in France until 1876. He suffered financially both from the war, and from the threat to wooden shipbuilding from the new steel industry. It was the defeat of Carlism in the 1881 Spanish election which stimulated Sabino Arana and his brother to defend the 'seigniorial tradition'. Arana was also a member of a marginalised class in the sense that he became politically active in Basque nationalism after having failed in his attempt at an academic career (Medrano 1995: 75–6). His first language was Castilian, but at this point he began learning Euskara (Sullivan 1988: 6).

21 Heiberg's subtle explanation of the construction of Basque identity is also summarised in Heiberg (1996). The merging of the two ideological strands of Basque nationalism was facilitated by the merging, in 1898, of Arana's PNV with the *Fuerista* bourgeoisie nationalist association of Sota y Llano (Medrano 1995: 71–5 and 81).

22 While 25 per cent in the Basque Country speak Euskara, 87 per cent wish their children to be taught it (31 per cent as the language of educational instruction, another 30 per cent as a compulsory subject and another 26 per cent as an optional subject) (Keating 1996: 142).

23 In response to the death of an ETA leader in a clash with the Spanish Civil Guard, ETA assassinated a police officer known to torture prisoners. The government imposed martial law and a repressive campaign. The Burgos trial of fourteen ETA members and two priests resulted in six death sentences (subsequently reprieved by Franco), and became a symbol of anti-Francoism which increased Basque unity in support for ETA (Letamendia 1995: 184–5, Sullivan 1988: Ch. 4).

24 Net in-migration was 44.5 per 1,000 in 1911–20, 31.1 In 1921–30, it was per 1,000, 12.2 per 1,000 in 1931–30 and 25.6 per 1,000 in 1941–50. It then rose dramatically to 174 per 1,000 in 1951–60, and 159.6 per 1,000 in 1961–70 (Medrano 1995: 120).

25 In 1981, 57.31 per cent of immigrants were blue-collar workers (compared to 36.51 per cent of natives) (Medrano 1995: 120–1). The shift in ETA ideology was a gradual and difficult one, moving, between the late 1960s and the early 1970s, from calls for the inclusion of migrants so long as they assimilated (in Krutvig's formulations), towards a more fully socialist call for solidarity with non-Basque workers.

26 The Basque Country GDP growth rate went from 7.6 per cent per year from 1960 to 1973, to 0.7 per cent per year for the 1973–85 period. The impact of this was to raise overall unemployment from 4 per cent in 1976 to 23.55 per cent in 1986 (Medrano 1995: 122).

27 These were provided for in the December 1978 Constitution and the 1979 'Statute of Guernica'.

28 For the factionalism within ETA, see Letamendia (1995), also Sullivan (1988). The argument presented here, that it was ideological ambiguities which engendered the intense factionalism of Basque nationalism in the 1970s and 1980s, can be compared with Conversi's explanation of the violence of radical Basque nationalism in this period. He argues that it was the cultural fragmentation of Basque nationalist identity, relating to its diverse racial, linguistic and religious bases, which engendered the ideological impasse of ETA, thus allowing the initiative to be taken by its most violent factions. Conversi also examines other factors promoting ETA violence (1997: 222–56).

29 ETA resumed violence in December 1999 in response to the lack of concessions from the Spanish government.

30 The PNV won 28.01 per cent of the vote, *Euskal Herritarrok* (the renamed *Herri Batasuna*) won 17.91 per cent, and *Eusko Alkartasuna* won 8.69 per cent. PNV and EA formed a minority coalition government, with the support of EH. In the March 2000 general elections, 30% voted for the PNV, and 28% for the PP; 36% abstained. If the level of support for HB is taken as a rough indicator of sympathy for ETA violence, then it is significant that it fell from 15–18% between 1977 and 1993 to 12% in 1996. In 1998 when ETA renounced violence, support for HB rose to 17.9%. In 2000, after ETA resumed violence HB's boycott resulted in 8% more abstentions in 1996. But since such abstentions rose throughout the country, support for HB appears to have fallen below 8%.

31 This point was made by Jaime Pastor and Maria Paz Felton in the session on Basque Nationalism at the September 1999 conference on Nationalism, Identity and Minority Rights, Bristol University UK.

32 The other factors include the impact of the post-1993 Spanish economic recovery in reducing unemployment, and thence in reducing tensions relating to immigration; and the impact of events relating to Quebec, German unification and the 1998 Northern Ireland pact, in promoting the reaction against political violence and in favour of attempts at negotiated independence.

33 Economic growth, the effective promotion of Euskara, and the gaining of further autonomy concessions for the region in 1996, have all facilitated the emergence of increased Basque self-confidence.

34 While only 26 per cent of those in the Basque Country are Euskara speakers, 35 per cent of parents choose to have their primary and nursery schoolchildren educated completely in the medium of Euskara, and another 28 per cent chose Euskara–Castilian bilingual (63 per cent overall). The figures are from Eustat 1996, and are cited in van Amersfoort and Mansvelt Beck (1999). Keating's figures indicate, that in 1994, over half of those parents not choosing Euskara as a language of instruction, nevertheless wished their children to be taught Euskara as a compulsory subject (1996: 142).

35 Heiberg (1989) and Hans van Amersfoort and Jan Mansvelt Beck (1999) are also pessimistic about the prospects for a 'depolarisation' of Basque politics. They suggest that the end of the involvement of Spanish parties in Basque governing coalitions, together with the promotion of Euskara, might promote polarisation between the nationalist parties and the Spanish parties.

36 This is specified in the September 1998 Declaration of Lizarra.

37 This includes those who give Basque as their sole identity and those who identify themselves as 'more Basque than Spanish'. Van Amersfoort and Mansvelt Beck (1999) derive their figure of 75 per cent from a 1995 survey by R.E. Bourhis. This figure represents a significant (20 per cent to 25 per cent) increase in Basque self-identification compared to figures for 1979 (47.7 per cent), 1988 (52 per cent) and 1991 (51.2 per cent) (Medrano 1995: 175).

38 It is important to note that while pride in the Euskara language is the main *symbol* of Basque nationalism, the main *marker* of Basque identity is residence or birth in the Basque Country. Only about one-third of Euskara speakers, and one eighth of non-Euskara speakers, give language as the main identity marker. These figures are quoted in van Amersfoort and Mansvelt Beck (1999).

5 Globalisation and nationalism

1 The quotation is adapted from Gellner (1983: 140). Gellner is important precisely because he brought together the idea of the nation as the political unit engendered by industrialisation, with the idea of the state as the key manager of national consciousness.

2 The concept of the mobilisation system derives from David Apter (1965).

3 In terms of homeland origin and linguistic affiliation, Singapore society is made up of mainly Hokkien, Teochew and Cantonese Chinese (78 per cent); Malays, incuding Javanese and Boyanese (14 per cent); Indians, mainly Tamils, Malayalees and Punjabis (7 per cent); Eurasians of mixed origins; and expatriates. Religious affiliations include Taoist, Buddhist, Islamic, Christian, Hindu and Sikh.

4 This comment by Tremewan might derive from accepting, at face value, the regime's own addiction to the language of crisis and insecurity, in which every hiccup is depicted as potentially fatal.

5 Hill and Lian's analysis of the PAP's 'nation building' strategies, is useful, but the depiction of the shift from the initial civic nationalism to the later focus on ethnocultural nationalism, is inhibited by their use of Breton's distinction between 'cultural–symbolic' and 'civic–instrumental' dimensions of the construction of the nation. This leads Hill and Lian to understate the PAP's use of civic symbolism, and to broaden their conceptualisation of ethnocultural nationalism so as to incorporate aspects of civic nationalism.

6 Direct state expenditure on social security programmes has been relatively low, although welfare funds are also distributed indirectly through the ethnic associations (Ramesh 1995b, Asher 1993).

7 Voting is compulsory. In 1997, the PAP got 64.9 per cent of the valid vote in the contested constituencies. This compares with 61 per cent in 1991.

8 See also Bruce Gale's comment on the 1997 election result that 'Singaporeans

appeared to have been voting for stability and material comforts as in (housing) upgrading' (*West Australian*, 8 January 1997: 15).

9 As in the annual National Day ceremonies, and in the government's glossy publication, *Singapore, The Next Lap* (1991).

10 The terminology is that employed by O'Donnell (1979).

11 The Chinese Development Assistance Council (CDAC) was formed in 1991. The Council for Malay Education (Mendaki) was formed in 1981. In 1989, it was strengthened and renamed the Council for the Development of the Singaporean Muslim Community (Mendaki II). The Singapore Indian Development Association (SINDA) was formed in 1991. The Eurasian Association was founded in 1994 (Brown 1994).

12 Tan Wah Piow, a student leader, was convicted in 1974 of inciting workers, and subsequently fled to London. Vincent Cheng was accused of leading the 1987 'Marxist conspiracy', for which Tang Fong Har and Teo Soh Lung was also detained. J.B. Jeyaretnam was elected the sole opposition MP in 1982. He was found guilty of contempt of parliament in 1986, fined and disbarred from standing for parliament. Francis Seow is a former Solicitor-General, who, as president of the Law Society, was critical of government legislation and acted as counsel for some of the 'Marxist conspiracy' in 1987. Tang Liang Hong was an opposition candidate in the 1997 elections, and Chee Soon Juan in the 1994 and 1997 elections. For details of the consequences for them, and others, see Chee (1998) and Seow (1994).

13 'Kiasu' is Hokkien for 'scared to lose', and refers to an anxious, anti-social selfishness (Chia *et al.* 1985).

6 Reactive nationalism and the politics of development

1 This chapter is a revised version of a paper delivered at the Annual Conference of the Australasian Political Science Association, Flinders University, Adelaide, 1997. I am grateful to John Dunn, Cherry Gertzel and Richard Jeffries for the comments on this paper.

2 The *Mfantsi Amanbuhu Fekuw* (Fanti National Political Society) was formed as a ethnocultural nationalist society in 1889. It developed into the Gold Coast Aborigine Rights Protection Society, formed in 1897 (Kimble, 1963: 150). The National Congress of British West Africa was formed in 1917, based primarily on emergent Pan-Africanist ideas (Kimble 1963: 150 and 358–403).

3 The official figure for the 1992 elections was a turnout of 48 per cent of registered voters, but Jeffries and Thomas suggest that the figure of 60 per cent would be more realistic (1993: 350). The turnout for the 1987/8 district elections was also high, at 59 per cent of registered voters. This compares with earlier, low turnouts of 18.4 per cent in the 1978 district elections and of 35.3 per cent in the 1979 parliamentary elections, which had been interpreted as evidence of public alienation from the previous regimes (Ninsin 1993).

4 Inflation rose from 27.7 per cent in 1993 to 70.8 per cent in 1995. Thereafter, it fell, to 20.8 per cent by 1997.

5 The issue of ethnic perceptions, noted here by Bawumia, is examined below (see pp. 122–3).

6 This discussion of garrison nationalism builds upon an earlier work (Brown 1984); and much of the material on the use of ideologies of Ewe tribalism in Ghana prior to 1982 derives from Brown (1982).

7 Ghana's administrative structure has meant that development resources have been allocated on a regional basis. Ghana's administrative regions were constructed so as to approximate the linguistic, cultural and political bases for traditional communities. Thus, the Asante, Brong and Fanti subgroups of the Akan (44 per cent) predominate in, respectively, the Ashanti, Brong-Ahafo and Western Regions; the Ga (8 per cent) are clustered mainly in Accra; the Ewe (13 per cent) predominate in the Volta Region;

and the Mole-Dagbani (16 per cent) predominate in the Northern, Upper-West and Upper-East Regions.

8 National solidarity had been mobilised after Rawlings's initial *coup* in 1979, in reaction to Nigeria's imposition of an oil embargo. Similarly, after the second *coup*, the regime mobilised national solidarity against Nigeria's deportation of Ghanaians in January 1983.

9 This 'house-cleaning' legitimation strategy is depicted by Hayward and Dumbuya (1984) as a case of the exploitation of charisma.

10 Rawlings has, however, continued to voice 'equivocation' concerning 'crookery in business', in order to retain his credibility with the subordinate classes (Tangri 1992). The term *kalebule* refers to the manipulation of state licences and controls in order to defraud the state and divert resources to oneself.

11 The quotation is from an election speech by Pat Pomary, the successful NDC candidate for Hohoe South Constituency.

12 In the 1969 elections, only the non-Ewes of the north of the Volta region, in Krachi and Nkwanta, had returned majorities for the Ashanti candidate, Busia, rather than for the Ewe candidate, Gbedemah.

13 Such patronage politics (and the failures of patrons to deliver on their promises) has contributed to ethnic conflict most notably as regards tensions between the Konkomba and various Dagomba, Gonja and Nanumba communities, in the northern and upper regions. Both in 1981 and in 1994, this resulted in violent conflicts. A similar outbreak of ethnic violence, this time over a land-ownership dispute, occurred in Brong-Ahafo in 1997.

14 Richard Sandbrook offers a brief summary of the regime's repressive stance towards civil society, but concludes 'that intermediary organizations [of civil society] can build their capacities even in difficult circumstances . . . the Ghanaian experience of institutional development gives some grounds for hope' (1997).

15 Many Akan traditions relating to chieftaincy, including the kente cloth, were adopted by the Ewes during pre-colonial periods of Ashanti domination, so that the employment of such regalia can symbolise the linkages between Ewe and Akan.

7 Contentious visions

1 In the discussion which follows, the term 'multiculturalism' encompasses the kind of claims made by immigrant minorities, as well as those made by distinct indigenous homeland communities.

2 One test of the acceptability, for liberals, of the state's support for ethnic minority group rights, is implied in the following passage from John Rawls (1993):

> The question is this, if some [ethnic minority] conceptions will die out and others survive only barely in a just constitutional regime, does this not by itself imply that its political conception of justice is not fair to them? . . . [W]e may regret some of the inevitable affects of our culture and social structure . . . there is no social world without loss . . . But these social necessities are not to be taken for arbitrary bias or injustice . . . If a[n ethnic minority] comprehensive conception of the good is unable to endure in a society securing the familiar equal basic liberties and mutual toleration, there is no way to preserve it consistent with democratic values as expressed by the idea of society as a fair system of cooperation among citizens viewed as free and equal.
>
> (197–8).

3 The main features of consociationalism, as elaborated by Lijphart, are government by grand coalition, segmental autonomy, proportionality and mutual veto.

4 As with Maori 'biculturalist' claims in New Zealand, discussed in Young (1995).

5 See Chapter 3.

6   Threats to a majority ethnocultural community, may come not only from perceptions of affirmative action in favour of ethnic minorities, but also from fears of a cultural globalisation process (usually thought of as Americanisation).

8 How can the state respond to nationalist contention?

1 In the discussion which follows, the politics arising from minority rights claims in Australia are illustrated with references both to the claims of migrant ethnic minorities, and also to the claims of Australian Aboriginals. This is based on the inclusion of both groups in the official multiculturalism policy, despite the fact that there are important differences between them in their circumstances and in government policies.

2 Maniolesco saw corporatism as an extension of Roman systems of state–society relationship, and Wiarda (1981) traces the concept to ancient Greece and to the Thomistic–Christian ideas of Christian hierarchy. Newman (1981) locates its origin in the 'spirit of feudalism' and then in the development of *Standestaat* (estate-based states) structured around the tripartite relationship between monarch, aristocracy and burghers.

3 Otto Newman notes intimations of such a version of the corporatist model, leading in the direction of the management of ethnic diversity rather than the management of economic strife, in the work of Spann (1938), who evinced 'distinctive veneration for the qualities characteristic of the ancient Teutonic tribes . . . Notions of 'blood' 'honour' and 'folk' (Newman 1981: 11).

4 Proponents of economic-focused corporatism would of course object to such a reversion of the concept to its earlier concern with the management of moral identities. Cawson suggests that the concept is only relevant to the state's relationship with producer groups because their collaboration with the state is crucial to this primary area of state policy, and because such economic interest groups are 'purposive–rational' in their willingness to enter into whichever relationships with the state best promote their interests, and are capable of membership-based political organisation (1986: 179). Williamson concurs with this, but recognises that corporatism 'may indirectly impinge upon [the state's] distribution and legitimation functions' (1985: 172). Moreover, Williamson is reluctant to restrict corporatism totally to the production sphere. He recognises that each of his three 'varieties of corporatism' share common elements, the most fundamental being the state's management of particular demands by identifying itself with 'a particular socio-economic order over and above popular and particular interests' (1985: 191). This seems to indicate that, even in the economic-focused version of corporatism, the state must structure the stratification of society so as to assert the moral priority of the nation, the embodiment of the common good, over its constituent parts.

5 There are various reasons for the shift to these pro-Chinese policies, but they relate to the fact that Singaporean national identity had previously been based mainly on the English language and Western culture, more than on the language and culture of its ethnic majority. This meant that the Chinese (dialect)-speaking majority have developed something of a 'minority mentality', so that the state has been impelled towards policies which will display its pro-Chinese credentials, using Mandarin to act as a bridge between the dialect-speaking populace and the English-educated élites.

6 An additional danger is that, the more the state takes the responsibility for managing ethnic rights claims, the more the relevant ethnic community loses a sense of responsibility for their own destiny, and develops a dependency mentality. Hence the claim in Australia that 'about three-quarters of the Aboriginal population is now totally dependent on government . . . The concept of volunteerism has disappeared' (Valadian 1990: 590).

7 Previously within the Prime Minister's Department, but absorbed into the Immigration and Ethnic Affairs Department by the new Liberal government in 1996.

8 Further festivals, which seem to offer symbols of national unity, but which instead

become focal points for disunity, are the 2000 Sydney Olympic Games and the 2001 Centenary of Federation.

9　The official principles of Australian Multiculturalism are laid out in the 1995 Report of the National Multicultural Advisory Council, and are similar to those previously indicated in the 1988 National Agenda. The ten 1995 principles are all compatible with the norms of civic nationalism, in that the calls for respect for cultural diversity refer only to the right of individuals to express their cultural heritage, and for this to be respected by all institutions. There is no advocacy of affirmative action, and no call for the public and political institutions to reflect and promote ethnic distinctions (NMAC 1995).

10　This issue is the subject of ongoing research, and these points are indeed only tentative conclusions derived from an initial pilot survey of university students, which cannot be regarded as constituting significant evidence. Respondents were offered five statements favouring each nationalist vision, and agreement with four out of five statements in one category was regarded as showing 'consistent' support for that vision. Accepting the provisional basis for the findings, the actual results were that 52 per cent consistently adhered to only one of the three nationalist visions, and within this category, 37 per cent adhered solely to the civic nationalist vision, while 14 per cent adhered solely to the multicultural nationalist vision. Sole adherence to the ethnocultural nationalist vision was extremely small (3 per cent), and consistent support for ethnocultural nationalism was low (12 per cent).

　　It is noteworthy, however, that as many as 78 per cent of respondents supported at least one ethnocultural nationalist statement, which is comparable with the various national surveys conducted in the 1990s indicating support for individual pro-assimilationist statements varying between 59 per cent and 87 per cent (NMAC, 1999, Statistical Appendix, Table 8). If it were accepted that support for a single pro-assimilationist statement is a weaker measure of adherence to ethnocultural nationalism than is consistent support for a set of such statements, then the implication would be that the extent of present support for the ethnocultural nationalist vision might have hitherto been exaggerated. But a fuller study is needed to confirm this.

11　An earlier version of this chapter was presented to a conference on Nationalism at Sydney University, in July 1996. This analogy was suggested by Liah Greenfeld in her comments on this paper, during her concluding remarks as keynote speaker at the conference.

12　This would not apply to the UK (as opposed to Britain), in that the presence of the UK state in Northern Ireland was perceived in ethnocultural (Protestant) terms, so that the minority (Catholic) response has indeed been a strident one.

13　The Australian case has been used to illustrate the corporatist politics of multi-culturalism, since the state deals with multicultural and Aboriginal affairs primarily by acting as the manager of the corporatist institutions inherited from previous governments. But the present government would clearly prefer a pluralist stance, and reverts to it wherever possible.

14　Some shift towards a pluralist stance has been evident in the area of Aboriginal 'reconciliation'. The Howard government retreated from its initial rejection of Aboriginal demands for a Constitutional Preamble recognising Aboriginal 'custodianship' of the land, and a formal government 'apology' for the impact of past policies on Aboriginals, by accepting (in August 1999) compromise wordings, suggested by others (most notably by the Aboriginal Senator, Aden Ridgeway), which might be understood differentially by the contending parties. The phrase 'kinship with the land' was intended to reduce the fears of those who saw 'custodianship' as suggesting an Aboriginal veto power over land use, while still being interpreted by Aboriginals as a strong term expressive of indigenous culture. Similarly, the parliamentary resolution expressing 'deep and sincere regret' was intended to satisfy those calling for a formal government 'apology' and 'restitution', while appeasing those who insist that present generations are not responsible for the sins of previous generations, and who suspect that calls for an apology might provide a legal basis for subsequent calls for financial compensation. It remains to be seen how effective such pluralist compromise will be in reconciling both sides.

Appendix

1 Pauline Hanson's maiden speech in the Australian House of Representatives, 10 September 1996. House of Representatives Official Hansard. Available HTTP: <http://www.penrithcity.nsw.gov.au/Services/hanson.html> (accessed 18 November 1998).

2 There is no consensus as to whether Australia's indigenous people should be referred to as one Aboriginal nation or as several distinct linguistic–regional nations (Noongar, Murri, Koori, etc.). When they are referred to as one community, there is similarly no consensus as to whether the term should be Aboriginal, Aborigines, Aborigines and Torres Strait Islanders, or Indigenous Australians.

3 Voting for Aborigines was voluntary after 1962, whereas voting had been compulsory for other Australians since 1925. It has only been since 1984 that Aborigines and other Australians have voted on the same compulsory basis.

4 The revision was to Section 51 xxvi of the Constitution. While it seems likely that in 1967 most Australians understood the referendum to be simply removing a constitutional clause which discriminated against Aborigines, it is significant that the predominant contemporary view of the referendum is that it empowered the federal government to make special affirmative action provision for Aborigines.

5 The assimilation policy was officially adopted by federal and state governments in 1937, and sought to "absorb" "half-caste" Aborigines into white society, while "full blood" Aborigines were assumed to be a dying race. The policy was reaffirmed in 1951 as applicable to all indigenous groups, and was only officially abandoned in 1972.

6 In the Australian context, the term 'multiculturalism' is used primarily to refer to the celebration of the different cultures of the various immigrant minorities, rather than to relations between settler and indigenous communities. Less frequently, it is used, as here, to refer to the recognition of the rights of all cultural minorities, both migrant and indigenous.

7 ATSIC was formed in 1989 to replace the earlier National Aboriginal Council. ATSIC functions both as a channel for the distribution of government grants and loans, and as an elected body representing the various Aboriginal communities.

8 The 1992 *Mabo* decision overturned the doctrine of *terra nullius* (that, at the time of European settlement, Aborigines had no land rights), and led to the 1993 Native Title Act, which sought to define Aboriginal land rights. When the 1996 *Wik* decision exposed an inadequacy in that Act by suggesting that Aboriginal native title could coexist with pastoral leases, the government moved to define the relationship between the two in the 1998 Native Title Amendment Act.

9 This made Australia the first Western government to be asked to explain its racial policies under the CERD's early warning and urgent action procedures.

10 It should be noted that some Aboriginal activists share the view that state provisions for Aborigines have generated a dependency mentality. Noel Pearson, the activist who had called the Howard government 'racist scum' in 1998, stated publicly in 1999 that 'Since the 1967 referendum, Aboriginal people have believed their right earned (in the referendum) was the right to drink . . . In the 1950s and 1960s, our people worked hard in the hot sun for red-necked pastoralists, and people placed value on every penny earned . . . Welfare is a resource that is laced with poison and the poison present is the money-for-nothing principle' (quoted in *The Weekend Australian*, 1–2 May 1999: 3).

11 Pauline Hanson, speech on 'The UN Draft Declaration on the Rights of Indigenous Peoples' 2 June 1998, House of Representatives. Available HTTP: <http: //www.gwb.com.au/onenation/landttle.html> (accessed 18 November 1998).

12 The Ulster Unionist Party 'requires the immediate unilateral withdrawal of the Irish Republic's territorial claim over Northern Ireland as contained in Articles 2 and 3 of their constitution'. Available HTTP:
<http://www.uup.org/text/static/policy.html> (accessed 5 May 1999).

13 'Symbols used in Northern Ireland – Unionist and Loyalist Symbols', CAIN Web Service. Available HTTP:
<http://www.cain.ulst.ac.uk/images/symbols/unionloyal.html> (accessed 5 May 1999).

14 <http://www.sinnfein.ie/documents/freedom.html1#civ/page2.html> (accessed 15 November 1998).

15 The Special Powers Act was repealed in 1973, but the Emergency Provision and Prevention of Terrorism legislation which replaced it was regarded by Sinn Fein as even more repressive. Available HTTP:
<http://www.sinnfein.ie/documents/freedom.html1#civ/page7.html> (accessed 15 November 1998).

16 Quoted in Jefferson (1992: 63).

17 Quoted in Hilsum (1994: 14).

18 Quoted in Mandami (1996): 21.

19 Quoted in Mutaboba (1994): 6.

20 Quoted in Mandami (1996): 5.

21 Quoted in Morrisby (1988): 34.

22 The Institute of History, Prishtina (1999) 'Expulsions of Albanians and colonisation of Kosova',
<http://www.kosova.com/expuls/conclus.html> (accessed 21 April 1999).

23 The Institute of History, Prishtina 'Expulsions of Albanians and colonisation of Kosova',
<http://www.kosova.com/expuls/conclus.html> (accessed 21 April 1999).

24 Serbia Info News – Kosovo and Metohia (1999) 'History',
<http://www.serbia-info.com/news/kosovo/facts/history.html> (accessed 21 April 1999).

25 Serbia Info News – Kosovo and Metohia (1999) 'Why a New Albanian State',
<http://www.serbia-info.com/news/kosovo/facts/state.html> (accessed 21 April 1999).

26 Serbia Info News – Kosovo and Metohia (1999) 'History',
<http://www.serbia info.com/news/kosovo/facts/history.html> (accessed 21 April 1999).

Bibliography

Acheampong, I.K. 1973. *Speeches and Interviews Vol.1*. Ghana, Information Services Department.

Adams P. 1995. 'Ghana: Cycle of Dependency?', *Africa Report* 40(2): 35–7.

Agyeman-Duah, B. 1987. 'The Politics of the PNDC', *The Journal of Modern African Studies* 25(4): 613–42.

Alagappa, M. (ed.) 1995. *Political Legitimacy in Southeast Asia: The Quest for Moral Authority*. Stanford, Stanford University Press.

Almond, G. and Verba, S. 1963. *The Civic Culture*. Princeton, Princeton University Press.

Alter, P. 1989. *Nationalism*. London: Edward Arnold.

Amin, S. 1980. *Class and Nation*. New York, Monthly Review Press.

Anderson, B. 1983. *Imagined Communities*. London, Verso.

Apter, D.E. 1963. *Ghana in Transition*. New York, Atheneum.

Apter, D.E. 1965. *The Politics of Modernisation*. Chicago, Chicago University Press.

Armstrong, J. 1995. 'Towards a Theory of Nationalism: Consensus and Dissensus' in S. Periwal (ed.), *Notions of Nationalism*. Budapest, Central European University Press.

Asher, M. 1993. 'Planning for the Future: The Welfare System in a New Phase of Development', in G. Rodan (ed.), *Singapore Changes Guard*. Melbourne, Longman Cheshire.

Austin, D. 1970. *Politics in Ghana, 1946–60*. London, Oxford University Press.

Barry, B. 1975. 'The Consociational Model and its Dangers', *European Journal of Political Research* 3(4): 393–412.

Bauman, Z. 1995. 'Searching for a Centre that Holds' in M. Featherstone, S. Lash, and R. Robertson (eds), *Global Modernities*. London, Sage.

Bawumia, M. 1998. 'Understanding the Rural–Urban Voting Patterns in the 1992 Ghanaian Election: A Closer Look at the Distributional Impact of Ghana's Structural Adjustment Programme', *The Journal of Modern African Studies* 36(1): 47–70.

Baynham, S. 1985. 'Divide et Impera: Civilian Control of the Military in Ghana's Second and Third Republics', *The Journal of Modern African Studies* 23(4): 623–42.

Bell, D., Brown, D., Jayasuriya, K. and Jones, D.M. 1995. *Towards Illiberal Democracy in Pacific Asia*. London, Macmillan.

Bellows, T.J. 1995. 'Globalization and Regionalization in Singapore: A Public Policy Perspective', *Asian Journal of Political Science* 3(3): 46–65.

Benjamin, G. 1976. 'The Cultural Logic of Singapore's Multiculturalism', in R. Hassan (ed.), *Singapore: Society in Transition*. Kuala Lumpur, Oxford University Press.

Benner, E. 1995. *Really Existing Nationalisms: A Post Communist View of Marx and Engels*. Oxford, Clarendon Press.

Bentsi-Enchill, N.K. 1980. 'Business as Usual', *West Africa* 10 March: 436–7.

Berberoglu, B. (ed.) 1995. *The National Question: Nationalism, Ethnic Conflict and Self-Determination in the 20th Century.* Philadelphia, Temple University Press.

Berman, B.J. 1998. 'Ethnicity, Patronage, and the African State: The Politics of Uncivil Nationalism', *African Affairs* 97(388): 305–41.

Betts, K. 1999. *The Great Divide: Immigration Politics in Australia.* Sydney, Duffy and Snellgrove.

Bienefeld, M. 1995. 'Structural Adjustment and the Prospects for Democracy in Southern Africa', in D. Moore and G. Schmitz (eds), *Debating Development Discourse: Institutional and Popular Perspectives.* London, Macmillan.

Birrell, R. 1995. 'The Dynamics of Multiculturalism in Australia', in D.W. Lovell, I. McAllister, W. Maley, C. Kukathas (eds), *The Australian Political System.* Melbourne, Longman.

Black, A. 1988. *State, Community and Human Desire.* Hemel Hempstead, Harvester-Wheatsheaf.

Blaut, J. 1987. *The National Question.* London, Zed.

Brass, P. 1985. 'Ethnic Groups and the State', in P. Brass (ed.), *Ethnic Groups and the State.* London, Croom Helm.

Brass, P. 1991. *Ethnicity and Nationalism: Theory and Comparison.* New Delhi, Sage.

Breuilly, J. 1982. *Nationalism and the State.* Manchester, Manchester University Press.

Brown, D. 1980a. 'Borderline Politics in Ghana: The National Liberation Movement of Western Togoland', *Journal of Modern African Studies* 18(4): 575–610.

Brown, D. 1980b. 'The Political Response to Immiseration: A Case Study of Rural Ghana', *Génève-Afrique* 18(1): 55–74.

Brown, D. 1982. 'Who are the Tribalists? Social Pluralism and Political Ideology in Ghana', *African Affairs* 81(322): 37–69.

Brown, D. 1984. *The Legitimacy of Government in Plural Societies.* Occasional Paper No. 43, Department of Political Science, National University of Singapore.

Brown, D. 1994. *The State and Ethnic Politics in Southeast Asia.* London, Routledge.

Brubaker, R. 1996. *Nationalism Reframed: Nationhood and the National Question in the New Europe.* Cambridge, Cambridge University Press.

Bullivant, B.M. 1989. 'The Pluralist Crisis Facing Australia', *Australian Quarterly* 61(2): 121–8.

Cable, V. 1996. 'Globalisation: Can the State Strike Back?', *The World Today* 52, (5): 133–7.

Campbell, A. (ed.) 1976. *The Portable Jung.* Harmondsworth: Penguin.

Canovan, M. 1996. *Nationhood and Political Theory.* Cheltenham, Glos., Edward Elgar.

Carr, R. 1966. *Spain 1808–1939.* Oxford, Clarendon Press.

Castles, S., Cope, B., Kalantzis, M. and Morrissey, W. 1990. *Mistaken Identity: Multiculturalism and the Demise of Nationalism in Australia.* Sydney, Pluto Press.

Cawson, A. 1986. *Corporatism and Political Theory.* London, Blackwell.

Cerny, P.G. 1994. 'The Dynamics of Financial Globalisation: Technology, Market Structure, and Policy Response', *Policy Sciences* 27: 319–42.

Chapman, M. 1993. 'Social and Biological Aspects of Ethnicity', in M. Chapman (ed.), *Social and Biological Aspects of Ethnicity.* Oxford: Oxford University Press.

Chazan, N. 1983. *An Anatomy of Ghanaian Politics: Managing Political Recession, 1969–82.* Boulder, Westview.

Chee, S.J. 1998. *To be Free: Stories from Asia's Struggle against Oppression.* Melbourne, Monash Asia Institute.

Chia, C., Wong, P.M., Seet, K.K., 1985. *Made in Singapore.* Singapore, Times.

Chin, J. 1997. 'Anti-Christian Chinese Chauvinists and HDP Upgrades: The 1997 Singapore General Election', *South East Asia Research* 5(3): 217–41.

Chua, B.H. 1993. 'The Changing Shape of Civil Society in Singapore' *Commentary* (Journal of the National University of Singapore Society, Singapore) 11: 9–14.

Chua, B.H. 1995. *Communitarian Ideology and Democracy in Singapore.* London, Routledge.

Clark, R.P. 1979. *The Basques: The Franco Years and Beyond.* Reno, University of Nevada Press.

Connor, W. 1994. *Ethnonationalism: The Quest for Understanding.* Princeton, Princeton University Press.

Conversi, D. 1990. 'Language or Race?: The Choice of Core Values in the Development of Catalan and Basque Nationalisms', *Ethnic and Racial Studies* 13(1): 50–70.

Conversi, D. 1997. *The Basques, the Catalans and Spain: Alternative Routes to Nationalist Mobilisation.* London, Hurst.

Dahbour, O. and Ishay. M.R. (eds) 1995. *The Nationalism Reader.* New Jersey, Humanities Press.

Davidson, A. 1997. 'Multiculturalism and Citizenship: Silencing the Migrant Voice', *Journal of Intercultural Studies* 18(2): 77–92.

Davis, J. 1996, 'Irrationality in Social Life', in J.A. Hall and I. Jarvie (eds), *The Social Philosophy of Ernest Gellner.* Amsterdam, Radopi.

De Rafael G.H. 1998. 'An Empirical Survey of Social Structure and Nationalistic Identification in Spain', *Nations and Nationalism* 4(1): 35–59.

De Tocqueville, A. 1840. *Democracy in America, vol. 1 and vol. 2.* New York, Vintage.

Deutsch, K.W. 1966. *Nationalism and Social Communication,* Cambridge, Mass., MIT Press.

Dietz, M.G. 1989. 'Patriotism', in T. Ball, J. Farr and R. Hanson (eds) *Political Innovation and Conceptual Change.* Cambridge, Cambridge University Press.

Dikotter, F. 1990. 'The Idea of Race in Modern China', *Ethnic and Racial Studies* 13(3): 421–31.

Drucker, P. 1997. 'The Global Economy and the Nation-State', *Foreign Affairs* 76(5): 159–71.

Dunn, J. 1980. *Political Obligation in its Historical Context.* Cambridge, Cambridge University Press.

Dunn, J. (ed.) 1995. *Contemporary Crisis of the Nation State?* Oxford, Blackwell.

Eller, J.D. and Coughlan, R.M. 1993. 'The Poverty of Primordialism: The Demystification of Ethnic Attachments', *Ethnic and Racial Studies* 16(2): 183–201.

Escobar, A. 1992. 'Reflections on Development: Grassroots Approaches and Alternative Politics in the Third World', *Futures* 24(5): 411–34.

Feuer, L.S. (ed.) 1969. *Marx and Engels: Basic Writings on Politics and Philosophy.* London, Fontana, Collins.

Finlay, D. 1967. 'Ghana and the Politics of Ideological Justification' in D. Finlay, Holsti and Fagen (eds) *Enemies in Politics.* Rand McNally, Chicago.

Finlayson, I. 1998. 'Psychology, Psychoanalysis and Theories of Nationalism', *Nations and Nationalism* 4(2): 145–62.

Folson, K.G. 1993. 'Ideology, Revolution and Development', in E. Gyimah-Boadi (ed.), *Ghana Under PNDC Rule.* Chippenham, CODESRIA.

Freeden, M. 1998. 'Is Nationalism a Distinct Ideology?', *Political Studies* 46(4): 748–65.

Frimpong, K. 1997. 'Structural Adjustment and the Myth of its Success in Ghana', in K. R. Hope (ed.), *Structural Adjustment, Reconstruction and Development in Africa.* Brookfield USA, Ashgate.

Fromm, E. 1955. *The Sane Society.* New York, Fawcett.

Frosh, S. 1991. *Identity Crisis: Modernity, Psychoanalyis and Self.* Basingstoke, Macmillan.

Frosh, S. 1997. *For and Against Psychoanalysis.* London, Routledge.

Geertz, C. 1963. 'The Integrative Revolution: Primordial Sentiments and Civil Politics in the New States', in C. Geertz (ed.), *Old Societies and New States: The Quest for Modernity in Asia and Africa*. New York, Free Press.

Geertz, C. 1973. *The Interpretation of Cultures: Selected Essays*. New York, Basic Books.

Gellner, E. 1983. *Nations and Nationalism*. Oxford, Blackwell.

Gellner, E. 1996. 'Reply to Critics' in J.A. Hall and I. Jarvie (eds) *The Social Philosophy of Ernest Gellner*. Amsterdam, Radopi.

Gil-White. F.J. 1999. 'How Thick is Blood?', *Ethnic and Racial Studies* 22(5): 789–820.

Government of Singapore, 1991. *Singapore: The Next Lap*. Singapore, Times.

Gray, J., 1993. *Post-Liberalism: Studies in Political Thought*. London, Routledge.

Gray, J. 1994a. 'Against the World', *Guardian*, 4 January.

Gray, J. 1994b. 'After the New Liberalism', *Social Research* 61(3): 719–35.

Greenfeld, L. 1992. *Nationalism: Five Roads to Modernity*. Cambridge, Mass., Harvard University Press.

Greenwood, D.J. 1985. 'Castilians, Basques, and Andalusians: An Historical Comparison of Nationalism, "True" Ethnicity, and "False" Ethnicity', in P. Brass (ed.), *Ethnic Groups and the State*. London, Croom Helm.

Group for the Advancement of Psychiatry. 1987. *Us and Them: The Psychology of Ethnonationalism*. New York. Brunner/Mazel.

Guibernau, M. 1996. *Nationalisms: The Nation-State and Nationalism in the Twentieth Century*. Oxford: Polity Press.

Hall, J.A. and Jarvie, I. (eds). 1996. *The Social Philosophy of Ernest Gellner*. Amsterdam, Radopi.

Hansen, E. 1991. *Ghana Under Rawlings: Early Years*. Lagos, Malthouse.

Hargreaves, J. and Keating, M. 1998. 'A Reply to Keating on "Stateless Nation-Building in Catalonia, Quebec and Scotland"', *Nations and Nationalism* 4(4): 569–77.

Hastings, A. 1997. *The Construction of Nationhood: Ethnicity, Religion and Nationalism*. Cambridge, Cambridge University Press.

Hayes, C. 1949. *The Historical Evolution of Modern Nationalism*. New York, Macmillan.

Haynes, J. 1991. 'Human Rights and Democracy in Ghana: The Record of the Rawlings's Regime', *African Affairs* 90(3): 407–25.

Hayward, F.M. and Dumbuya, A.R. 1984. 'Political Legitimacy, Political Symbols, and National Leadership in West Africa', *The Journal of Modern African Studies* 21(4): 645–71.

Hechter, M. 1975. *Internal Colonialism: The Celtic Fringe in British National Development 1536–1966*. London, Routledge & Kegan Paul.

Hechter, M. 1986. 'Rational Choice Theory and the Study of Race and Ethnic Relations', in J. Rex and D. Mason (eds), *Theories of Race and Ethnic Relations*. Cambridge, Cambridge University Press.

Hechter, M. and Levi, M. 1979. 'The Comparative Analysis of Ethno-Regional Movements', *Ethnic and Racial Studies* 2(3): 260–74.

Heiberg, M. 1989. *The Making of the Basque Nation*. Cambridge, Cambridge University Press.

Heiberg, M. 1996. 'Basques, Anti-Basques, and the Moral Community', in G. Eley and R.G. Suny (eds), *Becoming National*. New York, Oxford University Press.

Held, D. 1984. *Political Theory and the Modern State*. Cambridge, Polity.

Held, D. 1994. 'Inequalities of Power, Problems of Democracy', in R. Miliband (ed.), *Reinventing the Left*. Cambridge, Polity.

Herbst, J. 1993. *The Politics of Reform in Ghana, 1982–91*. Berkeley, University of California.

Hill, M. and Lian, K.F. 1995. *The Politics of Nation Building and Citizenship in Singapore*. London, Routledge.

Hilsum, L. 1994. 'Settling Scores', *Africa Report* May–June.

Hindess, B. 1992 'Citizens and Peoples', *Australian Left Review* 140: 20–3.

Hirst, P. and Thompson, G. 1995. 'Globalisation and the Future of the Nation State', *Economy and Society* 24(3): 408–42.

Hobsbawm, E. 1990. *Nations and Nationalism Since 1780*. Cambridge, Cambridge University Press.

Hobsbawm, E. and Ranger, T. (eds) 1983. *The Invention of Tradition*. Cambridge, Cambridge University Press.

Holbrook, D. 1971. *Human Hope and the Death Instinct*. Oxford, Pergamon.

Horne, D. 1996. '2001: A Forgotten Odyssey', *Weekend Australian*, 1–2 June.

Horowitz, D. L. 1985. *Ethnic Groups in Conflict*. Los Angeles/London, University of California Press.

Hutchinson, J. 1987. *The Dynamics of Cultural Nationalism: The Gaelic Revival and the Creation of the Irish Nation State*. London, Allen & Unwin.

Hutchinson, J. 1994. *Modern Nationalism*, London, Fontana, Harper Collins.

Ignatieff, M. 1993. *Blood and Belonging: Journeys into the New Nationalism*. London, BBC Books, Chatto & Windus.

Immerfall, S. 1998. 'The Neo-Populist Agenda', in H.-G. Betz and S. Immerfall (eds), *The New Politics of the Right: Neo-Populist Parties and Movements in Established Democracies*. London, Macmillan.

Innes, J.M. 1997. *Extreme Opinions, Racist Behaviour and the Importance of Maintaining Community*. Inaugural professorial address, Perth, Murdoch University.

Jakubowicz, A. 1984. 'State and Ethnicity: Multi-Culturalism as Ideology', in J. Jupp (ed.), *Ethnic Politics in Australia*. Sydney, Allen & Unwin.

James, P. 1996. 'As Nation and State: A Postmodern Republic Takes Shape', in P. James (ed.), *The State in Question: Transformations of the Australian State*. Sydney, Allen & Unwin.

Jayasuriya, L. 1990. 'Rethinking Australian Multiculturalism: Towards a New Paradigm', in D.W. Lovell *et al.* (eds), *The Australian Political System*. Melbourne, Longman.

Jayasuriya, L. 1993. 'Australian Multiculturalism and Citizenship', Occasional Paper no. 1. Perth, Ethnic Communities Council of Western Australia.

Jefferson, N. 1992. 'The War Within', *Africa Report* January–February.

Jeffries, R. 1991. 'Leadership Commitment and Political Opposition to Structural Adjustment in Ghana', in D. Rothchild, *Ghana: The Political Economy of Recovery*. London, Lynne Rienner.

Jeffries, R. 1992. 'Urban Popular Attitudes towards the Economic Recovery Programme and the PNDC Government in Ghana', *African Affairs* 91(363): 207–26.

Jeffries, R. 1998. 'The Ghanaian Elections of 1996: Towards the Consolidation of Democracy?', *African Affairs* 97(387): 189–208.

Jeffries, R. and Thomas, C. 1993. 'The Ghanaian Elections of 1992', *African Affairs* 92(368): 331–6.

Jones D.M. and Brown, D. 1994. 'Singapore and the Myth of the Liberalising Middle Class', *The Pacific Review* 7(1): 79–87.

Jordan, A.G. 1983. 'Corporatism: The Unity and Utility of the Concept?', Strathclyde papers on government and politics, Dept. of Politics, Glasgow University.

Junco, J.A. 1996. 'The Nation-Building Process in Nineteenth-Century Spain', in C. Mar-Molinero and A. Smith (eds), *Nationalism and the Nation in the Iberian Peninsula: Competing and Conflicting Identities*. Oxford, Berg.

Keating, M. 1996. *Nations against the State: The New Politics of Nationalism in Quebec, Catalonia and Scotland*. London, Macmillan.

Kecmanovic, D. 1996. *The Mass Psychology of Ethnonationalism.* New York and London, Plenum Press.

Kedourie, E. 1993. *Nationalism.* Oxford, Blackwell.

Kellas, J.G. 1991. *The Politics of Nationalism and Ethnicity.* London, Macmillan.

Kimble, D. 1963. *A Political History of Ghana: The Rise of Gold Coast Nationalism 1850–1928.* Oxford, Clarendon Press.

Koelble, T. 1995. 'The New Institutionalism in Political Science and Sociology', *Comparative Politics* 27(2): 231–43.

Kohn, H. 1944. *The Idea of Nationalism.* New York, Macmillan.

Kohn, H. 1962. *The Age of Nationalism.* New York, Harper & Row.

Kristeva, J. 1993. *Nations without Nationalism.* New York, Columbia University Press.

Kukathas, C. 1990. 'Democracy, Parliament and Responsible Government', *Papers on Parliament No. 8*, Department of Senate, Canberra.

Kukathas, C. 1991. in D.W. Lovell *et al.* (eds), *The Australian Political System.* Melbourne, Longman.

Kukathas, C. 1995. 'Are There Any Cultural Rights?', in W. Kymlicka, (ed.), *The Rights of Minority Cultures.* Oxford, Oxford University Press.

Kuper, L. and Smith, M.G. (eds) 1969. *Pluralism in Africa.* Berkeley, University of California Press.

Kymlicka, W. 1989. *Liberalism, Community and Culture.* Oxford, Clarendon Press.

Kymlicka, W. 1995a. *Multicultural Citizenship: A Liberal Theory of Minority Rights.* Oxford, Clarendon Press.

Kymlicka, W. (ed.) 1995b. *The Rights of Minority Cultures.* Oxford, Oxford University Press.

Kymlicka, W. 1999. 'Misunderstanding Nationalism', in R. Beiner, (ed.), *Theorizing Nationalism.* Albany, State University of New York Press.

Kymlicka, W. (forthcoming). 'Western Political Theory and Ethnic Relations in Eastern Europe', in M. Opalski and W. Kymlicka (eds), *Can Liberal Pluralism be Exported?* Oxford, Oxford University Press.

Lasch, C. 1977. *Haven in a Heartless World: The Family Besieged.* New York, Basic Books.

Lasch, C. 1995. *The Revolt of the Elites and the Betrayal of Democracy.* New York, Norton.

Laxer, G. 1992. 'Constitutional Crises and Continentalism: Twin Threats to Canada's Continued Existence', *Canadian Journal of Sociology* 17(2): 199–222.

Letamendia, M. 1995. 'Basque Nationalism and the Struggle for Self-Determination in the Basque Country', in B. Berberoglu (ed.), *The National Question: Nationalism, Ethnic Conflict and Self-Determination in the 20th Century.* Philadelphia, Temple University Press.

Li, T. 1988. *Malays in Singapore: Culture, Economy and Ideology.* Singapore, Oxford University Press.

Lijphart, A. 1969. 'Consociational Democracy', *World Politics* 21(2): 207–25.

Lijphart, A. 1977. *Democracy in Plural Societies.* New Haven, Yale University Press.

Lijphart, A. 1995. 'Self-Determination versus Pre-Determination of Ethnic Minorities in Power-Sharing Systems', in W. Kymlicka. (ed.), *The Rights of Minority Cultures.* Oxford, Oxford University Press.

Lipset, S.M. 1960. *Political Man: The Social Basis of Politics.* Baltimore, Johns Hopkins University Press.

Llambi, L. and Gouveia, L. 1994. 'The Restructuring of the Venezualan State and State Theory', *International Journal of Sociology of Agriculture and Food* 4: 64–83.

Lovell, D.W., McAllister, I., Maley, W. and Kukathas, C. (eds) 1995. *The Australian Political System.* Melbourne, Longman.

MacClancy, J. 1993. 'Biological Basques, Sociologically Speaking', in M. Chapman (ed.), *Social and Biological Aspects of Ethnicity*. Oxford, Oxford University Press.

MacClancy, J. 1996. 'Bilingualism and Multinationalism in the Basque Country' in C. Mar-Molinero and A. Smith (eds), *Nationalism and the Nation in the Iberian Peninsula: Competing and Conflicting Identities*. Oxford, Berg.

Maganga, V.V. 1988. 'Representing Efficiency: Corporatism and Democratic Theory', *Review of Politics* 50(3): 420–41.

Makinda, S. 1996. 'Sovereignty and International Security: Challenges for the United Nations', *Global Governance* 2: 149–68.

Mandami, M. 1996. 'From Conquest to Consent as the Basis for State Formation: Reflections on Rwanda', *New Left Review*, 216.

Mann, M. 1996. 'The Emergence of Modern European Nationalism', in J.A. Hall and I.C. Jarvie (eds), *The Social Philosophy of Ernest Gellner*. Amsterdam, Rodopi.

Mann, M. 1997. 'Has Globalisation Ended the Rise and Rise of the Nation-State?', *Review of International Political Economy* 4(3): 472–96.

March, J.G. and Olsen, J.P. 1989. *Rediscovering Institutions: The Organizational Basis of Politics*. New York, Free Press.

Medhurst, K. 1972. *Minority Rights Group Report No. 9: The Basques*. London, Minority Rights Group.

Medrano, J.D. 1995. *Divided Nations: Class, Politics and Nationalism in the Basque Country and Catalonia*. Ithaca, Cornell University Press.

Meinecke, F. 1963. *The German Catastrophe: Reflections and Recollections*. Boston: Beacon Press (original edition, 1950).

Meinecke, F. 1972. *Historicism: The Rise of a New Historical Outlook*. London: Routledge & Kegan Paul (original edition 1959).

Mill, J.S. [1859–61] 1970. *Utilitarianism, On Liberty, and Essay on Bentham*, (ed.) M. Warnock. London, Fontana.

Miller, D. 1995. *On Nationality*. Oxford, Clarendon Press.

Minogue, K.R. 1967. *Nationalism*. London, Batsford.

Montana, B.T. 1996. 'Language and Basque Nationalism: Collective Identity, Social Conflict and Institutionalisation in Spain', in C. Mar-Molinero and A. Smith (eds), *Nationalism and the Nation in the Iberian Peninsula: Competing and Conflicting Identities*. Oxford, Berg.

Moodley, K. 1983. 'Canadian Multiculturalism as Ideology', *Ethnic and Racial Studies* 6(3): 320–31.

Moore, B. 1966. *The Social Origin of Dictatorship and Democracy*. Boston, Mass., Beacon Press.

Morrisby, E. 1988. 'Rwanda and Burundi: Massacres in the Third World, *Quadrant* October: 33–7.

Mutaboba, J. 1994. 'I am Rwandese', *New Internationalist*, October.

Nairn, T. 1977. *The Break Up of Britain: Crisis and Neo-Nationalism*. London, New Left Books.

Nairn, T. 1997. *Faces of Nationalism: Janus Revisited*. London, Verso.

Newman, O. 1981. *The Challenge of Corporatism*. London, Macmillan.

Ninsin, K.A. 1991. 'The PNDC and the Problem of Legitimacy', in D. Rothchild (ed.), *Ghana: The Political Economy of Recovery*. London, Lynn Rienner.

Ninsin, K.A. 1993. 'Strategies of Mobilisation under the PNDC Government', in E. Gyimah Boadi (ed.), *Ghana Under PNDC Rule*. Dakar, CODESRIA.

Nkrumah, K. 1962. *Towards Colonial Freedom*. London, Heinemann.

NMAC (National Multicultural Advisory Council), 1995. *Multicultural Australia: The Next Steps: Towards and Beyond 2000, vols 1 and 2*. Canberra, Commonwealth of Australia.

NMAC (National Multicultural Advisory Council), 1999. *Australian Multiculturalism for a New Century: Towards Inclusiveness.* Canberra, Commonwealth of Australia.

Nugent, P. 1995. *Big Men, Small Boys and Politics in Ghana: Power, Ideology and the Burden of History, 1982–94.* London, Pinter.

O'Donnell, G. 1979. 'Tensions in the Bureaucratic–Authoritarian State and the Question of Democracy', in D. Collier (ed.), *The New Authoritarianism in Latin America.* Princeton, Princeton University Press.

O'Donoghue, L. 1996. 'Who's Accountable to Whom?', *Weekend Australian,* 15–16 June.

Ohmae, K. 1995. *The End of the Nation State: The Rise of Regional Economies.* London, Harper Collins.

Panitch, L. 1980. 'Recent Theoretizations of Corporatism: Reflections on a Growth Industry', *British Journal of Sociology* 31(2): 159–87.

Parsons, S. 1988. 'On the Logic of Corporatism', *Political Studies* 36: 515–23.

Patten, A. 1999. 'The Autonomy Argument for Liberal Nationalism', *Nations and Nationalism* 5(1): 1–17.

Pellow, D. and Chazan, N. 1986. *Ghana: Coping with Uncertainty.* Boulder, Westview.

Periwal, S. (ed.) 1995. *Notions of Nationalism.* Budapest, Central European University Press.

Pooley, S. 1991. 'The State Rules OK? The Continuing Political Economy of Nation-States', *Capital and Class* 43: 65–77.

Potter, D. 1992. 'The Autonomy of Third World States within the Global Economy', in A.G. McGrew and P.G. Lewis (eds), *Global Politics: Globalisation and the Nation-State.* Cambridge, Polity.

Ramesh, M. 1995a. 'Economic Globalization and Policy Choices: Singapore', *Governance* 8(2): 243–60.

Ramesh, M. 1995b. 'Social Security in South Korea and Singapore: Explaining the Differences', *Social Policy and Administration* 29(3): 228–40.

Rawls, J. 1993. *Political Liberalism.* New York, Columbia University Press.

Ray, D.I. 1986. *Ghana: Politics, Economics and Society.* London, Pinter.

Rex, J. 1994. 'The Second Project of Ethnicity: Transnational Migrant Communities and Ethnic Minorities in Modern Multicultural Societies', *Innovations* 7(3): 207–17.

Reynolds, V., Falger, V. and Vine, I. (eds) 1987. *The Sociobiology of Ethnocentrism.* London, Croom Helm.

Rimmer, D. 1992. *Staying Poor: Ghana's Political Economy 1950–90.* Oxford, Pergamon.

Robertson, R. 1995. 'Glocalization: Time–Space and Homogeneity–Heterogeneity', in M. Featherstone, S. Lash, and R. Robertson (eds), *Global Modernities.* London, Sage.

Rodan, G. 1989. *The Political Economy of Singapore's Industrialisation: National State and International Capital.* London, Macmillan.

Ronen, D. 1979. *The Quest for Self-Determination.* New Haven, Yale University Press.

Ross, C. 1996. 'Nationalism and Party Competition in the Basque Country and Catalonia', *West European Politics* 19(3): 488–506.

Ross, R. 1995. 'The Theory of Global Capitalism: State Theory and Variants of Capitalism on a World Scale', in D. Smith and J. Borocz (eds), *A New World Order.* New York, Praeger.

Rothchild, D. 1994. 'Rawlings and the Engineering of Legitimacy in Ghana', in I.W. Zartman (ed.), *Collapsed States: The Disintegration and Restoration of Legitimate Authority.* Boulder, Lynn Rienner.

Rustow, D.A. 1967. *A World of Nations: Problems of Political Modernization.* Washington, Brookings Institute.

Salecl, R. 1990. 'National Identity and Socialist Moral Majority', *New Formations* 12: 25–31.

Sandbrook R. 1997. 'Economic Liberalisation versus Political Democratisation: A Social Democratic Resolution?' *The Journal of Modern African Studies* 31(3): 482–516.

Sandel, M. 1982. *Liberalism and the Limits of Justice*. Cambridge, Cambridge University Press.

Schmidt, V.A. 1995. 'The New World Order, Incorporated: The Rise of Business and the Decline of the Nation-State', *Daedalus* 124(2): 75–106.

Schmitter, P.C. 1979. 'Still the Century of Corporatism?' in P.C. Schmitter and G. Lehmbruch (eds), *Trends Towards Corporatist Intermediation*. London, Sage.

Seow, F.T. 1994. *To Catch a Tartar: A Dissident in Lee Kuan Yew's Prison*. New Haven, Yale University Press.

Seton-Watson, H. 1977. *Nations and States: An Enquiry into the Origins of Nations and the Politics of Nationalism*. Boulder, Westview Press.

Shaw, M. 1997. 'The State of Globalization: Towards a Theory of State Transformation', *Review of International Political Economy* 4(3): 497–513.

Shaw, R.P. and Wong, Y. 1989. *Genetic Seeds of Warfare: Evolution, Nationalism and Patriotism*. Boston, Unwin Hyman.

Sherwood, M. 1996. *Kwame Nkrumah: The Years Abroad 1935–1947*. Legon, Ghana, Freedom Publications.

Shillington, K. 1992. *Ghana and the Rawlings Factor*. London, Macmillan.

Shubert, A. 1990. *A Social History of Modern Spain*. London, Unwin Hyman.

Smith, A. and Mar-Molinero, C. 1996. 'The Myths and Realities of Nation-Building in the Iberian Peninsula' in C. Mar-Molinero and A. Smith (eds), *Nationalism and the Nation in the Iberian Peninsula: Competing and Conflicting Identities*. Oxford, Berg.

Smith, A.D. 1971. *Theories of Nationalism*. London, Camelot.

Smith, A.D. 1981. *The Ethnic Revival*. Cambridge, Cambridge University Press.

Smith, A.D. 1986. *The Ethnic Origins of Nations*. Oxford, Blackwell.

Smith, A.D. 1991. *National Identity*. London, Penguin.

Smith, A.D. 1995. *Nations and Nationalism in a Global Era*. Cambridge, Polity Press.

Smith, A.D. 1998. *Nationalism and Modernism*. London, Routledge.

Smith, M. 1992. 'Modernisation, Globalisation and the Nation-State', in A.G. McGrew and P.G. Lewis (eds), *Global Politics: Globalisation and the Nation-State*. Cambridge, Polity Press.

Smock, D.R. and Smock, A.C. 1975. *The Politics of Pluralism: A Comparative Study of Lebanon and Ghana*. New York, Elsevier.

Snyder, J. 1993. 'Nationalism and the Crisis of the Post Soviet State', in M.E. Brown (ed.), *Ethnic Conflict and International Security*. Princeton, Princeton University Press.

Spencer, E.M. 1994. 'Multiculturalism, "Political Correctness" and the Politics of Identity', *Sociological Forum* 9(4): 559–70.

Sullivan, J. 1988. *ETA and Basque Nationalism: The Fight for Euskadi 1890–1986*. London, Routledge.

Tamir, Y. 1993. *Liberal Nationalism*. Princeton, Princeton University Press.

Tangri, R. 1992. 'The Politics of Government–Business Relations in Ghana', *The Journal of Modern African Studies* 39(1): 97–111.

Todorov, T. 1993. *On Human Diversity: Nationalism, Racism and Exoticism in French Thought*. Cambridge, Mass., Harvard University Press.

Tremewan, C. 1994. *The Political Economy of Social Control in Singapore*. London, Macmillan.

UN. 1993. 'World Conference on Human Rights: Vienna Declaration and Programme of Action'. General Assembly A/CONF. 157/23.

Valadian, M. 1990. 'Aborigines in the 1990s', in D.W. Lovell *et al.* (eds), *The Australian Political System*. Melbourne, Longman.

Van Amersfoort H., and Mansvelt Beck J. 1999. 'Institutional Plurality: A way out for

Basque Nationalism?', conference paper given at conference 'Nationalism, Identity and Minority Rights', Bristol University, UK, 16–19 September.

Van den Berghe, P. 1995. 'Does Race Matter?' *Nations and Nationalism* 1(3): 357–68.

Vasta, E. 1993. 'Multiculturalism and Ethnic Identity: The Relationship between Racism and Resistance', *Australian and New Zealand Journal of Sociology* 29(2): 209–25.

Vincent, A. 1997. 'Liberal Nationalism: An Irresponsible Compound?', *Political Studies* 45(2): 275–95.

Viroli, M. 1995. *For Love of Country: An Essay on Patriotism and Nationalism*. Oxford, Clarendon Press.

Volkan, V.D. 1998. 'Ethnicity and Nationalism: A Psychoanalytic Perspective', *Applied Psychology: An International Review* 47(1): 45–57.

Wade, R. 1996. 'Globalization and its Limits: Reports of the Death of the National Economy are Greatly Exaggerated', in S. Berger and R. Dore (eds), *National Diversity and Global Capitalism*. Ithaca, Cornell University Press.

Waldron, J. 1995. 'Minority Cultures and the Cosmopolitan Alternative', in W. Kymlicka (ed.), *The Rights of Minority Cultures*. Oxford, Oxford University Press.

Walzer, M. 1992. 'The New Tribalism: Notes on a Difficult Problem', *Dissent*, Spring: 164–71.

Walzer, M. 1995. 'Pluralism: A Political Perspective', in W. Kymlicka (ed.), *The Rights of Minority Cultures*. Oxford, Oxford University Press.

Weiss, L. 1997. 'Globalization and the Myth of the Powerless State', *New Left Review* 225: 3–27.

Wiarda, H.J. 1981. *Corporatism and National Development in Latin America*. Colorado, Westview.

Williamson, P.J. 1985. *Varieties of Corporatism: A Conceptual Discussion*. Cambridge, Cambridge University Press.

Williamson, P.J. 1989. *Corporatism in Perspective: An Introductory Guide to Corporatist Theory*. London, Sage.

Yack, B. 1999. 'The Myth of the Civic Nation', in R. Beiner (ed.), *Theorizing Nationalism*. Albany, State University of New York Press.

Young, C. (ed.) 1993. *The Rising Tide of Cultural Pluralism: The Nation-State at Bay?* Madison, University of Wisconsin Press.

Young, E. 1995. *The Third World in the First: Development and Indigenous Peoples*. London, Routledge.

Young, I.M. 1995. 'Together in Difference: Transforming the Logic of Group Political Conflict', in W. Kymlicka (ed.), *The Rights of Minority Cultures*. Oxford, Oxford University Press.

Index

Note: An 'n' after the page number
indicates an endnote.

Aboriginal community: corporatist strategy
  139, 140–3; multiculturalism and
  assimilation 155–7; *see also* Australia
Acheampong, Ignatius K. 117, 120, 121
Akan *see* Ghana
Albanians, Kosovo 164–7
alienation, and identity 26
Alter, Peter: Risorgimento and Integral
  nationalisms 66–7; will of the individual
  60
ancestry: and kinship 35; *see also*
  ethnocultural nationalism; primordialist
  approach
Anderson, Benedict: cultural ideas 32;
  print-capitalism 17
anti-colonial nationalism 33, 66
Arana Goiri, Sabino de 78–9, 80, 82,
  173n20
Asante, and Ewe 123
Ashanti 12–13, 20
assimilation: and civic nationalism
  170n5; ethnocultural 38–9; or
  exclusion 40–1; and loss of legitimacy
  of state 46; and multiculturalism:
  Australia 155–7
Australia 155–7; corporatism and
  multiculturalism 133, 139–47; ethnic
  minority rights claims 136; and identity
  16; pluralist strategy and
  multiculturalism 149
authoritarian nationalism: and liberal
  nationalism 50–69; *see also*
  ethnocultural nationalism
authoritarian rule, globalisation and civic
  nationalism: Singapore 95–8, 103–4,
  105

Basque country 9
Basque nationalism 27, 88, 171n3;
  constructivist approach 77–87;
  primordialist approach 70–3;
  situationalist approach 73–6
Basque Nationalist Party (PNV) 72, 74,
  83
Bawumia, Mahamadu 112
Benner, Erica: alienation and identity 26;
  class interests 32; German nationalism
  63
Boahen, Adu 122, 123
bourgeoisie, and rational nationalism 63
Brubaker, Rogers: primordialist approach
  168n3; social classification 21
Burgos trial 83, 84
Burma 47; nationalist movement 27

Canada 47; Quebec nationalism 57
Canovan, Margaret: civic and
  ethnocultural nationalisms 38; English
  and British identity 168n1; nationalist
  myths 27–8; nationhood 168n2
capitalism: rise of and formation of the
  state 17; and the rise of nationalism 26
Carlism 172n7
Carlist rebellion 74, 79, 80
Catalan nationalism 56
Catalonia 76, 79
Chee Soon Juan 104
China, Han identity 58–9
civic nationalism: and assimilation 170n5;
  Basque nationalism 81–7; and
  ethnocultural nationalism 34–8, 50–69;
  globalisation: Singapore 93–5;
  relationship with ethnocultural and
  multicultural nationalisms 126–34
civil society, and invention of national
  community 40–2

class: Basque nationalism 74–5; Marxism 16; and the state 32, 53–4
collective unconscious 7
collectivist–authoritarian nationalism, and individualistic–libertarian nationalism 55
colonialism, and spread of nationalism 18, 26, 33
common will, and the state 36–7
Connor, Walker: ancestry and nationalism 7; civic and ethnocultural nationalisms 35; ethnicity and nationalism 8; loyalty 10; perennialist approach 7; Soviet Union 35
constructivist approach 5, 20–9, 31–4; Basque nationalism 77–87
Convention People's Party (CPP) (Ghana) 109
corporatism: history of 136–8; and multiculturalism: Australia 133, 139–47
corporatist strategy 136–47, 178n4; Singapore 99–103
corruption, Ghana 119–21
cultural ideas, modernisation 32

decolonisation, fight for Ghana 109
democracy 41, 169n6
Deutsch, Karl: industrialisation and rise of nationalism 17; national integration 14
development 41; politics of Ghana 107–25; *see also* economy; globalisation; industrialisation
disruption, and nationalism 25–8
Dunn, John 4; globalisation 105; lies 16

eastern Europe: crisis of legitimacy 42; economic development and the state 39; nationalism – compared with that of Western Europe 54, 55
economy: Basque nationalism 74–5, 85; and crisis of legitimacy 42–5; Eastern European communist states 39; and legitimacy: Ghana 110–14; legitimacy of the state 38–40; Singapore 89–106; situationalist view of nationalism 13; *see also* globalisation; industrialisation
élites: constructivist view of role 28; and ideology of social justice 40, 41; insecure: illiberal nationalism 67; and legitimatory ideology of nationalism 31; primordialist view of role 10; Singapore and globalisation 100; situationalist view of role 16

emotions: ethnocultural nationalisms 59; and rational choice 15
England, origin of nationalism 33
ethnic exclusion, Soviet Union 40
ethnic identity 33; primordialist approach 6–13; situationalist approach 15, 16; *see also* primordialist approach
ethnic minorities 177n2; corporatist politics of 141–4; corporatist strategy towards 136, 144–7; exclusion or assimilation 40–1; fairness 138–41; marginalisation of 44–5; and multiculturalism 132–4; pluralist strategy towards 148–51; *see also* assimilation; multicultural nationalism; multiculturalism
ethnic nationalism 170n4
ethnicity 170n3; and ethnocultural nationalism 170n9; and loss of legitimacy of state 45–8; scapegoating in Ghana 114–18
ethnie 10, 33; *see also* ethnic identity
ethno-symbolism 169n6
ethnocultural assimilation, and political integration 38–9
ethnocultural nationalism 170n4; Basque nationalism 81–7; and civic nationalism 34–8, 50–69; and ethnicity 170n9; and globalisation 91–2; multicultural and civic nationalisms: relationship with 126–34; Singapore: corporatist rule 99–103
European Union, as manifestation of globalisation 19
Euskadi Ta Azkatasuna (ETA) 74–6, 84, 85–6, 87
Euskara language 71, 76, 82, 83, 84, 171n4
Ewe: accused of tribalism 116–18; and Asante 123; *see also* Ghana

false consciousness, nationalism as 1
fascist nationalism 66
Fichte, Johann G. 9, 53, 59; individual freedom 171n12
France 56; nationalism 64, 171n10
Franco, Francisco 71, 72, 83
Frosh, Stephen, language of the unconscious 23
Fueros 78, 79, 80, 82, 172n6
functional aggregations 14
functionality: modernisation and the state 31; *see also* situationalist approach

garrison nationalism, Ghana 114–18
Geertz, Clifford 169n6; conceptual
    ambiguity and nationalism 4; ethnicity
    and nationalism 8; modern states 12;
    primordial bonds 57
Gellner, Ernest 175n1; industrialisation 17;
    stress of modern life 23
Germany: fascist nationalism 66;
    nationalism 54, 63–4, 64; nationalist
    propaganda 33–4; race and nationalism
    59
gesellschaft, and *gemeinschaft* 137, 138
Ghana: constructivist view of
    nationalism and tribalism 28–9;
    primordialist view of nationalism
    and tribalism 12–3; reactive
    nationalism 107–25; situationalist
    view of nationalism and tribalism
    19–20
globalisation: effect on nationalism 18–9,
    26–7; Singapore 89–106
Goh Chok Tong 140
Goh Keng Swee 101
Gray, John 96, 147
Greenfeld, Liah 66; authoritarian
    assertions of collective will 59; civic
    nationalism 52; cultural ideas 32;
    French nationalism 171n10; German
    nationalism 64;
    individualistic–libertarian and
    collectivist–authoritarian nationalisms
    55; nationalism 171n14; *ressentiment* 65,
    171n17
group memories, and socialisation 7
group rights, and multiculturalism 130
Guibernau, Montserrat, civic and
    ethnocultural nationalism 55–6

Han identity 58–9
Hanson, Pauline 155
Hastings, Adrian, modern nations 8–9, 10
Hechter, Michael: choice 19; internal
    colonialism 18; structure and rational
    choice 14
Heiberg, Marianne 82, 173n21, 175n35
Herder, Johann G. 9, 53, 59, 66
Herri Batasuna 86
Hill, M., nation building 95, 175n5
Hobsbawm, Eric: capitalism and rise of
    nationalism 17; legitimatory ideology
    31
Horowitz, Donald 172n11; perennialist
    approach 7
Hutchinson, John 63, 145; civic and

ethnocultural nationalisms 63; Irish
    nationalism 68
Hutu, and Tutsi 160–4

identity: and alienation 26; management of
    45–6; and multiculturalism 129–30;
    situationalist view of 15; structuralist
    view 21
ideology: construction of national identity
    20–9; nationalism of state élites 31–4
individual liberty 59–60, 171n12
individualistic–libertarian nationalism, and
    collectivist–authoritarian nationalism
    55
Indonesia 56
industrialisation: and Basque nationalism
    74, 78; and modernisation 17; and rise
    of nationalism 13, 18; and the state:
    Ghana 39–40; *see also* economy;
    globalisation
insecurity, and legitimacy of the state 44
Integral nationalism, and Risorgimento
    nationalism 66–7
interests: and nationalist conflict 1; nature
    of the state 36; situationalist approach
    13–20; *see also* situationalist approach
internal colonialism 18, 33
international capital *see* globalisation
International Monetary Fund (IMF),
    Ghana 119
Ireland 57, 158–60
Irish nationalism 68; *see also* Northern
    Ireland

Janus 50
Jeffries, Richard, Ghanaian economy and
    politics 111, 112, 113, 119
Jeyaretnam, J.B. 104
Jung, Karl G., collective unconscious 7
justice *see* social justice

Keating, Michael: Catalonia 76; ethnic
    and civic nationalisms 55
Kedourie, Elie: frenzy of nationalists 23;
    legitimatory ideology 31; nationalist
    ideology 40
Kellas, James, western European and
    eastern European nationalisms 55
Kenya 67
kinship, and ancestry 35
kinship community, myth of 40–2
Klein, Melanie, splitting 24
Kohn, Hans 54, 57, 67; civic and
    ethnocultural nationalisms 63; reactive

nationalism 64–5; reactive and
optimistic nationalisms 66
Kosovo 164–7
Kymlicka, Will: criticises concept of
neutral state 132; ethnic
nationalism and ethnocultural
nationalism 170n4; individual liberty
59–60, 129

Lacan, Jacques, external structures and
identity 24
language: and modernisation 32;
Singapore 101, 103
legitimacy: corporatist state 146–7;
economic development and crisis of
42–5; and ethnicity 45–8; Ghana
108–14; and globalisation: Singapore
92–3, 94, 96, 105–6; social justice and
the state 38–40, 43
legitimatory ideology 31–4
Lian, K.F., nation building 95, 175n5
liberal nationalism: and authoritarian
nationalism 50–69; *see also* civic
nationalism
lies, credibility of 16
Limann, Hilla 117, 122

majority, and minorities 132–4
Mann, Michael: European nationalism
170n11; loyalty to the state 38
marginalisation, ethnic minorities 44–5
Marx, Karl: German middle class and
nationalism 63; nation and class
interests 53–4; social disruption and
nationalism 25
Marxism: class 16; and modernisation 32;
nationalism as ideology 25–6
Medrano, J.D. 172n12
Meinecke, Friederich 53–4, 67; German
nationalism 63
middle class: Basque nationalism 75;
nature of nationalism 63–4
Miller, David: civic nationalism 60–1; civic
nationalism and ethnocultural
nationalism 62; nationality and
nationalism 55; social justice 131
minorities, and multiculturalism 132–4
modernisation: optimistic view 30; role of
nationalism 31–2; theories of 17
multicultural nationalism, relationship with
civic and ethnocultural nationalisms
126–34
multiculturalism 11, 48–9, 56; and
assimilation: Australia 156–7; and

corporatism: Australia 138–47; pluralist
strategy 148–51
myth 28; common ancestry 58; psychology
and nationalism 23–5; *see also*
constructivist approach

Nairn, Tom: Basque nationalism 78; civic
and ethnic nationalism 56; identity
45–6
narcissism 24
nation-state, Singapore and globalisation
90–3
national community, invention of 40–2
national identity: corporatism 144–6; and
élites 10; ideological framework 20–9;
view of three conceptual languages 5
National Trade Union Congress (NTUC)
(Singapore) 97
nationalism *see* authoritarian nationalism;
civic nationalism; ethnocultural
nationalism; garrison nationalism;
liberal nationalism; reactive nationalism
nationality, and nationalism 55
nationhood 168n2
natural rights, and nationalism 6
neocolonialism, Ghana 115–16
Nkrumah, Kwame 63, 109–10, 115;
industrialisation and the state 39–40
Northern Ireland 9, 158–60

O'Donoghue, Lowitja 142–3

Pact of Ajuria-Enea 86
patriotism, Singapore and globalisation
98–9
People's Action Party (PAP) (Singapore)
93–4, 99, 102, 104
perennialist approach 7–8
pluralist strategy 148–51
political integration, and ethnocultural
assimilation 38–9
power, distribution and multiculturalism
131–2
Primo de Rivera, Miguel 71, 83
primordial character, ethnocultural
nationalism 57–8
primordialist approach 5, 6–13, 31–2;
Basque nationalism 70–3
print-capitalism 17
progress, and the state 39
Provisional National Defence Ruling
Council (PNDC) (Ghana) 112, 113,
119–20
psychological ideology 23–5

Quebec nationalism 57

race, and nationalism 59
rational choice 34; situationalist view 14–15
Rawlings, Jerry 117, 119, 120–4; legitimacy 110–14
Rawls, John, ethnic minorities 177n2
reactive nationalism 64–6; Basque nationalism 78, 80–1; Ghana 107–25
religion, Singapore 101–2
resources, distribution and multiculturalism 311–12
ressentiment 65, 67, 68, 171n17; Basque nationalism 78, 80–1
rights 41; *see also* group rights
Risorgimento nationalism, and Integral nationalism 66–7
Ronen, Dov, functional aggregations 14
Rustow, Dankwart: equality and achievement 30; margin for human choice 30–1
Rwanda 160–4

Scottish nationalism 56
self-fulfilment, and ethnocultural community 59
Seow, Francis 104
Serbs, Kosovo 164–7
Shubert, A. 172n10; ETA violence 76
Singapore 43–4, 67; Chinese chauvinism 52; corporatism and ethnic arithmetic 140; globalisation 89–106
situationalist approach 5, 13–20, 31–2; Basque nationalism 73–6
Slovenia 56
Smith, Anthony D. 170n13; civic and ethnocultural nationalisms 38, 54–5, 62, 63; civic nationalism 61; collective immortality 27; ethnic identity 33; ethnicity and the crisis of legitimacy 47; ethno-symbolism 169n6; globalisation and the nation-state 91; modern nations 8–9, 10–11; nationalist movements 171n7; nationalist myths 23; perennialist approach 7–8, 168n5
Snyder, Jack, crisis of legitimacy and rise of nationalism 43
social disruption 25–8
social justice: and crisis of legitimacy 38–40, 43; distribution of power and resources 131–2; and globalisation; Singapore 65–6, 92

socialisation: and group memories 7; and the state 36
South Africa 11, 170n7
Soviet Union: attempt to contain nationalism 21; civic and ethnocultural nationalisms 35; ethnic exclusion 40
Spain: Basque nationalism 70–88, 171–5n3–37; Catalan nationalism 56
Spanish Socialist Workers' Party (PSOE) 74
Spencer, Martin, multiculturalism 141
splitting 24
state 170n7; and class 32, 53–4; definitions of 36; formation as ethnically heterogeneous 9; modernisation and nationalism 17; as neutral 132; social justice and legitimacy 38–40, 43
Suharto, Thojib N.J. 56, 63

Tamir, Yael 66; ethnocultural nationalism as liberal 58
Tang Liang Hong 104
third world 33
Thompson, G., nation-states 91
Tito 164
Togo 12, 28
Tremewan, Christopher, Singapore and globalisation 94
tribalism: Ghana 12–13, 28–9, 116–18; and nationalism 5, 9
Tutsi, and Hutu 160–4

unconscious, and nationalism 23–5
uneven development 18, 32–3
United Kingdom 48; British and Welsh nationalisms 35; England and origin of nationalism 33; English and British 2, 168n1; English nationalism 64, 65; English supremacism 52; Northern Ireland 158–60; Scottish nationalism 56
United States of America: American and black nationalisms 35; civic nationalism and ancestry 61–2; civil rights unrest 9; economic development and legitimacy 42; multiculturalism 128, 148–9; nationalism 64, 65; and neutral state 132
universalism, ethnocultural nationalism 56
USSR: crisis of legitimacy 43

Van den Berghe, Pierre, culture and language 7

Wales 56
Walzer, Michael: ethnic minority cultures
148–9; neutral state 132
Weber, Max 53; German nationalism 64
Western Europe, nationalism – compared
with that of Eastern Europe 54, 55

Williamson, P.J., corporatism 178n4
World Bank, Ghana 111, 119, 124

Yack, Bernard, myth of the civic nation
60
Yugoslavia 11, 164